American Freedom and the Social Sciences

Critical Assessments of Contemporary Psychology
A Series of Columbia University Press
Daniel N. Robinson, Series Editor

American Freedom and the Social Sciences

James Deese

New York   **Columbia University Press**   1985

Columbia University Press
New York   Guildford, Surrey
Copyright © 1985 Columbia University Press
All rights reserved

Printed in the United States of America

Library of Congress Cataloging in Publication Data

Deese, James Earle, 1921–
    American freedom and the social sciences.

    (Conceptions in psychology)
    Bibliography: p.
    Includes index.
    1. Social psychology.   2. Liberty.   3. Free will
and determinism.   4. United States—Social conditions.
I. Title.   II. Series.
HM251.D359   1985   302   84-23683
ISBN 0-231-05914-0 (alk. paper)
ISBN 0-231-05915-9 (pbk.)

Contents

Preface

Some books have a way of evolving as if they had a life of their own. Certainly this one did. It began in postpartum ruminations about a bland little book I wrote in 1972. I first thought of this work as a revision of that book, but as the conception of it grew in my head it was clear that I had something very different in mind. I was concerned with the clash in assumptions behind most contemporary thought in the social sciences, particularly in psychology, anthropology, and sociology and the assumptions necessary for a democratic society.

The critical remarks I find necessary to make about the social sciences may mislead the reader into supposing that I am against the social sciences. Nothing could be more wrong. I am a social scientist, and I regard what I do and what I teach as being of value. However, the social sciences do need to be saved from themselves, and that is one of the purposes of this book. False assumptions, misdirected methods, and unexamined theory all contribute in various ways to the low intellectual esteem in which the social sciences are held.

My particular criticisms largely spare economics, not so much because it should be spared as because its methods and problems require a different sort of exposition. My general thesis, however, can be applied to economics, and the present disarray in which economic theory finds itself can be attributed to the same kind of mistakes in assumptions and methods that afflict the other social sciences. On the other hand, the disorder in economic theory, like the confusion in the house of psychology and that of anthropology, saves us from the follies that are committed daily in totalitarian states out of devotion to a single social theory.

The social sciences are at their worst when they pretend to be objective—that is to say, free of any kind of faith—and at the same time claim to be the source of ethical principles. The notion of an objective ethic suffuses the social sciences, from behaviorism to socio-biology, from psychoanalysis to cultural determinism, and, of course, in Marxism. Any pretense to real science disappears when social scientists (and here the economists are especially at fault) tell us what we *ought* to do. I applaud the social sciences when they tell us in sober voice what *is* and when they do not pretend to the implacable methodological certainties of the physical sciences. The social sciences are an essential part of our modern intellectual world, but if we are not to be ground down by them, we need to keep them in control.

I am indebted to various persons who have read portions of the manuscript for this book. In particular I am indebted to Ellin K. Deese, with whom I have spent many hours debating the ideas presented here. I am only less indebted to Daniel N. Robinson, editor of this series, because opportunities to debate were fewer. Professor and Mrs. Kurt Bergel of Chapman College provided me with a useful reading of an early version of the manuscript. There are many persons with whom I have talked about the ideas in this book, and they all have sharpened the arguments I present. Finally, my thanks to Marianne Walker, who did a splendid job of preparing the final manuscript.

James Deese
Charlottesville, Virginia
January 1985

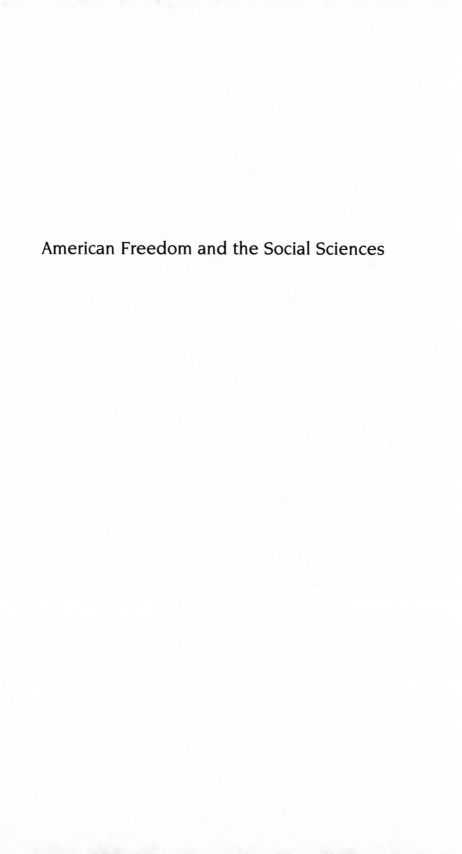

American Freedom and the Social Sciences

Chapter One

A Collision Course

W hy have I written this book? The answer to that question lies in the title to this chapter. When the simile of a collision of ideas first occurred to me, I had in mind something like the encounter between the *Titanic* and the iceberg. Now, after thinking about and making notes on the matter, I am inclined to the view that I am concerned with a collision between two mountains of mush. However the trope may be conceived, it is based upon an issue of great importance. Over the past few years I have become convinced that two influential and transcendentally overreaching ideas are competing to determine the future of American society. One of these ideas lies at the heart of the behavioral and social sciences. The other is centered in the most basic aspect of the rational for American political processes and for the procedures of the American judicial system. Both ideas extend far beyond their heartlands. They pervade our society. And they are mutually contradictory. They have coexisted in America for more than two hundred years and for a thousand years before that, but the increasing ascendancy of one in recent years threatens the balancing influence of the other.

The twin ideas of freedom and responsibility that govern our assumptions about political and judicial procedures have been challenged from the earliest times those institutions were adapted to the American landscape. But the challenge has only infrequently been intellectual and philosophical. Even H. L. Mencken's fusillades against democracy carefully spared the idea of freedom. Indeed, Mencken is something of a hero to the late-twentieth-century libertarian movement. No, the typical challenge has been ignorant and doltish. But in recent years those ideas, freedom and responsibility, have been undermined by what amounts to the working assumptions of the social sciences. Our conception of criminal justice has been on the defensive for the better part of the twentieth century, a state of affairs described by D. N. Robinson in his book, *Psychology and Law*.[1] Even more alarming is the fact that our faith in the validity of American political procedures has been eroded during the past generation. That erosion is widely recognized, and it is often attributed to the rough play in the political arena—Watergate and the like. However, I think a more insidious source of that erosion lies in our views of our own natures and our views as to how our actions, including political ones, are controlled.

It is hard to imagine a time in which cynicism and politics did not go hand in hand. But that companionship now leads to apathy in the electorate. Participation in the political process by the ordinary citizen declines at the very time that experts in political manipulation have come to dominate the electoral process. A month or so before I first drafted this chapter, Senator S. I. Hayakawa of California withdrew from the contest for his senate seat. His giving up early in the game was attributed by everyone to his poor showing in the public opinion polls. It was the unspoken but universally acknowledged consequence of those polls that he could not raise enough money to campaign. Without commenting one way or another about Mr. Hayakawa's merits (or his age), his political disappearance can only be described as managed, if not entirely by the pollsters, then at least by the pollsters and the press.

What are these ideas that are in conflict? They are the notion that all human action is determined and controlled by causes which operate upon individual human beings, and the contrary belief that we human beings are capable, from time to time, of exercising free choices undetermined by the operation of any universal material laws.

The first of these ideas is the assumption that pervades the world of official psychology, psychiatry, and their intrusions into the allied disciplines of political science and economics. It is surely a minority of psychologists who would not subscribe to the opinion that all behavior, at the bottom, has a physical cause, even though, all would agree the imperfect state of the science of psychology does not permit us to understand completely the nature of that cause.

The second of these ideas is essential to any conception of democracy, American or otherwise. Without the notion of free choice, democracy is a black joke. Less obvious is the fact that democracy entails a notion of individual responsibility. The erosion of a belief in responsibility, once again, is less evident in politics than in the judicial process, but it is there. The ideas of intention, premeditation, and psychological competence for responsibility, we all know, are at the very center of our theories of and processes for criminal justice. The outcry over John Hinckley's acquittal by reason of insanity for his assassination attempt has made everyone aware of the fact that these ideas are now threatened in the courts. However, it is equally important that these ideas—intention, premeditation, and competence—exist in the political process, and it is equally important that these ideas are threatened by the science of the "prediction and control of behavior."[2] The converse of the notion of responsibility not only threatens our political process, but it has come increasingly to dominate our notions of social justice and corporate—in the sense of the state's—responsibility for human conduct. Responsibility, removed from the individual, must reside somewhere, but allowing it to reside in a huge and unresponsive entity, the state, is perhaps the most ominous testimony to the effectiveness of the idea that human behavior is predicted and controlled by events beyond individual responsibility.

To be sure, the conflict between freedom and determinism, as these ideas have come to be called, has gone on almost from the origin of speculative thought. Every intellectual community that has considered them has evolved its own way of settling or ignoring the issue between them. As with most of our ideas, we have mainly resolved the issue by living with the contradiction. In fact, one of the ironies of this contradiction is that the conception of political freedom that came to fruition in the eighteenth century in America was fertilized by the notion that man was entirely at one with the physical, and in the special eighteenth-century sense, mechanical universe. Those two great documents of American freedom, the Declaration of Independence and the Bill of Rights, were written by men who were convinced that they lived in a clockwork universe in which human beings were very much part of the machinery.

The long history of the interweaving of these contradictory ideas tells us a great deal about the human mind. We human beings have an enormous capacity for simultaneously conceiving and believing in logically contradictory ideas. Of course, it is the case that one idea holds our attention in some particular context, and there it dominates. The contradiction reigns in some other domain, and we are made uncomfortable when the two domains are juxtaposed. The notion of freedom may not have to intrude itself when we think about the nature of the universe and man's place in it. But it does when we think about our moral obligations toward one another and the larger nature in which we live. Notice that I say may rather than cannot, for beginning in the nineteenth century and continuing at an accelerated pace into the twentieth century, the notion of a complete determinism has asserted itself in domains previously ruled by the notion of individual freedom.

With the beginnings of modern science in the seventeenth century, man's special place in the natural order of things came into question, particularly in Italy, France, and England. Man not only was obliged to live away from the center of the universe, he was increasingly understood as a material being, subject to the inescapable laws of mechanics. Almost every philosopher of importance in this century in these countries conceived of human conduct as being essentially physical in nature and caused by the same sort of conditions that caused the motion of inanimate objects. Even when, as with Descartes or more extremely with Pascal, there is an attempt to escape this conception, it provides the underlying *leitmotiv* of the philosophy of the century.

These ideas persisted and flourished in the eighteenth century. And a concomitant idea, though surely not a result, grew. It is the new conception of mental aberration. For the first time, mental disturbances were seen as diseases in the modern sense. The separation of disease and possession is nowhere clear in the ancient and medieval world, but the blithe optimism, mechanism, and rationalism of the eighteenth century allowed for a notion of mental aberration in the context of physical things. And it had its consequences. Pinel freeing the patients from their chains at Bi-cêtre is as much a phenomenon of the last quarter of the eighteenth century as is Jefferson drafting the Declaration of Independence.

However much the eighteenth century was receptive to mechanistic views of the universe and mankind and however much it was receptive to rational interpretations of madness, it differs from the twentieth century in one critical respect. Psychology as such did not exist. This is not to say that there was no body of empirical facts of a psychological sort or that there was not a body of attendant assumptions and superstitions about the mind. There were. Early in the century, the French materialists could write treatises describing, in exquisite detail, man as a machine. Hartley, who might be described as the father of hard physiological theorizing about the mind, could write, in almost as much detail as a late-twentieth-century physiological psychologist, how the senses affected the nerves and the nerves, in turn, the brain. All of these things existed, but there was nothing in them that would attract more than a glance from a reader of *Psychology Today*. It was all abstract and theoretical. It is true that La Mettrie's famous description of the soul as an "enlightened machine" got him in trouble in 1748, but by the late years of the century, such ideas scarcely raised a murmur. They were accepted by the philosophers, but they had little or no practical consequences in the creation of the modern conception of freedom. Those persons, who in Garry Wills' phrase invented America, accepted without hesitation these kinds of ideas, but at the same time they defended and enlarged human freedom in a way that has never been equaled. If the contradiction occurred to them, it was quietly suppressed.

Simply put, there was no psychology in the modern sense in the eighteenth century. The materialism of the age was abstract and ritualistic. The connection between the brain and mind had been established, but beyond that there was—Hartley excepted—only a weak attempt to bring the scattering of known psychophysiological facts together. The control that pleasure and pain exerted over the actions of human beings could be commented upon, and the similarity of the passions of animals to those of people could be alluded to (much as Aristotle could allude to the similarity between man and other mammals that dissection revealed). But no one talked about the prediction and control of behavior, even when allowance for eighteenth-century diction is made. To assert that thought is the secretion of the brain is one thing. To discover concrete and particular chemicals that the body produces, hormones, capable of influencing moods, actions, and even thinking is quite another. The late twentieth century knows all about such possibilities, and it has lived with them for fifty years or more. The philosophers of the eighteenth century could talk heady abstractions about psychological materialism as easily as parlor revolutionaries can talk about the revolution. The concrete realities of modern psychological sciences make the ideas of eighteenth-century *philosophes*, like the ideas of parlor revolutionaries, seem, at best, to be quaint.

The difference between the eighteenth century and the twentieth is that the latter is the age of psychology. It is not the age of politics, as was the eighteenth century; it is the age of psychology. To be sure, many modern intellectuals are nearly as fascinated with politics as were eighteenth-century thinkers, but the fascination is of a radically different sort. Now the interest is not so much in political theory as such (unless the theory happens to be Marxist) as it is in the bringing of *empirical knowledge* to politics. Politicians, of course, have always interested themselves in bringing knowledge of human nature to statecraft, but today's student of politics has a fundamentally different attitude. He or she wants to bring the whole theoretical-empirical warehouse of the modern social sciences to bear on the everyday business of day-to-day politics. What makes the machinery of politics work? Often this question focuses, in the manner of modern scholarship, upon only small parts of the process. A student of politics may address himself or herself to the question of accounting, in some psychosocial way, for the pattern of votes in the Virginia General Assembly.[3] But whether it is the study of some grand political system or some parochial part of it, the assumption is that the actions of those who engage in politics are caused and therefore open to prediction and control. Intellectuals, particularly those on the left, don't like to openly acknowledge the fact that much of political science is dedicated to means of control, but when the issue is put, they admit to it.

I have already alluded to the fact that the practical management of politics requires politicians to be psychologists in the sense understood by the man in the street. That is to say, they must be able to understand and, in some unarticulated way, be able to influence people. Or so, lore has it, were the skills of the old-fashioned political boss. The new bosses, however, have interested themselves in the ways of the social and behavioral sciences. How can a campaign be scientifically designed so as to get an unpopular figure elected? Or, on the other hand, how can one make use of an inexplicably popular figure to get unpopular policies adopted? In short, the new managers of politics ask how they can make use of the methods and results of the behavioral and social sciences.

The manipulation of votes of a crude and simple sort —a pint of whiskey for a vote—has been going on since the Neanderthal age of American politics, and it is hard not to believe that something similar has always been a part of the politics of genuinely democratic states. Though such practices may have had, from time to time, the blessing of a cynical political philosopher, they have not been canonized by the establishment of the social sciences until recent time. Social scientists buying votes? That is not the only way to interpret the interests of social scientists in politics and social reform, but it is one way. Politicians in totalitarian states, of course, have considerable interest in the manipulation of public opinion, but their methods, of necessity, are different and little open to free investigation. It is hard to determine whether or not they believe in or rely upon the methods of the social and behavioral scientists. There was a certain pretension among the Nazis in so doing, and, after all, Dr. Goebbels was a Ph.D. in what may be broadly conceived as social philosophy.

Be that as it may, the old-time American political boss knew what he knew, and he used his craft and experience to get things done. But he was a bumbler by comparison with those media experts who run the smooth machinery of large-scale modern campaigns. Image polishing may have been an implicit notion in the old days, but the application of the techniques of the social sciences in providing the polish is something that has developed in the last sixty years. In short, psychological determinism, almost unconsciously, has entered our views of how politics works at its most fundamental level. And so it is perceived by the ordinary voter, who often gives expression to feelings of helplessness and alienation in the face of blatant manipulation. That such manipulation is done and that it is done through the systematic scientific study of man and his world is one of the fundamental givens of our psychological age.

There is no necessary reason why the psychological age should be the age of material determinism, but it is. Even so wise a psychologist as William James[4] argued that psychologists as scientists must accept complete determinism, even if they think it is not true. James could say that, of course, and still hold to notions completely antithetical to it. But the way in which James puts the matter tells us that he was all too aware of the contradiction. Modern psychological scientists are not. They will take for granted, on the one hand, the assumption of complete psychological determinism while arguing, on the other, a passionate defense of intellectual freedom. Not many of them are defenders of economic freedom and only a tiny minority see any connection between economic freedom and intellectual freedom or the inherent contradiction in their assumptions of psychological science and their belief in unfettered free expression.

However, the assumptions behind psychological determinism are not limited to the psychological scientist. They have, to a surprising degree, penetrated the thinking of the ordinary American citizen. It is not that we say to ourselves: "All human action and ideas are determined or caused by natural events." What we do is to act as if that were the case, and we accept those legal judgments and procedures that appear to presume it. The unease that exists between the psychological community[5] and such groups as Alcoholics Anonymous is in no limited way the result of AA's distrust, rare in the helping professions, of the notion of complete determinism. Because AA seems to be, by the standards established by the helping professions, so spectacularly successful, there is a certain grudging acceptance among the professionals that whatever AA is doing, it is doing it in the right way. AA, on the other hand, resists being put under the psychological microscope, perhaps because it wishes to protect its assumption that human beings, to rescue themselves from a particular compulsion, must transcend their own most obvious limitations.

What stood at the very center of the American enlightenment in the eighteenth century was the view that human beings were free and were entitled to that freedom by right, unrestrained by the various bondages of tyranny that had held them for ages past. What stands at the center of the mainstream of social thinking in twentieth-century America is the notion that individual human action can be "explained" by the individual's experiences and his heredity. It is true that, in this explanation, heredity is currently in disfavor, but that may change tomorrow. The important point is that freedom of choice can be explained, if the social scientists are correct.

In the next few chapters I review something of the history of the rivalry between freedom, usualy expressed in the phrase freedom of the will, less often by volition, and determinism. This history is important, but what is more important is the context of the late-twentieth-century within which confines we review it. The context for twentieth-century humanity is the fearsome knowledge that has now come to be the common heritage of us all. The notion of evolution pervades the intellectual world of the twentieth century in countless powerful and irresistible ways, as does our understanding of the vastness and strangeness of the universe. A commonplace observation of the past seventy or even hundred years points to the fact that such discoveries seem to diminish our image of ourselves. Humanity is a vastly less important aspect of the modern universe than it was to Dante or even to Milton. The eighteenth century knew something of that diminishment, and its philosophers were firmly convinced that we were part of a large and indifferent (the twentieth century might claim hostile) universe. But the eighteenth century knew nothing of human biological development and could only speculate about our possible connection with fabulous creatures such as gorillas and orangutans. The nineteenth century showed, in sufficiently concrete detail to be painful, our place in nature to be a far more ignoble place than even the most materialistic of the eighteenth-century philosophers could have imagined.

Evolution and its psychological implications are now so much a part of the popular culture that mass audiences can be enchanted by movies on the theme. *Quest for Fire* surely has its appeal in the violence that it shares with the more conventional westerns, *Star Wars*, and the countless spy pictures of the last twenty years. But its reason for being is not that conventional violence of the cinema but the transformation of not-man into man. It even used the services of a popularizer of the behavioral sciences, Desmond Morris, to give some sense of authenticity to its speculations. I suspect that such a portrayal of the origins of humanity would have shocked Thomas Jefferson or even perhaps Locke or Voltaire. Now it receives no objection save from the lunatic fringe of the fundamentalist movement.

The eighteenth century accepted hedonism as the universal motive, but even that most eighteenth-century–like thinker among contemporary psychologists, B. F. Skinner, employs the pleasure-pain theory of human motivation in a sense vastly different from that used by eighteenth-century philosophers. If in no other way, his views differs fundamentally from his philosophic predecessors because he accepts the pragmatic point of view discovered by the early twentieth century psychologists (e.g., E. L. Thorndike) that pleasure is what organisms seek and pain is that which they avoid. But we know far more than this now. We know about centers in the brain that, when stimulated, produce pleasurable not to say ecstatic feelings, and we know about others that appear to produce unbearable pain. Furthermore, we know that pain, in the conventional sense, is often attractive to organisms, perhaps more than ordinarily so to human beings. Finally, we know that pleasure and pain are often so inextricably mixed as to be impossible of separation. In short, we know more about pleasure and pain than did the eighteenth-century *philosophes* and their British counterparts of the nineteenth century. And we know about such things in a context that has been profoundly altered by the universal intellectual acceptance of evolution—of the descent of man, to use Darwin's title.

Even those eighteenth-century thinkers who surely must have speculated on the possibility of evolution could not envisage the revolution in our thinking about ourselves that a firmly established theory of evolution created. In fact, the very evidence for evolution was resisted by the most characteristic eighteenth-century rationalist, Thomas Jefferson. Jefferson could argue that the fossils he found in the mountains of his Virginia were not fossils but merely curious kinds of rocks. He knew this because his rationalism instructed him to make calculations to show that the biblical account of the flood, then universally accepted as explanations for fossils on mountain tops, could not have been possibly correct.[6]

Thus, the tables have turned. Ideas that were on the periphery of the great movements of the eighteenth century are now at the center. This is the context of modern determinism. It is not so much that we occasionally must act as if we are free to make decisions as that such decisions are increasingly isolated from the main thrust of the intellectual life of the twentieth century. We no longer go to the priest to be forgiven and to receive advice. We go to a therapist whose magic is that of somehow altering or influencing the bad events that have made us what we are.

As we shall see in the next chapter, there are vast gulfs, indeed contradictions, in the varieties of determinism that dominate modern psychology. The irrational theory of instinct that lies at the heart of modern psychoanalysis has little in common with and perhaps is antithetical to the calculus of hedonism that characterizes much of the behavioristic movement and that lies at the heart of nearly all attempts in microeconomic theory to come to grips with human desires. Despite these discrepancies—incompatibilities—the whole is pervaded by notion that free choice, at the bottom, is foreordained by our nature. We cannot escape the Oedipal situation, and its outcome is determined by things that happen to us, not by what we do about it. We cannot cure our own neuroses, but we must be led by the skilled manipulator (for that is what the analyst is) to a state in which we are no longer consumed by our neuroses. Nor can we escape the calculus of rewards and punishments. The merchant, the politician need only play on the balance of our desires and what we have received thus far. To be sure, in economic theory at least, the calculus is a rational one —that is to say, we strive to maximize something or minimize something or adopt some reasonably rational combination of the two. But the calculation is not because we are rational beings free to make erroneous choices. However rational the choice, it is simply because we are made that way—perhaps shaped that way by evolution.

In our daily lives we may not allow these notions to intrude, though anyone who has ever known anyone undergoing psychoanalysis will know that the intrusion is insistently there. But even without the intrusion of psychological determinism into our ordinary commerce with ourselves and with other people, the faith in psychological determinism chips away at those aspects of our lives that are away from our personal centers but which are vital to the society in which we live. There is a vast difference between accepting the corruptibility, the venality of politicians and accepting the notion that the whole political process is simply a matter of manipulating the right motives and producing the right rewards. And perhaps not very far distant is a time when many of us will accept complete psychological determinism in a way that will allow it to envelope our lives with a terrifying fatalism. In a later chapter I shall touch upon the kind of fatalism that comes from religious belief. Suffice it to say here that religious fatalism, because it endows the whole universe—the individual included—with a kind of purpose, is vastly different from the purposeless fatalism that sees us as the mere victims of impersonal forces shaped only by the evolution of matter.

In the next few chapters I shall examine the varieties of determinism and the varieties of conceptions of freedom that have been advanced from time to time. I shall try to segregate those into notions that are in the mainstream of psychology and those that come from religion, philosophy, and literature. The reader will surely understand that such a separation cannot be accomplished neatly, for, as the last few pages have suggested ideas leak and merge into one another. Nevertheless, in order to impose some order on the history and varieties of versions of these two ideas, I have treated both determinism and freedom in the context of several categories.

In later chapters I shall examine contemporary psychology. Here I shall deal, of course, with such famous deterministic manifestos as Skinner's *Beyond Freedom and Dignity*, but I shall also deal with the humbler propaganda that is slipped into the four-color, heavy-stock, slick-paper introductory textbooks in psychology. I shall try to persuade the reader that the term propaganda is not too strong when applied to much of the material one finds there. Finally, I shall present my views as to the nature of psychology and to argue that a complete determinism is not only scientifically unjustified but reprehensible, given the almost pious belief in the objectivity of much of what passes for current psychological knowledge.

If all of this implies that this book is simply a polemic attack on modern psychology, the implication is wrong. I have argued elsewhere[7] that the behavioral and psychological sciences are absolutely essential to the functioning of any complex, over-developed society. They will emerge in one form or another because they are necessary. But they are badly used by a pretense that they can lead to understanding of things that are beyond their techniques and theories. We need to perceive that they, at various places and times, falsely intrude themselves, that they offer systems of values in the guise of value-free science, and that they offer values at variance with values built into the foundations of our society. The least we can say is that the values of the behavioral and social sciences are there. They intrude themselves into our lives in ways that few of us stop to think about. Even some of us in the psychological community are taken aback by the vast influence of modern psychology and the implicit system of values behind that influence. Any belief that we have, to a degree, some control over our own lives must reckon with that influence.

Chapter Two

The Rise of Scientific Determinism

The belief that all human action is fixed and determined by some cause or another has its foundation in an astonishingly wide variety of assumptions, some of which come from the most discrepant sources imaginable. The notion that all human action is, in principle at least, determined by natural events is the cornerstone of modern, materialistic behavioral science. In equal degree, the notion that all human action is determined, like everything else, by the nature of God has been the cornerstone of Muslim theology for a thousand years.

Nor is there any consistent set of beliefs that easily characterize all psychological determinisms as opposed, say, to theological determinisms. There is an irreconcilable gulf, for example, between the determinism of radical behaviorism and that of classical psychoanalytic theory. Even within behaviorism, basic assumptions and consequences vary. Modern psychobiology is built on the assumption that the way to understand behavior is to study the relation between the physical nature of the organism and what it does. The behaviorism advocated by B. F. Skinner, to the contrary, advocates the understanding of how behavior is controlled by study independent of the study of the physical nature of the organism.

The one thing we can say about all deterministic views is that belief in them has important social, political, and ethical consequences. The nature of these consequences, of course, will depend upon the assumptions behind any particular variety of determinism, and so it is to an examination of those assumptions that we turn in order to understand the consequences. In this chapter I shall deal with psychological determinism in its scientific context.

The Rise of Scientific Determinism

We might characterize most psychological determinism as being scientific because psychological determinism is mainly rooted in the methods and assumptions of science. The one big exception is psychoanalysis, and though psychoanalysis has to a remarkable degree been assimilated to the mainstream of psychology, both in its method and theory, it still lies outside of the ordinarily accepted rules of science. Therefore, I shall reserve my treatment of psychoanalysis for the next chapter rather than this one.

As with all aspects of science, psychological determinism has its first stirrings in speculative philosophy. Commentators from time to time have professed to see a connection between scientific determinism and theology,[1] but I think the connection to be forced. Psychological determinism is always hand in hand with the development of materialism and the effort to establish empirical truths about the nature of mind. It also, of course, is the intimate companion of the development of biology.

In the following pages I shall discuss some of the philosophic and biological origins of materialistic determinism in psychology. I do not intend this chapter to be a major essay in the history of ideas, but the complex and sometimes contradictory nature of modern psychological determinism can be understood best in the light of history. In the next chapter I shall examine some of the nonscientific brands of determinism; my purpose in this comparison is to illustrate the contrasting social and moral consequences that different assumptions about determinism produce. In that chapter I shall comment upon psychoanalysis, historical determinism, and theology. In this chapter I write only about scientific determinism.

Scientific determinism, as contrasted with theological determinism, is psychological in nature. That is to say, the varieties of scientific determinism attempt to characterize the actions and ideas of human beings so as to claim that these actions and ideas grow out of a few principles that govern human nature and the place that nature has in the order of things. Even historical or economic determinism is basically psychological in nature even though the aims of these two children of the enlightenment may not be to account for individual human actions but for the activity of whole societies or cultures.

Psychological determinism arises on the twin assumptions that man is, with no exceptions, a part of the natural order of things and that all nature is governed by some laws or principles, accessible, to a degree, by the physical sciences. Though, as I shall show later, determinism is not a necessary or inescapable inference from these assumptions, these may be regarded as premises for a logical argument to that effect. The plausibility of such an argument depends upon more fundamental assumptions.

Twentieth-century man is apt to think of the basic laws of nature as being physical. The more difficult natural laws, such as those of biology and psychology, are, by the common consent of the intellectual world of the late twentieth century, reducible to physical principles. That attitude did not come into existence until the seventeenth century. Natural law, before the seventeenth century, had at least the possibility of a very different basis. It is the seventeenth century, with its reduction of everything to mechanics, that places a very different interpretation on man and his nature that had, however objective it may have been, existed from ancient philosophy on.

Aristotle and the Biological Metaphor

The origins of modern science and hence scientific determinism are with Aristotle, though those origins have to be considered in a special sense. It is difficult to argue that Aristotle was a scientific determinist in the modern sense. As Esper,[2] among many others, has pointed out, Aristotle is fundamentally a biologist. He thought like a nineteenth-century biologist. He was obsessed with dissection and classification. The best of Aristotelian science is rooted in biology. His physics is, at best, clumsy. He is most at home as a describer and classifier of the natural world. Despite the primitive and all too often erroneous nature of his physics, he is a natural philosopher. He is not a metaphysician or epistemologist in the modern sense. That is to say, Aristotle accepts man and everything in the world as a natural and explainable whole. Whatever special characteristics are to be attributed to man, they are a part of the natural whole.

J. R. Kantor, in many places,[3] has argued that Greek philosophers were completely objective—positivists—in their view of man. He asserts that the notion of an inextensible soul or mind separated from man's physical being was imported into western philosophy from Persian sources, the Neoplatonists being the principal transmitters. His argument cannot be entirely correct, for the notion of a disembodied mind is universal among human societies. All peoples everywhere, after all, dream and experience visions of distant or dead persons. The notion that there is a kind of entity in a person independent of the body is as natural to human experience as dreams themselves, though, of course, the modern psychologist will have a natural, in the Aristotelian sense, explanation for dreams. In any event, the notion of a nonmaterial soul, free from the restrictions of the physical world, is common in Greek thought, particularly among those Greeks influenced by the Orphic or Pythagorean notions.

Nevertheless, it is entirely correct to say that Aristotle, in Kantor's sense, was an objective philosopher. The rational soul, as the phrase is usually translated,[4] is simply the name for rationality as a working principle, or, as Kantor would have it, rational activity. Conation, or action, is impelled by two agencies, impulse and will. Impulse acts through sensations in such a way as to cause human beings to avoid pain and seek pleasure. Will is rational, though the results of its actions may not necessarily be rational. There are, according to Aristotle, four souls, or functions, that control living things, but only a small portion of creation possesses the rational function.[5] That only certain beings, namely human beings, possess the rational soul is simply a result of the architecture of nature. It does not imply any special status accorded to man.

My point, in reminding us in this sketchy way of Aristotle was a classifier, and he believed that to classify objects was to understand them. Hence the importance of defining souls so that organisms may be classified according to the special functions they exhibit. Each soul has its own *telos*, or purpose, and the purpose of rationality is to guide the human being in achieving its ends (the final cause). The rational organism is conscious of a principle of ultimate good, and its rational function can be used to guide that organism toward the ultimate good.

My point, in reminding us in this sketchy way of Aristotle's psychology, is simply to show that the modern notion of scientific determinism is not a category that applies to Aristotle's views. We see this even more clearly when we learn that the wisdom of practical reason in Aristotle's psychology is not only to provide knowledge of the right but also the ability to achieve it. Sometimes, of course, rational individuals act badly, and Aristotle wrestled with this problem. The answers he gives to it are complicated and varied. In one place he argues that desire "rises into action" before deliberation is complete. More significantly for my present concern, he also argues that the individual reasons to a conclusion that he or she strongly desires, even though it may not be ultimately good. This certainly sounds like the freedom to make a moral choice. But once again, we must remember that the notion of freedom of will and the possibility of conflict between determined actions and free actions does not emerge in any clear form in Aristotle. Aristotle did not invoke the notion of freedom of moral choice in any of its modern ethical and theological senses. Moral choice is simply a consequence of rationality. He meant to say that it is possible to think right, but not to act right, for action is not identical with reason. It is only guided by reason, as it is guided by other principles.

Aristotle was, in the best modern sense, a naturalist,

and he takes a simple, functional view of will and reason. But, because he classified the nature of beings in the way in which he did, he could not conceive, as the modern thinker can, of all of nature being governed by one principle, aim, or to use Aristotle's word, entelechy. The notion of freedom of choice is simply a part of his naturalism. That there might be something to the contrary never arises in Aristotelian thought.

The Mechanical Metaphor and the Rise of the Modern Age

Leaping from Aristotle to the seventeenth century is a matter of great convenience to my argument, for it places into most elemental contrast Aristotle's organic, goal-directed view of nature, with its consequences for psychology, and the mechanical view of nature that emerges in the seventeenth century and comes into full flower in the eighteenth. The mechanistic view provides a metaphor for psychology that is still with us (consider the ease with which such phrases as "defense mechanism" occur to us).

If the contrast between free will and determinism hardly mattered for Aristotle, it stood near the center of things for the seventeenth century, for the seventeenth century was a time when Christian theology still mattered. The issue of free will and determinism had been firmly set in place by theological argument, both Christian and Muslim. The main outlines of this theological issue properly belong in the next two chapters. Here I simply point out that modern philosophical or scientific determinism (as opposed to theological determinism) arises in an age still dominated by theology. Scientific determinism receives its earliest treatment in the seventeenth century.

Certain mystics aside, those who wrote about psychology in the seventeenth and eighteenth centuries wrote from a point of view that accepts man as part of nature. But it is a vastly different kind of nature than that of Aristotle's. It is the nature of the emerging science of physics, incarnate in classical mechanics. When seventeenth-century philosophers began to think of man as part of nature, they did so in the sense that twentieth-century philosophers do, not in Aristotle's sense. That is one reason why it is so hard for us to see Aristotle as essentially a naturalistic philosopher.

The seventeenth century, then, is the beginning of the attempt to make psychology a part of physics. It is easy, from our vantage point, to be condescending about the clockwork universe that dominated the conception of nature in the seventeenth and eighteenth centuries. Though it permeated the grand Baroque and the Enlightenment, and though we live with its inheritance in the form of mechanistic thought in biology and psychology, it seems quaint. Hydraulically driven statues as a metaphor for human action simply seem bizarre. The trouble is that we know too much biology now. With one great exception, the seventeenth century knew scarcely more physiology and anatomy than did Aristotle.

The one great exception was important, not only in itself, but because no discovery could have better played into the notion of man as mechanism. It was, of course, Harvey's discovery of the circulation of the blood. That the very organizing principle of the body itself was a mechanical device of the highest but simplest sort could not have been more adventitious to the theory that man was a part of the clockwork universe and nothing more. It is true that the principle behind the operation of the heart eluded seventeenth-century science, but that the body was interconnected by a pump operating upon a closed hydraulic system was discovery enough. The very coordination of the body was built on the same principle that ruled the stars in their heaven.

It was both a symbol of the age and an argument for those who, for the first time, could properly utter the reductionistic argument: "Man is nothing but. . . ." In Aristotle's nature, everything had its place. But now man could be reduced to something simpler, the laws of mechanics. Ever since the seventeenth century, the Aristotelian notion of a description of each thing in its place and each thing with its function has given way steadily to the notion that the complex, the organic, reduces to something simpler The unity of the sciences is a realizable goal. Everything, in the end, reduced to physics, even if the reduction is only in principle. Not everyone in the seventeenth century could accept this reduction; indeed, more often than not, it was the privately held view of a tiny minority of thinkers. But in the twentieth century, one must search to find a psychological scientist who would dissent.

Harvey's discovery must surely have been responsible for the notion, commonly advanced in one form or another in the eighteenth century, that the nerves were tubes filled with fluid. This was the conception of David Hartley, the English physician who makes strong claim to be the father of physiological psychology.[6] Hartley's speculation about how the brain and its nerves coordinate the body was based upon the notion of vibrations in a fluid medium. These speculations were important because, for the first time, a theory of the physical action of the body, vibrations in the nerves, was united with a theory of psychological action, namely associationism. But the hydraulic analogy is not only in Hartley; it is everywhere. We all know that Descartes was supposed to have come to his view of organisms as machines by observing the hydraulically operated statues in the royal gardens. It gave a metaphor for organic movement that was to last for more than a century, well into the beginnings of modern biology.

There were determinists among the post-Aristotelian philosophers, even among those who count as being pre-Christian. But these philosophers, for the most part, were not physicalists in the seventeenth-century sense, neither were they naturalistic in the Aristotelian sense. Their concerns were primarily ethical. The Stoics, for example, made determinism a keystone of their ethics. Freedom was reduced by them to assent. But little of this was significant for the rise of psychological or scientific determinism in the seventeenth century. Materialism arose in the context of the beginnings of modern physical science, and it reaches it fullest fruition in the late nineteenth century and early twentieth century under the impetus of the great biological discoveries of that era. But there is another way in which the seventeenth century is the wellspring of modern psychological and scientific determinism.

Brett[7] describes the seventeenth century as the gateway of method. What he meant was that the great arguments about how knowledge is acquired began then. To be sure, philosophers have always made speculations about the origin and nature of knowledge, but in the seventeenth century the argument becomes focused upon the question of method, indeed one might almost say, of scientific method. It was the time of the great insight, variously and differently seen by Descartes, Galileo, Hobbes, and others, that the method of investigation defined the nature of knowledge. Hence, here is one more sense in which the seventeenth century provides the cradle for modern psychology. Psychology in the twentieth century swears its allegiance to the scientific method and abjures speculative philosophy. The split between science and philosophy begins in the seventeenth century and it begins with method.

There is still another respect in which the seventeenth century is critical to the development of modern psychology. It is in this century that dualism receives its modern form.[8] Dualism in the twentieth century has fallen on evil times. It is something that neither contemporary philosophers nor contemporary psychologists like to talk about. Nevertheless, its ghost is very much with us. Dualism is only marginally of significance for determinism. Late in the nineteenth century, when psychology came into full bloom, monists, dualists, and those who regarded the whole question as irrelevant were all determinists. Nevertheless, there is a kind of accidental significance of dualism for determinism, if only in the sense that it is psychologically easier to accept a deterministic position if one is a materialistic monist.

Descartes, of course, is the father of modern dualism. His celebrated view that mind, without physical extension, interacts with the body at a particular locus, the pineal gland, is a very untidy one from the point of view of systematic philosophy. It is the source of terrible paradoxes. Nevertheless, Descartes' dualism is very probably the dualism of the man in the street (the pineal gland aside), who regards mind and body as separate kinds of things that nevertheless influence one another. Fastidious philosophers preferred one or another version of parallelism, even though the whole issue is an embarrassment for the mainstream of modern philosophy and psychology. Despite the mentalistic language of psychoanalysis and some contemporary cognitive the-

orists, as well as the contemporary concern with states of consciousness, dualism has almost disappeared both in psychology
and philosophy.

Medicine, because it both theorizes about states of the
body, and, from the seventeenth century on, is responsible for
many fundamental discoveries in biology, has provided another
framework for the doctrine of determinism. Medicine was not always scientific in the modern sense. It was a fundamental subject,
however, in the medieval universities both in Christian Europe and
in Islam. Paracelsus and a few others argued for the physical nature of medicine, but to a remarkable degree there was an aura of
magic to the practice of medicine. In the seventeenth century
medicine went through the gateway of method to genuine science,
and physicians, both in France and England, were in the forefront
of the development of a materialistic and deterministic psychology.

I shall comment in greater detail in a later section on
the full flowering of the contributions of medicine to the psychological sciences. Suffice it to say here that its great advances at
the end of the eighteenth and beginning of the nineteenth centuries saw the abandonment of the mechanical metaphor. Medicine
gradually returned to the organic metaphor of the ancient world.
Chemistry rather than mechanics became the science of ultimate
reduction.

It was not until the early years of the nineteenth century that material speculations about how ideas were formed and
communicated to muscles in order to create movement had any
foundation in fact whatever. But the early nineteenth century
began to appreciate the electromechanical nature of nerve propa-
gation, and, following Bell and Magendie, it knew that sensory and
motor impulses travel separate routes. The reflex, invented by
Descartes out of the hydraulic analogy,[9] comes to have something
like a foundation in empirical investigation in the early years of
the nineteenth century. The stage is set for a psychological materialism well grounded in physiology, chemistry, and the emerging
science of biology. With these, determinism leaves the restrictions
imposed upon it by the mechanical metaphor and comes to have

a solid foundation in the totality of science, or, to use the twentieth-century phrase, the unity of the sciences.

However, this is probably not the most important aspect of the impact of medicine upon the psychological sciences so far as the subject of this book is concerned—that is to say, the impact of psychological determinism upon political and moral questions in the American context. I refer to the development of what we now call the "medical model" of mental aberration. It is a natural child of the liberal spirit of the Enlightenment, as natural as the Declaration of Independence and the Bill of Rights.

Pinel's removal of the chains from the insane at Bicêtre is one of those great symbolic acts of the age, one that justifies the name Enlightenment. Though it was an act of great humanity, like so many similar actions and theories of the late eighteenth century, it grew out of a materialistic determinism which, when carried to its logical conclusion, places frightening shackles upon the notion of freedom. Thomas Szasz, in various places,[10] has reminded us how the application of the medical model has already begun to erode our notions of political and personal freedom.

I need say only a brief word about one other great figure of the seventeenth century, Thomas Hobbes. Hobbes was more nearly the complete materialist than anyone of his time, though he did not, so far as I can discover, embrace the metaphor of mechanism. His autobiographies, however, imply an influence of Galileo, an influence ordinarily regarded as affecting Hobbes' view of method. Hobbes does speculate about the physiology of the mind. He reduces thinking to some internal substance in the head—the hoary ancestor of all those ideas that describe thought as a secretion of the brain. Hobbes, however, is more important for his political philosophy and his pessimistic view of human morals than for his materialism. Once again, I shall have to defer discussion of a fundamental paradox—the influence of Hobbes upon American political philosophers, particularly those responsible for the Declaration of Independence and the Bill of Rights.

Brett reminds us that Hobbes could talk like a physiologist and yet preserve the common touch of psychological description.[11] That combination—talking like a physiologist while preserving the common talk of everyday psychology—is one of the principal tools in the trade of the propagandist for modern behaviorism, whether of the ordinary variety or the more exotic kind to be found in sociobiology. It is one way of preserving a complete materialistic reductionism in the absence of the empirical evidence to make such a reductionism plausible.

The Nineteenth Century and the Metaphor of Adaptation

Modern determinism becomes only remotely plausible from the scientific point of view in the nineteenth century, and this is chiefly the result of developments in the biological sciences. I have already alluded to the great discoveries in anatomy and in the physiology of the nervous system made in the early years of the nineteenth century. The important consequence of these discoveries for my thesis was to make a clear biological distinction between reflexive and voluntary action. I deal with the distinction between reflexive and voluntary action in a later chapter.

The great climax of nineteenth-century biology was not in anatomy or physiology but was the publication in 1859 of *The Origin of Species*. That book is one of the most compelling testimonies to the importance of ideas in the conduct of men and the ability of ideas to influence almost every aspect of human life. Given the monumental importance of Darwin's invention of the theory of natural selection, it is almost trivial to point out that it transformed psychology. But the importance of psychology in the daily commerce of life in the last quarter of the twentieth century is simply one more testimony to the influence of Darwin and his book.

Biology has become a "reduced" physical science only in the late twentieth century. The biology of the nineteenth century is a biology almost independent of physical *concepts*. This requires a word of explanation.

I use the word physical in two senses. One describes the materials of ordinary experience. Thus, we say that rocks, cells, and houses are physical objects. To describe them as physical in the full epistemological and metaphysical sense requires subtle argument of course, but the ordinary man in the street, with his cheerful simplification of experience, simply accepts them as physical. The other sense of physical makes use of the theory of physics. I use the phrase, "theory of physics" broadly, I mean to encompass the complex network of theory and evidence that exists in those sciences intended to describe the nature of matter and energy.

Until recently, biology was a physical science only in the first sense, not the second. Concepts like cytoplasm, chromosomes, and mitosis are physical only in the first sense. However, DNA chains, semipermeable membranes, and ATP are physical in the second sense. Nineteenth-century biology made use of certain tools discovered by physical and chemical research, but it was not ready to be reduced to physics and chemistry. Those who, like Jacques Loeb, thought it could be had only a few things here and there to point to by way of example. Resistance to reduction is still true of evolution, which, more than a century after the publication of Darwin's book, evokes controversy among physical scientists. Doubts among physicists about the theory of natural selection are not new. Many important nineteenth-century physicists, including Kelvin and Rutherford, had reservations about organic evolution because the time scale demanded by evolution (then on the order of millions rather than billions of years) exceeded any age that nineteenth century physics could grant to the sun.

However, it was the theory of natural selection more than anything else that reintroduced the organic metaphor into psychology and provided for a modern interpretation of Aristotle's entelechy. The new entelechy was survival. And survival was achieved through adaptation. Here is the origin of functionalism in modern psychology, and it is a functionalism not very different in principle from the functionalism of Aristotle. What was new about it was the portrayal of the organism as something buffeted by its environment and so shaped into something that managed to survive and perpetuate itself. This notion of functional adaptation permeated much psychological thinking, particularly in America, in the first quarter of the twentieth century. What is perhaps more important, the notion dominated German biology. Haeckel transformed German biology, and when, late in life, he wrote *The Riddle of the Universe* (1899–1900), he gave popular intellectual voice to the uncompromising notion that all life, including man's, was material. Haeckel's book had a vogue in the early years of the twentieth century, and it was more influential in the spread of materialism among the American writers of naturalistic fiction in the early twentieth century than were writings of Marx or Nietzsche.

The first generation of American psychologists were mainly German educated, not in biology, but in Wundt's experimental psychology. American psychology, to paraphrase Boring,[12] had a German body, but its mind was closer to Spencer's evolutionary psychology. Under the influence of Darwinism, as it was then called, the Americans introduced animals into the psychological laboratory, thus blurring the distinction between biology and psychology.

The Americans were also eager appliers of psychology, even before there was much to apply. In a strange way this eagerness to be practical was a characteristic American transformation of functionalism. Under the influence of functionalism, American psychologists began to leave the traditional problems of sensation and perception, reaction time, and the like and interested themselves in things like personality and motives. They were the first in the wider world to see the importance of Freud. It was G. Stanley Hall who brought Freud to America in 1904 and hence to the attention of the world.

In America psychological *science* became triumphant in a way in which it would not in Europe for another fifty years. There was a heady mixture of evolutionary theory, experimentation in the laboratory, the study of individual differences, applications, the invention of personality and personality theories, and the utter lack of distinction between human beings and animals as tools for psychological research. In such a confusion there can be no single clear set of principles but only an ever-changing sense of consensus. Behaviorism was born out of that mixture. John B. Watson thought he had forever freed psychology from mind. Before, however, we examine the implications of the behavioristic movement, we need to pick up one more thread in that rich American mixture.

Physiological Psychology and the Medical Metaphor

David Hartley was the first physiological psychologist in the sense that he was the first of the long line of theorists who combine speculation about activity in the central nervous system with psychological theory. Real physiology relevant to the study of behavior does not begin until the nineteenth century, and two insights, just about two thirds of the way through that century really gave impetus to physiological psychology. There was the discovery, by Broca, of the specific linguistic deficit associated with damage to the area in the third frontal convolution forever associated with his name. The other, less adventitious—for Broca's notion was but a lucky guess—was made possible by the invention of ether. It was the discovery by the German physiologists Fritsch and Hitzig that electrical stimulation of particular regions in the prefrontal cortex of dogs will elicit movement in particular regions of the body. Evidently the cortex was arranged so that specific cortical cells controlled the movement of particular muscles. The speculations of Gall and Spurzheim appeared to be confirmed, but that was clearly an illusion, for the degree of specificity of cortical tissue is an issue that is still with us. However, the search for the anatomical, physiological, and later, chemical correlates of behavior was on.

All of this is important to the view that behavior can be reduced to its biological and physical substrates. But, except for what was once called psychosomatic medicine and now appears to be rechristened medical psychology, it has had only marginal influence upon the practical side of psychology. The practical side of psychology, including a belief in the complete determination of behavior has, however, received great impetus from medicine. The influence comes not so much from particular medical discoveries as it does from a revolution in medical attitude that took place all through the nineteenth century. One of the great results of the enlightenment was the triumph of the belief that diseases of the mind were diseases of the brain. Even faraway colonial America provided figures in this movement. In the eighteenth and early nineteenth centuries, it was Benjamin Rush (a signer of the Declaration of Independence). Rush's last book was *Diseases of the Mind* (1812), in which he argued that mental disorders were the result of underlying physiological disorders. The physician turned novelist, S. Weir Mitchell, was responsible for the first popular treatment for that most characteristic of nineteenth-century mental disorders, hysteria. Mitchell's "rest cure" held the field until it was displaced by the ideas of Pierre Janet. I note that Mitchell's cure was much more obviously based upon a belief in the physiological cause of the disorder (save for the ancient Greek belief) than anything that preceded it and for most ideas on the subject that immediately succeeded it.

In short, the Americans were among the leaders in the notion that the diseases of the mind were really physical disorders. They were leaders even as early as the establishment of the Republic. Such a view was followed by the notion of neurosis, which appears, in the past ten years or so, to have dropped from popular use if not from the official nomenclatures of the two APAs.

The idea of neurosis, while not originating with them, was popularized by psychoanalysts. It held brief competition in the 1920s with the behavioristic "bad habit"[13] theory, only recently revived in the surge of various therapies based upon behavioral modification. Though much of the naive physicalism of early American psychiatry has disappeared, it has left its legacy in the overwhelming commitment of the American laity to the medical metaphor as the answer to various social problems. We all know that alcoholism is a disease. So is compulsive gambling. Even illicit sexual activity is a disease.[14]

It should be noted that public outrage and a certain amount of political pressure has forced minor retreats in this advance of the medical metaphor. Homosexual advocacy groups have recently and successfully brought pressure upon both the American Psychiatric Association and the American Psychological

Association to remove homosexuality from the list of official disorders. The acquittal of John Hinckley has brought some pressure from the opposite side of the political spectrum. In any event, there is reason to believe that at least the issue of the universal application of the disease principle to aberrations of behavior will at least be debated.

While this movement towards characterizing all manner of social problems as diseases has been protested from time to time by a few literal-minded logicians,[15] it is so engrained in modern American attitudes as hardly to be challenged. I once tried to dissuade an intelligent young undergraduate student in a seminar on ethics and psychology from the belief that anyone who committed a murder was *ipso facto* "sick." I failed. Almost anyone who commits any breach of the prevailing ethical principles, or even anyone who is merely eccentric runs the risk of being described as "a very sick person." In a later chapter I shall explore the effects of this metaphor (that of mental illness) upon our society. Suffice it to say now that it fits the notion of human action as being completely determined as perfectly as anything could.

Behaviorism and the Abolition of Mind

Almost every student of psychology knows that the behavioristic movement began with John B. Watson. Watson had his predecessors, though I do not think that we can count the French materialists of the eighteenth century among them. Also we should note that some of his contemporaries came simultaneously to remarkably similar views. Nor should we discount the influence of H. H. Donaldson and Jacques Loeb upon the young Watson, a graduate student at Chicago at the turn of the century. It is fair to say that behaviorism was in the air. But it is a matter of great importance to label Watson as the father of behaviorism. At the same time we need to realize that Watson's almost messianic vision (in his later propagandist years) fell upon eyes already opened. I need only mention E. L. Thorndike and his hardheaded and down-to-earth functionalism in this respect. Thorndike had an enormous influence, not only upon American psychology, but upon American education (and I suspect educational practices worldwide).

It is not fair to say that Watson discovered Pavlov for the Western world, but he surely popularized him. Pavlov and his contempt for psychological experimentation (as he knew it) and his insistence on physiological experimentation (as it was understood at the end of the nineteenth century) might well have been lost on the Western world for many years if it had not been for Watson's insistence that the conditioned reflex stood at the center of all mentality (an insistence that was only to be undone—within the behavioristic fold—by the great student of behavior of the next generation, B. F. Skinner).

Watson did burst upon the scene with a splash. At age thirty-five he had presented his major manifesto before the psychological establishment in America,[16] and in 1915, at thirty-seven, in his presidential address before the American Psychological Association, he enthroned the conditioned reflex at the center of American and later international behavioristic theory, where it remained for more than a generation.

But, as I have pointed out, his way was prepared by a host of John the Baptists. In every respect, the American blind acceptance of experimentation as *the* tool for psychological research came, if not before, at least contemporaneously with the influence of Watson. And it came from strange and out-of-the-way places. Max Meyer, immigrant German and former student of Stumpf at Berlin, found himself teaching at the University of Missouri in the early years of the century. He preached behaviorism before there was such a thing. He gave his major book the arresting title, *The Psychology of the Other One*. I am told that Meyer used the simile of a train guided by the railroad tracks to describe the life of a person.[17] No more strikingly deterministic metaphor could be found.

Thus, I must argue that the importance of Watson in preparing the ground for the near universal acceptance of scientific determinism cannot be underestimated. We now have three generations of college students who have absorbed the Watsonian ethos much as their forefathers absorbed the Bible. It is altogether ironic that Watson moved in two worlds, the world of the mind (as embodied in the University of Chicago and Johns Hopkins), and the world of advertising, for he spent the last twenty-five years or so of his working life as an executive in the services of two of America's largest and most prosperous advertising firms.

The duality shows in all of his work. His earliest experimental investigations drip with impatience. Later, he and Karl Lashley studied the behavior of migratory birds in the field, something that anticipated by more than a generation the work of the scientific ethologists. He was always impatient to get to human beings, and his last scientific work—before his scandalous divorce made academic life all but impossible—concerned the development of human infants. His bold and forthright environmentalism was a battle cry almost to equal that of Marx's about workers having nothing to lose but their chains: "Give me a dozen healthy infants, well-formed, and my own specified world to bring them up in and I'll guarantee to take any one at random and train him to become any type of specialist I might select—doctor, lawyer, artist, merchant, chief, and yes, even beggar-man." [18] No one, not even Marx, could have been either more dramatic or more wrong.

Watson's determinism and its real influence is often now overlooked as we smirk at his simple-minded environmentalism. I have the impression that his environmentalism developed much as an inspired political orator or preacher might gradually bring himself as well as his audience into the conviction of the rectitude of so absurd a position. I hasten to point out that the absurdity of the position has nothing to do with what used to be called the nature-nurture controversy as it does with the insanity of anyone ever achieving that degree of control over another. It might be possible to produce a vegetable of sorts. But Watson's list?

The most important and best known of Watson's many successors is B. F. Skinner. I shall not say anything about Skinner's brand of behaviorism here because I deal with it extensively in later chapters. Suffice it to say that, Skinner aside, Watson's environmentalism has been muted, and with the so-called sociobiologists apparently turned on end. But Watson's influence is not to be measured by the ideas of his psychological and scientific successors; it is to be measured by the extent to which behaviorism has come to permeate not only psychology but the totality of American society. Most textbooks define psychology as the study of behavior; *Time* magazine has a feature section labeled *Behavior*. As with many departments of psychiatry, the department of psychiatry at the University of Virginia has been renamed the Department of Behavioral Medicine and Psychiatry. The behavioral sciences is now the collective term by which we refer to psychology and all of its allied disciplines. There is no doubt; Watson's victory is a real one.

Psychology: The American Synthesis

The worldwide enterprise we call psychology was born in Europe, but it received its present heterogeneity and preeminence in America. Its very heterogeneity is its saving grace, for a discipline that speaks with so many voices would find it difficult to impose dogma. That the diversity sometimes leads to contradictions is also a virtue, for it saves the bulk of us from many a messiah. Consider the case of individual differences and the heredity-environment issue. Given the present climate it is hard to recollect that, in the early days of mental testing, there was almost universal agreement among the testers that intelligence, or whatever the test measured, was determined by heredity. H. H. Goddard's *The Kallikak Family*, which contrasted the bad and good psychological genes respectively in the descendents of the Kallikaks, is now forgotten. The sterilization laws have either entirely disappeared or are no longer enforced. Perhaps we should not be surprised that the strong egalitarian streak in American life won out over the hereditarians. Perhaps it matters only to a few of us that the issue of heredity and environment in abilities as well as other psychological characteristics is essentially unsolvable given present techniques. However we have been saved from a rigid hereditarian determinism by the fact that—whatever the genetic contribution may be to the outcome of individual psychological test results— heredity cannot completely determine performance. That we have moved in the direction of an equally rigid environmentalism should not be surprising. Excess in matters of psychological de- terminism are commonplace. One of the things this book pleads for is a humble confession of ignorance where the available facts and techniques justify little else.

The myriad theories of psychotherapy and the various practices, including group dynamics, that have grown out of the American melting pot really fall outside of the purview of science, however loosely that term may be applied within psychology. Therefore, I treat these things in the next chapter, devoted to deterministic views outside of the scientific tradition.

Chapter Three

The Varieties
of Determinism

The notion that human action can be explained in some way or another is a cultural universal. It pervades myth, religion, philosophy, literature, and, as we have just seen, it has become the most fundamental article of faith in the scientific study of human beings and their ways. Because all of these various ideas about how we are controlled impinge on at least some of us some of the time, they are worth making explicit and worth comparing. That is what this chapter attempts to do. Once again, the purpose is not to review the history of determinism so much as it is to provide a context for the growing ethos in American society that accepts our actions as controlled and therefore beyond both blame and praise. The closest continuity to the previous chapter is provided by psychoanalysis and the growing interest in psychotherapy. Therefore, I begin with a discussion of these.

Psychoanalysis and Psychotherapy

I have chosen to treat psychoanalysis and psychotherapy separately from the treatment of the antecedents of modern scientific determinism. I have so chosen because to call psychoanalysis scientific is to abuse the language. Psychoanalysis, to put it simply and baldly, has none of the characteristics of true science. Its so-called facts cannot be established by independent and objective investigation. Its theories cannot be objectively related to any body of facts, as scientists understand the notion of fact, and its fullest appreciation comes only with a faith in the correctness of its assumptions and beliefs. It is couched in metaphoric, indeed in mythic terms, and its most important intellectual consequences are literary. At best it is a *Geisteswissenshaft*.

It is a little more arbitrary to treat psychotherapy as if it had no scientific basis. As everyone now knows, there is something called behavioral therapy, which, for good or ill, derives from a branch of scientific psychology, and, largely under the impetus provided by the National Institute of Mental Health, there have been some attempts to assess objectively the outcomes of the myriad varieties of psychotherapy now available. Nevertheless, psychotherapy is best viewed as a kind of personal relationship, perhaps based upon one or another psychological theory or even simply based upon some intuitive understanding of human nature possessed by the therapist, but it is at the bottom a personal relationship. I wish to point to the fact that the kind of knowledge that goes into psychological treatment owes far more to opinion, faith, and intuition than it does to scientific investigation. The transition from priest to therapist has done little to alter that fact.

Psychoanalysis and the Metaphor of Tragedy

Stanley Edgar Hyman, in his fascinating treatment of Darwin, Marx, Frazer, and Freud, *The Tangled Bank*,[1] reminds us that Freud's writings in the original German are not only of an intensely literary nature but are of a very high order of literary quality. Hyman compares Freud to Goethe. If the English translations of Freud are, more often than not, heavy-handed, the literary nature of his work is still obvious.

Scientific writing, except for essays in the most abstract regions of mathematics, is often metaphoric in nature. But the metaphors of science are those of the easily comprehended physical world. The Rutherford-Bohr model of the atom is that of a metaphoric solar system; to be sure, no one of us yet has seen the solar system in its entirety, but, 300 years after Galileo, we understand and live with it. To cast the atom into the form of a nuclear sun with its revolving electronic planets, however naive, fits what we can already understand. Sometimes, in contemporary physics, the concrete metaphor disappears into coy abstraction. Consider the use of the word *colored* in connection with the Joycean-named particles invented by Gell-Mann, quarks. But mainly the metaphors of science are intended to aid human intuition in understanding some process or structure not immediately apparent to the senses.

The metaphors of psychoanalysis are of a very different character. They are anthropomorphic and demonic, and they are contained within the framework of a view of human life as drama, specifically tragic drama. As everyone knows, Freud drew heavily upon Greek tragedy as the source for the metaphors that riddle his theories. A central element in the psychoanalytic theory of psychosocial development is described as Oedipal. It is perhaps less obvious that the relations among the id, the ego, and the superego (which is properly not a character but a chorus) are portrayed by Freud as actors in a drama. It is easy from reading Freud to extract the image of the id and the ego as demons warring over the possession of the human soul, as the Deity and Mephistopheles warred over Faust's soul. And the warfare is ritualistic. It repeats in each person, and it results, in every family, in the same story.

What did Freud accomplish with these strange metaphors? First of all, he invented, in its modern form, the concept of the unconscious mind. This is an historical misfortune, for the peculiar constraints Freud both directly and by implication put upon his notion of the unconscious inhibited for nearly three quarters of a century a proper understanding of the range and depth of unconscious processes in human mentality. One can only speculate upon how things might have been if the world had paid attention to the innovative investigations (often incorrectly called experiments) of the Würzburg psychologists,[2] who were Freud's contemporaries.

The psychologists at the University of Würzburg stumbled, as it were, upon the unconscious. As a consequence they did not see it as the power-source, so to speak, of the mind, but simply as a mode in the process of thinking. Almost all German psychology of the time was based upon introspective (more accurately, as the criticisms of the Würzburgers by orthodoxy made clear, retrospective) inspection of the contents of the mind when some simple mental action was undertaken. What the Würzburgers discovered, to their astonishment, was that when asked to think through some simple problem (such as giving a supraordinate association to a particular word), the solution came without any intrusion into consciousness *of the process that led to the solution*. There was no image, as the tradition of the British empiricists would have had it. There was simply nothing. Just a brief period of time and then the solution. The Würzburgers correctly reasoned that there *must have been an intervening process*, but it was simply not available to conscious inspection.

Because all orthodox psychologists of the time believed that all mental processes were conscious, there was a great controversy between the Würzburgers and their critics. That controversy threw the then reigning instrument of experimental psychology, introspection, into doubt and disrepute, and very probably hastened the acceptance of behaviorism. But in the last years of the twentieth century, largely through some insights provided by generative linguists, who remind us that we invent sentences requiring mental activity of some high and unknown degree of complexity entirely unconsciously, we accept the notion of unconscious thinking. In fact, I suspect that most cognitive psychologists would now agree that nearly all mental processes are unconscious.[3] Freud thought so too, of course, but he so invested operations of the unconscious with primitive, demonic power, that it would be difficult, from his perspective, to see that so prosy a matter as solving easy arithmetic problems is the result of processes as unavailable to conscious inspection as the motivation for being rude to a close friend.

The fact of the matter is that Freud, so far as the world

is concerned, did invent the unconscious. He is also credited with discovering the sexual interests of children, though surely no one could deny that this was not only obvious but borrowed wisdom. Freud differs largely from his predecessor, Moll, in this matter by the fact that Freud was not content merely to describe case histories. Freud invests childhood sexuality with the elaborate garments of his theory.

He also invented the notion that the earliest experiences of life are the most important in *determining* character. Other thinkers had, of course, hinted that such was the case, but it was Freud who gave it dramatic status by incorporating it into his universal tragic drama. In this same connection, Freud developed a theory of the ontogenesis of the human psyche. But what is important is not that he did all of these things but that he did them together. He pulled all of these ideas together into a system. To be sure it is the most ramshackle system imaginable, but it is a system. Its internal contradictions are, perhaps, no more a problem to its explicators than the problems of dogmatic theology are to those who explain it, but it surely is a problem of a very different order than the problems of those who try to make sense of scientific theory.

For good or ill, the twentieth century has lived with the consequences of Freud's ideas for all of its allotted span. Fortunately, perhaps, these ideas were set down over a long period of time in what can only be described as an eternal process of becoming.

Freud frequently changed his mind, and to the extent that he did, we are freed from the constraints of a monolithic system forever engraved in stone. That, together with the literary and metaphoric quality of Freud's writings makes it possible to live with the enormous influence of psychoanalysis.

Freud, like Marx, was dogmatic, and he was an egotist. He was also paternalistic to the extent of being authoritarian. It is not surprising that much of his work has come down to us in the spirit of dogmatic theology. His writings are treated, not as, say, those of Descartes or of Darwin but as living realities, much as the Bible is treated by fundamentalist preachers.

Much of what he did thus remains unchanged by time.

As always, however, dogmatism breeds heresies. And there have been attempts at various times and places to absorb the Freudian legacy into other traditions. At Yale University's Institute of Human Relations in the thirties and forties there was a considerable effort, ludicrous both in intent and results, to wed psychoanalysis to Yale-style behaviorism. In more recent years, there has been an absorption and softening of the faith so as to make it generally compatible with the ideas and results coming out of the ethological study of infant-parent interactions in man and other mammals.

Be that as it may, classical psychoanalysis was rooted in one firm notion. It was that mental life was completely determined by the processes described in psychoanalytic theory. The extent of this determinism is so vast as to defy any simple summation. It suffuses the works of Freud, his followers, his apologists, and even his apostates. However, to make my point plausible, I shall illustrate by example.

The Determination of Everything and Unconscious Thinking

I choose my example from one of the most influential, important, and revealing of the works of Freud, *The Psychopathology of Everyday Life*.[4] The example occurs in the first chapter, and it was drawn from a paper published in 1898. It concerns an anecdote taken from a vacation trip that Freud made in the then Austrian provinces of Bosnia and Herzegovina. Freud converses with a stranger on the trip. He asks the stranger if he had ever been to Orvieto to see the frescoes painted by. . . . Freud could not remember the name, *Signorelli*, and instead he thought of *Botticelli* and *Beltraffio*. Freud attributes his failure of memory to the disturbance in his mental life produced by the preceding topic of conversation. He and his acquaintance had been talking about the fatalism of the Turks in Bosnia and Herzegovina. Freud remembered that if you tell them nothing can be done for a sick person, they reply: "Herr, what is there to be said?" Freud then goes on to explain to the reader that these Turks prize sexual enjoyment above everything, and he recalled a colleague's Turkish patient once saying

"Herr, you must know that if *that* comes to an end then life is of no value." Though Freud remembered this piece of ethnic misinformation he suppressed it because he did not want to refer to such indelicate matters to a stranger. Finally, Freud was, he tells us, much under the influence of some news that had arrived while he was staying at *Trafoi*. The news was that a patient, suffering from "an incurable sexual disorder" had committed suicide.

Freud then explains that the forgetting of Signorelli's name was not a chance event. There was a motive. The unconscious machinery worked as follows: The name *Signorelli* was divided in two. The *Signor* part is translated as Her(r) as in Herzogovina and Bosnia. The *Bo* part of *Bosnia* unites with the *elli* fragment from *Signorelli* to produce the false memory, *Botticelli*. The transformation is under the influence of "Herr, what is there to be said?" In addition, the *Bo* fragment of Bosnia leads to the false name, *Boltraffio*. But that is helped by the repression of the bad news at *Trafoi* (the similarity of *traffio* to *Trafoi* is the medium).

Thus we have the unconscious in a very short time doing an elaborate linguistic and semantic analysis of a series of names and words and linking them in such a way as to prevent the hapless Freud from remembering the name of an artist. What is implausible about the whole account is not the elaborateness of the process, nor indeed even the associations among the names and the name-fragments, but simply that *a particular analysis is correct*. There are countless ways one could imagine the presumed repression to take place. We are a bit limited in constructing alternative scenarios to Freud's, for like the writer of detective fiction, Freud can hold back or tell us what he pleases in describing such an incident. Freud has, however, simply given us one of many possibilities.

There is nothing too complicated for unconscious mental processes, for all but a trivial part of our ordinary thinking, including problem solving, can be accomplished without the least intrusion into consciousness. Furthermore, it is not implausible to suppose that many errors of speech, instances of forgetfulness, or wrong memory are motivated. What is implausible is *any particular* version of almost any such example and the assumption that these, along with every twist of ordinary thought, are rigidly controlled by a set of motives.

Stanley Edgar Hyman makes comparison between Freud and that creation of A. Conan Doyle, Sherlock Holmes.[5] He sees a remarkable resemblance between Freud and Holmes. Conan Doyle wrote fiction, and therefore he could use all of the puppet-tricks of the novelist to exhibit the certitude and rectitude of Holmes' inspired guesses, incorrectly labeled as deductions by Doyle. Holmes appears to be infallibly correct simply because the novelist doesn't just know the right answers, he *creates* them.

In the same way, Freud can, with an air of infallible brilliance, create the correct interpretation of some bungled action or slip of the tongue. As with some of Holmes' guesses, some of Freud's interpretations seem, on close analysis, to be more plausible than others. The point is, however, none of them, even the most plausible, can be verified by anything that a working scientist would accept as reasonable empirical evidence. On the other hand, it is possible to speculate upon the influence an analyst may bring to bear in creating in a patient a set of symptoms, or even in creating a case history. *There is simply no way to know* the extent to which such imaginative processes go on in the course of psychoanalysis.

Psychoanalysis, Marxism aside, is the purest example that I know about of the assertion of the scientific correctness of a point of view in the absence of any method of proof. Freud regarded himself as a scientist, and he occasionally uses the metaphor, dissection, for what he did. But can anyone tell where the dissection ends and creation begins? There is nothing by way of the usual canons of science to justify not only the system as a whole but modest exemplifications of it as in the anecdote about the vacation in Bosnia and Herzegovina. Everything must be taken by faith, and only the complete absence of any theology together with Freud's implacable atheism kept me from placing this whole discussion in the section on theological determinism.

It is true that, from time to time, there have been timid and largely unsuccessful efforts to establish links between something close to genuine science and psychoanalysis. The difficulty in this matter can be appreciated when one considers the problems inherent in any effort to associate the major psychoanalytic constructs, the libido, the ego, the id, and the superego, with anything that grows out of biological or psychobiological investigation. True, people have occasionally murmured about the libido and "sex drives," but any careful examination of comparative sexual behavior reveals subtle complexities that elude such an easy identification. Most efforts bring a smile to the knowledgeable. I remember an old undergraduate text (I mercifully have forgotten the author's name) that argued, tentatively to be sure, that the id was located in the thalamus (the author might better have chosen the hypothalamus), the ego in the parietal lobes, and the superego in the frontal lobes (the latter identification still persists in some out-of-the-way places). As quaint as all of this seems, who has a better scheme for uniting the major structural notions of psychoanalysis with the nervous system?

The fact of the matter is that in many ways psychoanalysis was born two centuries too late. Were it invented in the sixteenth century, its extravagant metaphors, the absence of any real contact with science, and the high tragedy of its determinism would have made it at home. Only its Darwinian functionalism and its insistence upon the libido as the wellspring of action would have made it alien to that century. Why did it spread so, particularly in America? That is a question, of course, that admits only speculation as an answer. However, it must have touched something very important in the intellectual context of the times.

Psychotherapy

I have only the briefest word to say about psychotherapy. Ironically, it is here that the psychoanalytic description of processes in human interactions come closest to being plausible. The whole elaborate machinery of psychoanalytic therapy, with its transfer, countertransference, etc., must have some reality in what, after all, is an intense personal interaction of a particular sort. There is no doubt but that the peculiar features of psychoanalytic practice are likely to induce in people who would otherwise be quite different similar patterns of reactions. Partly, I suppose, this is because one must believe in order to persist in the process, and if one believes, then certain consequences will follow. Nor is this matter limited to psychoanalytic therapy. Various other kinds of specialized, systematic therapies produce patterns of similarity among those patients who accept them.

There is nothing necessarily deterministic about psychotherapy. In fact, several of the better-known systematic therapies place great stress on spontaneity. However, those therapies, like psychoanalysis, which search for causes in order to "cure" a patient must make use of imaginative reconstruction of what the patient's life must have been like. The notion that a particular pattern of neurotic behavior must have a particular cause and thus be "cured" in a particular way makes assumptions that, like all assumptions about historical causes, are impossible of proof.

This focus upon particular causes is a feature that psychoanalysis shares with various behavioral therapies. These therapies, and in particular those that are aimed at phobias and the like, assume that deviant behavior is the result of a particular kind of learning. Phobias are peculiar things; even so ascribing their cause to the process of classical conditioning has a certain appeal about it. We do know that such conditioning can produce profound aversions, and many phobias date from particular experiences. But then, phobias are peculiar, and they are complicated. Assigning them to classical conditioning is probably an oversimplification.

Psychotherapists who advocate one or another of the various "deep" therapies argue that behavioral therapy for the purpose, say, of "curing" a phobia is hopelessly oversimple. It attacks the symptoms, not the real cause. And apparently it sometimes is the case that the attempt to eliminate a phobia with behavioral techniques fails, and it even sometimes happens that the removed phobia is replaced by another one. Nevertheless, a certain degree of plausibility attaches to the behavioral theory of phobias. And, as behavior theory argues, phobias appear to arise precisely in that system which cannot easily if at all be subjected to voluntary control, the system governed by the principles of

Pavlovian or classical conditioning. There is a literature that one must label as scientific which deals with this matter. Because, however, case histories are unique events—historical events—we can never really be as certain about this matter as we can, say, of a diagnosis arrived at by making a throat culture.

Even if the conditioning theory of phobias is correct, we must remember that it applies to *involuntary behavior*. Behavior therapy, or any therapy applied to *voluntary behavior*, is quite another matter. Psychotherapy, in any event, is a complex interaction between two people, or in the case of group therapy, among many people, the nature of which we only dimly understand. It is an art and not a science. There are good therapists and bad ones, no matter what their persuasion. And it is even possible that holding a particular point of view does give the therapist a place from which to start. The notion, however, that the process is completely under the control of some theory is one that cannot help but get in the way of sensible treatment.

The Determinism of Historical Necessity

Now we leave psychological matters for a while and turn to a larger framework of human experience. We turn to history. One of the striking features of social thought in the nineteenth and twentieth centuries is the rise of the notion of historical necessity. It had surfaced here and there before, but it is invented in its modern form by Hegel and, of course, redefined by Marx. Hegel might be said to be the father of the philosophy of history, but it is Marx's ideas about history that have dominated the twentieth century.

Marx and the Metaphor of Struggle

The main features of Marx's views of the nature of history are well known. A struggle between the proletariat and capitalists is the inevitable result of the rise of capitalism itself.

That struggle is preceded by the ever falling state of the workers and the ever growing wealth of the capitalists. Out of the struggle comes some kind of synthesis that leads to an earthly paradise beyond history itself. The struggle grows out of the inevitable control of political and social events by the forces and conditions of production. Capitalism itself is a natural process, the result of the evolution of the forces and conditions of production. Equally inevitable is the class struggle that results from the cumulation of capital.

The Marxian view of historical necessity is Hegelian. But Marx substitutes a materialistic economic determinism for Hegel's idealistic historical dialectic. And in so doing, he, by implication, becomes a psychological determinist as well as an historical determinist. The will of the capitalist and the will of the worker are in helpless conflict. It is so decreed by the inescapable laws of economic history.

But there is in Marx a strange mixture of Hegelian philosophy and revolutionary fervor. In the *Manifesto*, the bourgeoisie are portrayed as some ravenous beast impelled by hideous instinct. Such a vision takes some of the edge off the icy historical necessity that suffuses much Germanic philosophy of history. The metaphor of the struggle is, in a curious way, reassuring. As inevitable as the outcome may be, there are always unexpected elements in a struggle. It is not, as in Hegel, merely a matter of a confrontation of disembodied ideas, it is a conflict between a ravenous capitalism which must "nestle everywhere, settle everywhere, establish connections everywhere"[6] and the increasingly restive exploited proletariat. Capital itself as a beast is, so far as I know, never explicitly stated in Marx, but certainly the image is latent in his polemic writing.

But bourgeois society is also "like a sorcerer, who is no longer able to control the powers of the nether world whom he has called up by his spells." The death which the bourgeoisie has called into existence for itself comes from the very class it has created, the proletariat. As in Freud, the metaphor of high drama is always in the background of Marx's writings. The demon wills its own destruction. That destruction is, of course, inevitable, and so the will is inevitable. Though the powerful polemics of Marx make us momentarily forget the iron grip of determinism, it is there.

Marx's materialism, and hence his psychological determinism, is of a very special sort. For Marx everything—social organization, spiritual values, what have you—is determined by the material conditions of production. It is not just that man is material, a part of nature, it is that his special characteristics are determined by the fact that *human beings are productive*. Humanity itself is defined by the production of the means of life. It is this fundamental character of Marx's determinism that places him squarely in the tradition of historical necessity rather than in the tradition of psychological determinism.

Finally, we should note that Marx, along with many other determinists, is not above using the rhetoric of freedom. Brenkert,[7] in his essay on freedom and private property in Marx, argues that Marx condemned private property precisely because he prized freedom. But this notion of freedom is a very different one from the notion of political freedom espoused by the American founding fathers. It is, among other things, freedom from fortuity. It is useful, from time to time, to remind ourselves that notions like freedom have very different meanings in different contexts.

Spengler and the Metaphor of Organic Growth and Decay

Spengler may stand as the most characteristic representative of philosophers of history. Spengler is often regarded as being at the other end of the political spectrum from Marx. If so, that is not nearly so important as is his unrelieved pessimism. Spengler is in the Hegelian tradition without being a Hegelian. And he is the most thorough exponent of the doctrine of historical necessity. He does not equivocate in the faith, as does Marx, by calls to action. No action is possible. The very last words of *The Decline of the West* (in the translation by Atkinson) are:

For us, however, whom a Destiny has placed in this Culture and at this moment of its development—the moment when money is celebrating its last victories, and the Caesarism that is to succeed

approaches with quiet, firm step—our direction, willed and obligatory at once, is set for us within narrow limits, and on any other
terms life is not worth the living. We have the freedom to do the
necessary or do nothing. And a task that historic necessity has set
will be accomplished with the individual or against him. D*ucunt Fata*
volentem, nolentem trahunt.[8]

These words were written in 1918 amidst the apocalyp-
tic scenes of the end of World War I. And in the light of subsequent
history, who is to say that Marx is a better prophet than Spengler?
However, I produce the quotation to make a different point.

I use the quotation to illustrate the fact that the doctrine of historical necessity does not necessarily imply complete
psychological determinism. "With the individual or against him."
Within the limits of the tragic drama of the growth and death of
civilizations, individuals may live out their lives in peace and judgment. This point is particularly important because within the
framework of theology a similar distinction has grown up, particularly in Christianity. The complete determination of everything by
God does not absolve the human being from making free choices.

But within the larger political and social sphere, Spengler tells us, whatever we do and however we do it, the result is
always the same in the end, for that end is determined by where
we are in the life cycle of a particular civilization. While Spengler
uses the metaphor of organic growth and decay to a degree that
suggests he believed that cultures really were organisms of a kind,
he also uses the metaphor of the passing year. There are several
charts at the end of vol. 1 of *The Decline of the West*, and one of these
shows four "contemporary" cultures, Indian, Classical, Arabian,
and Western, with their various events listed in the spring, sum-
mer, autumn, and winter of existence. The very last entry for winter
is "spread of a final world-sentiment." For Indian culture it was
Indian Buddhism, for the classical culture it was Hellenic-Roman
stoicism from 200 on, for Arabian culture it is practical fatalism in
Islam after 1000, and for our Western culture it is ethical socialism
after 1900.

So it is that all cultures die with a faith in fatalism or

practical determinism, and Spengler thought that he had pointed to the end of Western culture by invoking an ethical system that was materialistic and deterministic. As with all of his comparisons, critics were quick to point out, this one was based upon a very elastic scheme for determining "contemporary" events and values. Nevertheless, one must admit that Spengler gives voice to a widespread attitude, more evident among European intellectuals than among Americans (for perhaps appropriate reasons) in our time. It is the belief that the Western world is near its end. With the beginning of the nuclear age, that belief is only periodically superseded by a belief in the imminence of a worldwide nuclear holocaust.

In any event, the modern world finds many expressions of a "practical fatalism," to use Spengler's phrase. Spengler himself has never been very influential among American intellectuals, but there is justification for including him in the context of a discussion of American values and ideas because the idea of inevitable decline is widespread. One hears it voiced by blue-collar workers and by managers. Also, Spengler reminds us of the potency of ideas in human life in a curiously inverted way. The deep content of ideas, according to Spengler, is determined by the place in the cultural life cycle, but the particular manifest contents of ideas inspire and stir men to action.

I cannot resist a further editorial comment on Spengler. Perhaps it is not the final world sentiment that is important in decline as much as it is the absence of one. It is often said that the intellectuals and leaders, perhaps even the common people, in the Soviet Union no longer believe in the cliches of Marxism-Leninism. Perhaps so, but in the Western world and in the third world one finds plenty of intellectuals who still fervently believe in the destruction of capitalism and the triumph of the proletariat, even though one suspects that much of this belief is fueled by a fury of hate against America. What is more important for our concerns, however, is to inquire whether or not Americans still believe in personal and political freedom, and if they do, whether or not they simultaneously accept the notion that we are controlled by implacable forces.

Theological Determinism

Theological determinism, in the higher religions, rests upon one fundamental assumption, the omnipotence of God. God is not only omniscient; He is omnipotent, and, therefore, He not only knows everything that is to happen but also causes all things. This assumption creates a fundamental problem, not to say a paradox for Christianity, with its twin notions of sin and salvation. If there is sin, we must be free to commit it, and if we are to be saved, we must make a deliberate decision to do so.

The attempts to solve this problem are almost as numerous as theologians. The most famous solutions are those by Augustine and Calvin, who both call upon predestination. We must remember that determinism and predestinarianism are not the same thing. We also must remember that not all Christian theologians accept the notion. Hans Küng tells us that the Church's theologians have wrestled with the question, "without being able to lift the veil of mystery."[9]

Christian Predestination and the Freedom of the Will

It is a matter of choice whether to deal with the predestination-freedom-of-the-will problem in this chapter or the next. I do so here chiefly to show that, contrary to misconception, the doctrine of predestination is not an ordinary kind of determinism.

I shall sketch out, in far too few words, Augustine's notion of predestination.[10] Augustine solved the problem by supposing two kinds of freedom to exist: the freedom to make choices, and the freedom to achieve ends. The ability to choose makes one ethically responsible for one's own actions. In this, Augustine agreed with Pelegius. But Augustine analyzed the second kind of freedom into a subtle set of distinctions. There were three fundamental states: the ability to sin; the ability not to sin; and the inability to sin. Only Christ possessed the last. In his fall, Adam, and all of the rest of us, lost the ability not to sin. But despite the necessity of sinfulness which results, God in his mercy graciously predestines salvation for some of us. This neither removes our ability to sin, nor does it excuse us from erroneous choices. Though our sinfulness and possible salvation are foreordained, we are free to make choices, even though God knows what those choices are beforehand and foreordains them as He foreordained everything. God must witness a human tragedy in which He not only knows the end but which He created. At the same time the human actors must choose their own lives and actions.

In this way the Augustinian doctrine divorces determinism and predestination. But from the very beginning, Augustine's solution led to problems. If our destiny is prearranged, what is the value in doing anything? In particular, why should we strive to do right? These questions have been answered in various ways by other theologians, and in the next chapter, I shall briefly touch on some of these answers. The point here is that predestination does not mean determination. Christian theology would be impossible without the freedom to sin.

I make this point in order to introduce a proposition fundamental to this book: Complete psychological determinism is incompatible with any notion of moral or ethical principle, and to the degree that we accept *degrees* of determinism, we diminish the possibilities of moral choice. The notion of psychological determinism is not the only conception in the modern world that threatens moral and ethical choice and freedom, but it is one of the most important. And, because it comes in our day clothed in the beneficence of the social sciences, it is insidious.

Having said that, I hasten to point out that we always face paradoxes in dealing with such ultimate questions. One of the most rigidly moralistic of the world's great religions has been, for a thousand years now, committed to a complete theological determinism. Before commenting upon the example provided by Islam, however, I shall say a brief word about Calvinism, for conventional wisdom in the study of American culture says that it was Calvin's notions that molded a basic theme of American ethical and political thought.

Calvinism and the American Experience

We think of Calvinism in connection with the notions of determinism and predestination in American thought not so much because, on these questions, Calvin differs from Augustine or because of Calvin's notion of total depravity (it is this notion that is supposed to be so important to the Puritan foundations of American thought). I shall comment shortly on determination in American fiction, but it is my view that determinism as reflected among American writers (taking a certain genre to be a reflection of the common thought) is not so much Christian as it is utterly atheistic or pagan. That applies even to Hawthorne (consider *The Marble Faun*). I shall try to point out that a major component in American determinism lies in popular science rather than in Calvinism. Calvinism is important. However, a whole spectrum of authors of the late nineteenth century and early twentieth century— Dreiser, London, Jeffers, and Crane—owes more to science than to theology. Even Hawthorne is more fascinated with the notion of depravity than he is with that of predestination.

No commentary on determinism and predestination in America could be complete without at least a mention of Jonathan Edwards. The question of the extent of Edwards' influence in the American mind is an important one, and I deal with it altogether too quickly and superficially. Suffice it to say that Edwards adds a new dimension to American puritanism. or perhaps more accurately, provides us with a convenient doctrinal source for another dimension of American puritanism. To the Calvinistic notion of total depravity, he adds the burden of moral responsibility, moral responsibility in the absence of any sense of reward. It is, of course, the ultimate reduction of the predestinarianism of Augustine. If Christianity was to combine God's will with moral responsibility, the individual Christian was left with the necessity of being moral in the face of the bleakest of prospects.

Islam and the Determination of Fate

Wherever possible, I have limited myself to discussing intellectual and ethical themes close to the mainstream of American life. And while there are to be found in the late twentieth century significant numbers of Americans who are followers of Islam, Islam has never played in this country the important role that evangelical Christianity, Roman Catholicism, or even Judaism have. I turn to a brief account of Islam in order to provide an example of complete theological determinism and at the same time to show that it is possible for a theologically driven determinism to be associated with a moral standard of the most unbending sort.

Islam was not always so deterministic. Muslim theology was in steady ferment during the first three centuries after the death of the prophet, Mohammed.[11] One of the earliest conflicts was over freedom and necessity. Moore tells us that this conflict had its origin in practical matters rather than in the theological question of the omnipotence of God. The rulers argued for determinism, Moore claims, because their authority came from God, and, therefore, resistance to that authority was a form of impiety. The Caliphs, went the argument, were "irresponsible instruments of the inscrutable divine will," and they were to be obeyed as a kind of obedience to God.

By the death of the most famous of all orthodox Muslim theologians, al-Ashari in 935, a determinism of the most rigid kind became virtually the only position possible for a Muslim. God is both the creator of men and their acts. Voluntary action is created in us by God. While, as Moore points out, one can find similar passages in Luther, they are never central to Luther's theology as they were to al-Ashari's. God not only causes human actions, he creates human sensations. As an orthodox catechism has it, if He were so inclined He could cause us to feel heat upon touching ice. Similarly, right and wrong are known only through revelation.

My major point in providing this brief account of Islamic determinism is to show that piety and a rigid code of moral standards are not incompatible with a strict theological determinism. I have heard rumors of various faiths in which a strict and complete theological determinism has been used to excuse the most licentious and depraved behavior on the grounds that what-

ever is done is the will of God. I have not been able to find any
serious reference to such sects in the major religions, though I
have seen various popular accounts that argued the monk Raspu-
tin so believed. In any event, Islam is a monument to the contrary.
Practically, in one society at least, and in one in which theology
pervades every aspect of life, a strict and complete theological
determinism has been for a millennium compatible with both a
strict moral code and a high degree of observance of that code. It
reminds us of a fundamental truth: the nature of the effects of any
particular idea depend upon the historical context in which that
idea has its influence.

Finally, a word of comment on one other aspect of
Islam and its theological determinism. I have argued in an earlier
work[12] that social-psychological studies cannot be, in the strictest
scientific sense, causal. Causal investigations in social psychology
are, almost without exception, either trivial or fraudulent. Given
that view, I cannot easily subscribe to popular views about national character and its determination. Ascribing particular features of a culture to some prevailing custom or pattern of human
relations, ignores, among other things, the fact that all things in
the world of human relations occur in particular contexts. So I
resist the temptation to examine the vulgar presuppositions that
are behind the view that Islam is inherently fatalistic. Islamic determinism is embedded in a complex social matrix. And, furthermore, Islam is not all of a piece. There is an Arab culture, to be
sure, but at one end of the Islamic world there is the independent
Berber culture and at the other end Indonesia. The extent to which
a cultural ethos of fatalism pervades Islam must remain a matter
of opinion. The psychosocial observer, at best, can only note con-
fluences and contradictions in cultural features. Any attempt to
draw causal inferences replaces the neutral eye of the observer
with the faith of the believer.

Furthermore, I hasten to add, the world of Islam, as I
write, is in the midst of a convulsive revolution unprecedented in
its history. From the tenth century through the nineteenth, Islam
survived more or less intact, at least in its heartland. Turkish and
Iranian variants and the golden age of the Western Caliphate left

the center of Islam untouched. In our own time, the very core of Islam has been pierced by the modern world, and any observer who is astute enough to detect an emerging pattern in Islam runs the risk of being labeled a false prophet.

Determinism in American Fiction

I almost placed this section in the chapter on scientific determinism. That requires a word of explanation. Conventional wisdom has it that the American ethos is fundamentally puritanical and that pessimistic determinism in America stems from that source. To the contrary, I shall argue that determinism in American thought, as it is revealed in American literature, owes more to a faith in science than it does to some residual Calvinism.

Writers of fiction are often among the most thoroughgoing of determinists. They can afford to be, for in the sense of Muslim theology, writers of fiction have the omnipotence of God. They create and control their characters. The last words of Thackeray's *Vanity Fair* are: "Ah! *Vanitas Vanitatum!* Which of us is happy in this world? Which of us has his desire? Or having it, is satisfied? Come, children, let us shut up the box and the puppets, for our play is played out."

The perceptive writer, dealing as he or she does with the tragedies, major and minor, of life, is an easy victim to pessimism and determinism. The puppets do what the puppet master wants. So it is not difficult in the world of literature to find important works, more or less the common property of the civilized world, in which psychological determinism is expressed. In fact, it is hard, as we shall see in the next chapter, to find significant writers who seem to express something to the contrary.

American fiction is particularly rich in the expression of determinism. This, as I pointed out, is the result of something more than just the Puritan ethos. The great flowering of determinism in American fiction is in the age of naturalism. The age of naturalism is, almost by definition, the age of scientific determinism. As Commager[13] reminds us, it was a shameless mixture of Darwin, Haeckel, and Nietzsche that fed American naturalism. It was certainly not the Puritan divines. To his list of ingredients he might have added, though he did not, European socialism and positivism. So constructed it could almost be construed to be a reaction against Puritanism.

If the Puritan predestinarians would not do as sources for American naturalism, neither would, by themselves, any of the European borrowings be sufficient. Dreiser, in his more advanced years, professed Marxism, and Jack London professed at a variety of times scientific—that is to say, positivistic—socialism and the cult of the superman. Sources for Stephen Crane and Frank Norris are harder to name. But whatever the sources, there was an ethos in American naturalism that was different from that in Europe. European ideas, to adopt the rhetoric of Spengler, found their ultimate expression of pessimism and determinism in a much more self-conscious and less revealing form. Some European decadents, Huysmans and Brandes, have not aged well. Others, Ibsen and Dostoyevsky, have become the darlings of our age.

The Americans were more direct, simpler, and in the literary sense far more "scientific." For these reasons they often seem more old-fashioned to us than the Europeans, for in the meantime we seem to have acquired many of the ideas that suffused Europe prior to World War I.

Darwin and Marx: Dreiser, Norris, and London

Of the various alien ideas that infiltrated America, it was the most familiar—those of Darwin (who after all wrote in English)—that were the most important. Though Dreiser and London, and perhaps even Norris, claimed to be socialists, they were really Darwinian materialists. It is one of the ironies of the history of ideas that Darwinian notions took hold in two vastly incompatible ways in America in the last years of the nineteenth century. One was in William Graham Sumner's defense of the robber barons of capitalism in his social Darwinism. The other was in the socialism of the radical Westerners, in the case of London and only less so in the case of Dreiser described more accurately to our contemporary sensibilities as fascism.

Darwin provided both the imagery and the plots. That Dreiser's heroes were often capitalistic plunderers only reinforces the connection to Sumner's capitalists. However, the simplest and most naive expression of Darwinism in American literature is generally regarded, with some justice, as being in the works of Jack London.

London read everything, at least everything that was available to a sometime student at Berkeley living in Oakland in the last years of the nineteenth century.[14] Spencer, judging from the record, made the greatest impression upon him. But, with due regard for the influence of old Europe upon new America, what was important was not the particular ideas of Spencer, or Haeckel, or Nietzsche, or Boas, or Frazer, as much as it was the life that writers like London led. His life was as bizarre as it was thoroughly American. True, the disorders attendant upon a rapid change in the conception of the nature of human life everywhere intruded itself in the western world by the 1890s. But living, as London did, on the margins of society in a still raw west made the mixture of all of these changing conceptions an especially important experience. London's early life had no real foundations. In the absence of anything to the contrary, I can only suppose that all of the nineteenth century biological materialism and positivistic socialism that London read tumbled with particular force into the crater that had been left by his disordered childhood and youth. All of this, however, must be supposition, as any implication of causation must be in psychological studies of particular people, of society, and of social history. But such a supposition, while not capable of verification in any scientific sense, does provide us with a framework by which we can understand how Darwinian determinism found acceptance not only in Jack London but in that larger aspect of American life for which London stands as a synecdoche.

So it was with Norris, another Westerner. Both Norris and London were pamphleteers, a feature that makes even the most powerful of their novels difficult to read today. *The Sea Wolf*, in my view London's masterpiece, is disfigured by the sophomoric philosophizing of Wolf Larsen. *The Octopus*, similarly Norris' masterpiece, is even more disfigured by the rantings against the Southern Pacific Railroad and the hosannas for the effects of truth upon malefactors. Only Dreiser is free from the need to turn a novel into a philosophic-sociological tract. Suffering through Dreiser's prose—the literary equivalent of being trapped in the La Brea tar pits—is difficult for the modern reader, difficult enough to make one doubt that Dreiser is the great psychologist that he is credited with being. But he is a tragedian, at his best comparable to Dostoyevsky. He is less clearly the biological materialist than London, but he is the greater interpreter of human life. And he sees it as gripped by the iron hand of circumstances.

All three wrote with a message. For London it was that life is determined by the material struggle for existence and that it is a brutish business. For Norris it is that life is grim and hemmed in by the iron bounds of the social order, by man's nature embodied in society. For Dreiser it is simply the iron law of history now made into psychological determinism.

Because no one can make strong causative claims in such matters, I cannot argue that American naturalism, as exemplified by these three writers or by the larger field created by the addition of Stephen Crane, Sherwood Anderson, and Edgar Lee Masters, has in any sense been responsible for the receptive posture of late twentieth century America to a working practical determinism. To the contrary, modern psychological determinism, with all of its excuses for deviant behavior, is soft and muddled compared to the clearer vision of the naturalists. But there is a deep strain in America of the will to believe in the determination of life by circumstances. It turns up not only in literature, but in the early enthusiasm, represented by Rush and Mitchell, for the medical conception of psychological disorders, and the wildfire acceptance of the ideas of John B. Watson.

There is a general belief that we Americans are a pragmatic, practical people. There is even a more naive notion that we, more than other peoples in the world, require hard evidence as being necessary to belief. But the ease with which we and our intellectual forebears have and continue to accept the various doctrines of determinism, including psychoanalysis, behaviorism, social Darwinism, and similar ideas, show both of these notions to be false.

The Unbelievers: Twain and Mencken

The last paragraph sets the stage for discussion of another important feature of certain American minds, namely skeptical disbelief, often in the face of a great longing to believe. The American literary landscape is strewn with representative results of this attitude. Two persons provide perfect examples: Mark Twain and H. L. Mencken. They are the boys who come to the revival tent and then sit in the back row to chew tobacco and scoff.

Twain is the more interesting on all counts but especially in the present context because determinism rides so heavily upon him. His famous essay *What Is Man?* is generally dismissed by critics as an embarrassment—a kind of testament from the village atheist. I dissent from that view, but my point in evoking it is to show how hard it is, even for those who know better, to accept the unrelieved pessimism of Twain's last years. His last works express not only pessimism and disbelief, they do so in not muted tones of despair. Not that Twain did not, at the same time, cultivate the image of the wise, old sage, the kindly, mellow old grandpa, but in Twain despair reaches nihilism.

Consider the end of *The Mysterious Stranger*.[15] Satan continues his visits to Theodor after the events of the story have ceased. The last chapter is an account of the reasons for Satan's visits to the boys of Eseldorf. It is to show Theodor and the others the nonentity of existence. At the end Satan says to Theodor: "It is true, that which I have revealed to you: there is no God, no universe, no human race, no earthly life, no heaven, no hell. It is all a dream—a grotesque and foolish dream. Nothing exists but you. And you are but a thought, a vagrant thought, a useless thought, a homeless thought, wandering forlorn among the empty eternities."[16]

If Twain had been a writer given to obscurity and subtlety, rather than being given to the forthright rhetoric of American English, this kind of thing, common in the late Twain, would have proclaimed him as a forerunner of modern existentialism. But it lacks the obscure indirection of existentialism. It is thoroughly American and direct in its expression, and it is at least as valid a reflection of an important current in American thought of the time as is the rhetoric of Russell Conway.[17]

Mencken is better contained. He mocks rather than lashes out in fury, but the message is not very different. Like Twain, Mencken maintained a lifetime interest in the church, in clergy, and in the Bible. He confessed that as an adolescent he had a "vast and unhealthy interest in theology." But he remained the convinced skeptic, like Twain a determinist and a pessimist.

Mencken was also a behaviorist, though he would have resisted the label. He reflects in countless ways the behaviorism of the twenties, not only in his own writings but in the kinds of things he accepted for the *American Mercury*. He and John B. Watson shared a provincial city, with a very limited intellectual circle, for many years, and it would be astonishing if their paths had not crossed, but if such were the case there is no record of it. Mencken heaps his characteristic scorn on the professors of the Homewood campus of the Johns Hopkins University, and he reserves what faint praise he can muster for academic people for the doctors in east Baltimore at the Johns Hopkins Medical School. Perhaps that is the reason that he never mentions Watson. It would have required him to break faith with his carefully prepared image as the sworn enemy of the academy.

In any event, Mencken, like Twain, reflects an important and often, when the matter of national character is the topic of discussion, neglected aspect of American thought. It is one that is equally well exemplified by those figures of American folklore, Colonel Robert Ingersoll and the village atheist. Mencken and Twain tell us how ready America was, despite its mask of evangelical piety, for an acquiescence to the iron grip of determinism. What they did not tell us was that it would come in the guise, not only of the hard sciences, but in the sentimental belief in the improvability of man through man's own efforts, of the notion if something is contrary to accepted psychological principles, then it is not worth defending.

Robinson Jeffers and Predestinarianism

Robinson Jeffers' name does not win instant recognition today. To a small group he is something of a cult figure. But in the larger world he is kept alive by his splendid free version of *Medea*, though a few of his shorter poems are still to be found in current anthologies. He enjoyed a passing success among the intellectuals in the twenties, for, I fear, the wrong reasons. There would be no reason to mention him at all as a representative of any strand of American thought save for one thing. Of all of those who have been so accused—Sherwood Anderson, Dreiser, Sinclair Lewis, and even James Branch Cabell—Jeffers is the only important literary figure of the past one hundred years who can correctly be identified as a carrier of Calvinistic predestinarianism into modern American literature. In fact, he comes close to refuting my thesis that predestinarianism is not really deterministic, for as I read Jeffers, he is deterministic.

Jeffers was the first of two children born to a fifty-year-old professor of Bible and theology in the Western Theological Seminary (Presbyterian) of Pittsburgh and his bride in her early twenties.[18] Jeffers grew up in Europe and Pittsburgh, a lonely child studying Greek and the modern European languages when most of his contemporaries were struggling with the light demands, even in those days, of American public education. Out of what must have been one of the most appalling childhoods since that of Samuel Butler came an absorption to the marrow of Greek drama (though not of Greek philosophy) and a bitter Calvinistic sense of the damnation of mankind. This latter was unrelieved by a belief in God. Jeffers views and talents matured into what is perhaps the grandest and most Miltonian sense of the rhythm of American English and a philosophy that has, in my view incorrectly, been labeled by students of Jeffers as "inhumanism."

Jeffers so-called inhumanism is no less a pessimistic

judgment on humanity than Mark Twain's despair and Mencken's scoffing. What gives it its special flavor is his love of nature, particularly the nature of the California coast. But Jeffers' nature is not the nature of the Sierra Club, despite that organization's exploitation of him, nor is it the nature of Coleridge. It is the nature of Jack London—fierce and unyielding. Here Darwin and Calvin meet.

I will not draw a causal connection between Jeffer's childhood and his mature views except to point to the most superficial and mundane things. Jeffers' erudition was the result of an education supervised by his elderly father who, for the most part during Jeffers' youth, was retired. But to engage in the sort of speculation favored by Bruce Mazlish and other so-called psychohistorians would do a great injustice both to Jeffers and his views. He was by all accounts a happy and fulfilled man. He spent a lifetime with a devoted wife. He reared two stable sons. There is nothing in his published letters,[19] or any of the currently available biographical information, to suggest the sort of disordered mental life that a dedicated psychohistorian would have constructed on the evidence of the facts of his childhood and his poetry. We need only report the known facts. His father was a Presbyterian theologian of formidable learning. Jeffers became, like Freud, a theological determinist without a God. He is one more representative of both the actuality for and the potential for the varieties of determinism in American life.

The Living Presence of Determinism

When, a few years ago, I first contemplated this study, I seriously considered basing it in part upon the results of an attitude survey. I am very happy that I early abandoned that notion. I do not wish to demean attitude surveys. They have their proper place, but in the detection of what in the lingo of survey research are called latent traits, they are miserable. For their results are at the mercy of the questions asked. The questions I would have put into such a survey *before* I undertook this survey of the varieties of determinism would have born no relation whatever to the questions I would have used after I had made the examination. Furthermore, I don't know what I would have made of the fact that, say, 66 percent of a sample of Americans endorsed the statement: "I have no control over the main features of my life," or that 22 percent or 1 percent so endorsed. The interpretation of any such result would have been rendered indefinite by the particular context in which the inventory was presented—on Monday morning? Just after learning of a handsome raise? The death of a child?

Nevertheless, attitude surveys have been very important in the spread of determinism. I shall later discuss the matter in some detail, but here I restrict myself to one particularly pernicious example.

I suppose that the least attractive among the many unattractive influences of the Frankfurt school on American intellectual life is something called the *Authoritarian Personality Scale*.[20] Perhaps it is unfair to attribute the *Authoritarian Personality* to the Frankfurt school, but the fact is that the first author on the most important publication on the matter was T. W. Adorno, and he appears as coauthor of the lesser publications.

The Authoritarian Personality was written in the immediate post–World War II era by a group of Americans and refugees from Nazi Germany, all associated with the University of California at Berkeley. Senator Joseph McCarthy was about doing his mischief, and the overwhelming bulk of liberal Americans still regarded Soviet Russia as a friend only to be won over by kindly acts. The attempt to mute the communist movement in the United States alarmed American liberals, and it even more alarmed the refugees from the unspeakable horrors of Nazi Germany. It is therefore an irony almost too macabre to contemplate that what this group came up with was a personality inventory designed to tell the good guys from the bad guys, the generous, open personalities from those who favored authority, totalitarianism, and, by implication, Nazism and Fascism. In short, a way of telling those kinds of *personalities* subject to feelings of hatred toward the rest of us.

If in a different place and with only a slight shift in emphasis, these authors had come up with a comparable way of differentiating the typical Aryan personality from the devious Jew personality, they would have at least earned a medal from Dr. Goebbels.[21] That the irony of this fact escaped these earnest souls is difficult to imagine, but it is all the more reason for writing about the matter here and writing about it firmly.

That the California F-Scale (F for Fascism), as it came to be called, had anything to do with personality (remember, the book was called *The Authoritarian Personality*) is something only that Dr. Goebbels and his henchmen would have appreciated. However, so basic an issue aside, what these people stumbled onto was a set of items for an attitude inventory that could distinguish people with traditional, often small-town, American values from those with liberal, cosmopolitan values. Could anyone doubt on which side the person who positively endorsed such items as: "Obedience and respect for authority are the most important virtues children should learn?" "If people would talk less and work more, everybody would be better off!" Some of these items now bring a smile: "The businessman and the manufacturer are much more important to society than the artist and the professor."

Milton Rokeach fortunately punctured the whole business in his excellent book, *The Open and Closed Mind*.[22] Aside from the vastly greater wisdom and tolerance evident in Rokeach's work, it had the positive effect of showing that one could play the authoritarian game with any political attitude. Rokeach demonstrated that there was, within the framework provided by the Berkeley group, authoritarian personalities on the left as well as on the right. As is often the case, the real world in the form of Students for a Democratic Society and the Weathermen made Rokeach's demonstration academic.

More to the point, the notion of an *Authoritarian Personality* is something out of the Nazi era, or at least out of the kind of grandiose mystical determinism thought to be inspired by Spengler. But despite Rokeach's demonstration and the concrete evidence supplied by Students for a Democratic Society, the point of view that spawned the *Authoritarian Personality* remains with us.

Americans, on reading their Sunday supplement magazines, learn, without doubting or rising in indignation, that their political decisions can be predicted by their "personalities," and that people who drink too much or gamble too much do so, not out of any *wish* to do so but because they are "sick."

 I cannot, given my views as to the limitations of the methods of any social investigation, ascribe particular causes to the shift that has been and is still occurring in American thought away from notions of responsibility and freedom toward notions of determinism and lack of personal responsibility. I can only point to the long history of movement between the two historical antipodes of determinism and freedom, and variety of forms each takes, and to the conceivable harm that would result from a world irretrievably committed to one, determinism. Before exploring this question further, I shall have something to say about the comparably rich history of the varieties of conceptions of freedom of the will. To that question the next chapter is devoted.

Chapter Four

Free Will, Voluntary Action, and Freedom

We use the word free, when applied to human actions, in three different but related senses. The terms free will, voluntary action, and freedom cover these senses. This chapter will describe each and show the relation between the first two and our conception of the third. First, however, I point to a fundamental difference between theories of determinism and theories of freedom.

All concepts of freedom differ from concepts of determinism in that everyone recognizes that we are not nor should we be totally free. It is simple enough for a determinist to argue that all of our actions are controlled by our physical nature and the circumstances of our life. That argument is easy, almost cheap, because, in the absence of positive evidence, one can always postulate hidden or unknown causes. The advocate of free will cannot so argue, for it is abundantly clear that many of our actions are caused. That fact has given rise to an important tradition in the history of psychology, the distinction between reflexive and voluntary behavior. Finally, even the most extreme of the rational libertarians (I exclude the Marquis de Sade) recognizes that each of us must be under some kind of restraint, that we cannot be completely free to act and say what we please. The libertarian only wants lesser constraints placed upon actions than do most of us.

Theology and Freedom of the Will

The entry in the eleventh edition of the *Encyclopaedia Britannica* on the will is by the Reverend Henry Herbert Williams, then a Fellow in Philosophy at Hertford College, Oxford. It begins as follows:

> "The Problem of Freedom" provides in reality a common title under which are grouped difficulties and questions of varying and divergent interest and character. These difficulties arise quite naturally from the obligation, which metaphysicians, theologians, moral philosophers, men of science, and psychologists alike recognize, to give an account consistent with their theories of the relation of man's power of deliberate and purposive activity to the rest of the universe.[1]

I cannot imagine a more accurate statement of the problem, and I shall use the Rev. Mr. Williams' article as a point of departure for this section. The article goes on to tell us, "There is some ground nevertheless for maintaining, contrary to much modern opinion, that the controversy is fundamentally and in the main a moral controversy." I suppose that the Rev. Mr. Williams had to say "contrary to much modern opinion" because when he wrote the article textbooks on psychology still carried chapters labeled "The Will" or something similar. That has not been the case for the past three quarters of a century. It is commonly said that the topic of motivation has replaced that of the will, and while that may be so, the psychological issues generally discussed under headings like will have disappeared as well. In any event, the Rev. Mr. Williams was correct. This issue was and still is mainly a moral one.

The Classical Origins

The issue of freedom of the will, as it has been honed by centuries of Christian theology, hardly existed for Aristotle, as Williams reminds us. Aristotle is content to tell us that we can be held accountable only for those actions that are the result of purposive choice. Aristotle sometimes uses the notion of purposive choice to refer to the choice between divergent moral ends, and sometimes he uses the notion to refer to choice of means rather than ends. In Aristotle, as in Plato, the power of making a right choice is limited by knowledge, and thus morality becomes almost synonymous with wisdom. It is also based upon rationality.

The problem of the will begins to take on something like the form it has in Christian theology with the Epicurean philosophers. Epicurus ties the freedom of the mind to make choices to the ultimate freedom of the atoms which compose it, but the important point is that he argues for the existence of freedom of choice as opposed to the Stoic notion of fate. And, of course, the Epicureans developed a kind of utilitarianism. It is not, of course, the utilitarianism of modern psychology, or even of those nineteenth-century figures with whom the term is usually identified. In the modern sense, pleasure and pain are kinds of biological compulsions. In the Epicurean sense, they are themselves the basis for the idea of the Good, or criteria of the Good, as they were for many figures that followed, including Thomas Aquinas.

But, as Williams tells us, it was not until the rise of Christianity and Christian theology that the world becomes aware of the difficulty of reconciling a belief in human freedom with a belief in the Divine governance of the world. We have, in the last chapter, examined some of the difficulties that arise from the Christian doctrine of redemption when we looked at the notion of predestination, and we shall reintroduce the topic near the end of this section. First, however, we should look at the medieval synthesis.

The Medieval Synthesis

The Middle Ages based what might be called the psychology of Christian theology upon the twin pillars of reason and will. Various philosophers intervening in the years since Aristotle had tried to reduce knowledge to sensation and the consequences of sensation. This, of course, would not fit the Christian notion of

salvation by faith, for there was, though occasional medieval philosophers tried to argue to the contrary, no basis for faith in experience. Reason was the mark of man's superiority to the beasts,
but reason alone was not sufficient for salvation. There had to be
belief, which was supplied by the will. The medieval notion of
reason, as it reaches its most refined statement in Albertus Mag-
nus and Aquinas, owes much but not everything to Aristotle. It is
an oversimplification but one that conveys the spirit of the matter
to say that Aristotle's objective psychology becomes spiritual in
the interests of Christian theology. In this transformation, the will
is a new, non-Aristotelian element. It depends upon reason for its
guidance, but it is the aspect of human nature that permits choice.
The freedom of the will, then, is for Aquinas the freedom to choose
what is necessarily determined by reason to be worthy of choice.

Despite the complete secularization of psychology in
the nineteenth and twentieth centuries, resisted only in a few
Catholic strongholds in Europe and America, the preservation and
indeed transformation of Aristotelian psychology by the school-
men is one of the great inheritances for the whole of psychology.
The distinction that emerged, following Aristotle, among the veg-
etative, the sensitive, and the rational souls is no longer with us,
but something very much like it has been reinvented, time and
time again, and it, or something very like it provides a foundation
for most of what I have to say.

The moral requirements of freedom of the will also
survive in several guises. In their most important form they survive
in the development of the political philosophy of freedom, the
kind of political philosophy that culminated in the American experiment. In a lesser, duller, and indeed deadlier form, they survive
in the various controversies in psychology in the nineteenth century. I shall not deal with the dispute over act and content in
nineteenth-century psychology, but I shall try to sketch out the
psychological conception of the will in the nineteenth century.
While that conception was devoid of theological content, like the
determinism of Freud and Jeffers, it maintains many features of its
origin.

The Psychology of the Will

Nothing could be less rewarding than reading the segment in a psychology text of the late nineteenth century devoted to the will. Partly by way of defending that statement and partly by way of explanation as to why the concept of will disappeared from psychology, I discuss three authors in a thoroughly jumbled chronological order. Two of these authors provide us with convincing examples of the discomfort psychologists of the nineteenth and early twentieth centuries experienced with the notion of the will. The third provides us with some sensible notions about the idea. They all too readily see its theological origins.

The first author is William James. He is first in this discussion because, among other reasons, his treatment of the will is so famous. The second is a thoroughly obscure figure, Frederick A. Rauch. I chose him partly because he writes the first treatise published in America under the title of *Psychology* but more to the point he writes a much more sensible account of the problem than does James. Finally, I shall briefly summarize the views of William McDougall, who juxtaposes the theological (which McDougall calls moral) notion of the will and his anticipation of the modern theory of motivation.

James and the Will. There are two principal sources for James's ideas about the will, his essay *The Will to Believe* and the chapter on the will in the *Principles*.[2] I shall deal mainly with the latter and then briefly comment upon the former.

In his chapter, James argues that voluntary movements stand in contrast with primary or reflexive behavior. In a later section of this chapter I shall comment on the voluntary-reflexive distinction. Suffice it to say here that it was new enough in James' time to be exciting. James then goes on to give an example of involuntary behavior that leads one to think that he did not understand the distinction as it had developed in physiology. It is that of a child fleeing into the arms of an adult when a train approaches. James uses this example to get to the heart of the conception of voluntary action. In order for an action to be voluntary, it must be *foreseen*. "When a particular movement, having once occurred in a random, reflex, or involuntary way, has left an image of itself in the memory, then the movement can be desired again, proposed as an end, and deliberately willed" (*Principles*, 2: 487). This conception of voluntary action James shares with the German introspectionists of the period.

There is, then, nothing unique about James' conception. It simply reflects the belief, common among late-nineteenth-century psychologists, that to be willed, behavior must be *consciously* planned. To this James adds only a component of learning; the initial performance of an act is random. The initial random movement must leave some conscious trace through kinesthesis. James, however, disputes the notion of a feeling of innervation, a notion favored by the German psychologists. Instead, he elaborates upon the notion of an image of a "remote kind."

James does make one major departure from many of his nineteenth-century predecessors. He dismisses the notion that pleasure and pain provide the only "comprehensible and reasonable motives for action." James remarks that such might be the case for an ethical system but not a psychological one! James argues that the heart of the matter of volition is the effort of attention. Attention is the most essential phenomenon of the will.

Later in the chapter James deals with the question of the freedom of the will. It obviously makes him uncomfortable. After some preliminary discussion which identifies the sense of freedom with the effort of attention, he says that the "question of free-will is unsoluble on strictly psychological grounds" (*Principles*, 2:572). The moral philosopher (read theologian) wars with the scientific psychologist. James refers us to his paper, *The Dilemmas of Determinism*, and in so doing he appears to sweep the whole question under the table. He does take Spencer to task for saying that psychic processes either conform to nature or they do not. If they do, then they are determined and if they do not, then a science of psychology is not possible. "Psychology will be Psychology and Science Science, as much as ever (as much and no more) in this world, whether free will be true or not. Science, however, must be constantly reminded that her purposes are not the only purposes, and that the order of uniform causation, which she has use for, and is therefore right in postulating, may be enveloped in a wider order, on which she has no claims at all" (*Principles*, 2:576).

This is a thoroughly Jamesian passage in which he shilly-shallies in his charming way. He fails to see that any "order of uniform causation" is valid only so far as it can be applied with empirical reference; otherwise it is no science.

The Will To Believe, as we might suppose from the title, is an essay upon the psychology of belief. It is full of James' intriguing paradoxes and it is written in that style of guilelessness that makes James so irresistible. The important point here is that it reveals James' flirtation with but inability to appreciate the full significance of the medieval synthesis: reason and will. He says: "*A rule of thinking which would absolutely prevent me from acknowledging certain kinds of truths if these kinds of truth were really there, would be an irrational rule.* That for me is the long and the short of the formal logic of the situation, no matter what the kinds of truth may materially be" (*Pragmatism and Other Essays*, p. 212; the italics are James').[3]

He goes on to use phrases like: "if we were scholastic absolutists.... But if we are empiricists ... We ought, to the contrary, delicately and profoundly to respect one another's mental freedom." In short, James cannot decide. His loyalty is both to his belief in religious truths and his faith in science. He cannot see that he betrays the latter by granting to it, at least in its guise as psychological science, more than it can bear.

Rauch: A Pragmatist Before There Was One. Frederick A. Rauch is many things. The most astonishing, if one reads him, was that he was perhaps the earliest representative of the German psychological tradition in the United States. He is not a functionalist, and his account of the will is not constrained by functional considerations. In short, he does not, as do Spencer and Bain, use the notion of the will to presage the modern concept of motivation. But he does use the modern concept of motivation, though not in those words. He writes a kind of descriptive, practical psychology that is the forerunner of the twentieth-century popularization of psychology.

Rauch received a Ph.D. degree in philology from Marburg in 1827.[4] He moved very rapidly. He was *Privat Docent* and later *Professor Extraordinarious* at Giessen. In 1831 he was on the brink of being appointed *Professor Ordinarious* at Heidelberg, when he fled Germany for political reasons. As a refugee in America he had difficulty at first in finding a suitable position, but by 1836, at the age of thirty, he was the first president of Marshall College (later Franklin and Marshall). He became an important theologian for the Reformed Church in America. More to the point, he published in 1840, the year before his death, his *Psychology or a View of the Human Soul, Including Anthropology*. It was an enormously successful work, and it was widely used as a textbook for many years afterwards. Its influence is almost certainly underestimated by the historians of psychology, and in many ways it reads like a more modern book than James' but hardly so fascinating.

There is a whole section devoted to the will, and unlike James, Rauch delivers himself from the question of the freedom of the will at the outset. But Rauch obeys the medieval principle, and his section on the will follows that on reason. The important point, however, is that, theologian though he was, he manages to avoid the will in the essentials of his psychology.

The first section in the book is a long discussion of anthropology, and though it is in the Kantian tradition, it has a very modern flavor. Rauch discusses national differences and "qualities of mind produced by sexual differences." There is a section on developmental psychology and one on the "powers of the mind over body." Rauch's background in philology causes him to write a long section on language—what today would be called psycholinguistics—something totally absent in James' almost retrogressive text of fifty years later.

But my major purpose in reviewing Rauch's work is to present his conception of the will and its freedom, a conception vastly more forthright than James'. Will and reason complement one another (so much is the inheritance of medieval philosophy clarified by the German enlightenment). But at the outset—in the second paragraph of his discussion of the matter—Rauch makes a distinction. "Will may be viewed in a twofold aspect, as nature and as moral will; in the latter respect it is to be viewed in the closest connection with *law, moral obligation, duties,* and *rights;* in the former it manifests itself by *desires, inclinations, emotions,* and *passions.*" [5]

This distinction is one of the few things in Rauch, the antique diction aside, that would not appeal to a modern devourer of the psychological literature. Almost everything he has to say would receive a nod of approval from the most devoted reader of Rollo May. Rauch treats of such uncharacteristic topics for the time and place as self-hatred. And such insights! "Thus *self-hatred* originates only in self-love." He even discusses sexual love. It is small wonder that this text was popular and influential all out of proportion to the attention given it by the historians of psychology.

But more to the point, the whole question of freedom of the will is solved by the distinction between natural and moral will. Only the moral will is truly free, Rauch tells us. "The merely natural will is wholly dependent on external objects or internal passions, it does not determine itself by its own nature, but by the nature of that which is different from itself. In the sphere of the natural will we can recognize nothing but *determinism.*" [6] Could Watson have put the matter better? Rauch's diction is not that of Watson, but the sentiment is. We can relegate the moral will to being outside of psychology. In short, it shows us that American secular determinism came not only from the utilitarians, the atheistic and agnostic British empiricists, and the biology of evolution, but it came from the heartland of idealism itself, transplanted to a new world. Furthermore, it shows us that morals and values lie outside of psychology.

Rauch's solution to the problem of the will is a very American one, even more American than James' agonizing. He simply declares that there is such a thing as moral freedom, and then he goes on for fifty or more pages discoursing on natural determinism. Except for the fact that modern psychologists do not feel the need to make his apologetic gesture in the direction of moral freedom, the whole treatment by Rauch is very modern. We are Americans, a modern psychologist might say instead, and therefore we believe in freedom, but on the other hand we are psychobiologists and scientists and.... Each aspect of life from "self-hatred" to "sexual love" can be described as caused naturally and apart from moral choice. A more thoroughly American or pragmatic account could not have come from a native son. Rauch, as the archetypical representative of the German intellect in a new land turns out to be, if not the progenitor then surely the anticipator of modern American psychobabble.

McDougall and the Transition to Motive. William McDougall's Social Psychology was one of the best known psychological works of its generation. It was first published in 1908. My edition, the fourteenth, is dated 1921.[7] Along with E. A. Ross' Social Psychology,[8] it is regarded as founding the modern study of social psychology. Its content, however, bears little relation to the content of contemporary books on social psychology. That, however, does not mean that the book does not have a certain modern flavor; it does. It is just that the title, Social Psychology, is out of place in the modern context. What it is, simply put, is an explanation of human behavior, incidentally including social interactions, in terms of a list of instincts, or what we would now call motives. These instincts have both motivational aspects and conscious (affective) aspects, and they served for McDougall as biologically based explanations for all human actions. I do not think that McDougall's arguments would be very convincing to a modern student of psychology, but the notion that human conduct was to be explained by a set of fundamental drives and motives is one that would be very familiar to the modern student. This is the legacy of McDougall's book.

What makes it important, however, is that he has a separate chapter on volition. One would have supposed that the list of instincts would have made such a chapter superfluous, but it is there. It is there because McDougall, in contrast to Rauch (and probably James, who consider the matter outside of psychology) wants to describe moral actions and sentiments.

"I do not propose to go at length into the world-old dispute between libertarians and determinists. But the acceptance of the libertarian doctrine would be incompatible with any hope that a
science of society, in any proper sense of the word "science" may
be achieved; for in the face of each of the most important problems
of such a science, we should have to content ourselves with the
admission of impotence.[9]

Despite this disavowal, McDougall spends several
pages at a critical point in the chapter arguing the respective
merits of the *moral* position of libertarians and determinists. He
says that the libertarians are totally wrong on the issue of moral
responsibility. Responsibility means accountability, and the social
system of rewards and punishments makes any action accountable. Punishment makes no sense, McDougall argues, if a man's
voluntary actions are outside of the "system of his mental constitution," i.e., his psychologically determined nature.

On the other hand, McDougall argues, an argument for
free will based upon *moral need* cannot be so easily dismissed. If,
he asks, my actions are completely determined by my heredity and
my history, why should I make any moral effort? This argument, he
concedes, may not be serious for those "who believe that their
own natures are above serious reproach, but not to those who can
point to undesirable ancestry and unmistakable flaws in their native dispositions." "Nothing," he continues, "is more difficult than
to give any helpful answer to one who adopts this line of justification for moral slackness; we can only hold him responsible and
punish him."[10]

Having raised the question, which in an altered form
may be said to be the problem at the basis of this book, McDougall
airily dismisses it. "But psychology must not allow its investigations and theories to be biased by moral needs."[11] Perhaps, but
when the "investigations and theories" of psychology, to use
McDougall's phrase, become public policy, then indeed some
question may be raised.

McDougall's solution to the problem of volition, ignoring, as it does, the moral issue is only slightly more interesting

than the waffling of James and much less interesting than the outright disclaimer advanced by Rauch so far as psychology is concerned. It is only a slight exaggeration to say that McDougall anticipates the behavioristic theories of the 1930s. Volition, Mc-Dougall tells us, is the condition that arises when the personality as a whole throws itself upon the side of a weaker motive in some conflict. This has the effect of eliminating the moral question, for morality may well be on the side of the stronger motive. What he says is that there is a special kind of effort that a person can exert, and this effort influences action. McDougall, in later pages, goes on to speculate that this "self-regarding sentiment" that throws its lot in with the weaker side of a conflict is under some kind of social control (the social contract, though McDougall makes no reference to the concept by that name). Character emerges when the sentiments are organized by volition into some harmonious system of hierarchy.

Here we have three psychologists struggling with the notion of moral decisions and free will. All three seem to accept the idea that our passional (to use James' term) volitions are determined by our natures and our environment, but all three also seem to agree that we ought, somehow, to except moral decisions from psychology. Rauch simply says so; James agonizes over the problem, and McDougall tries to provide a psychological explana-tion (the weaker side of the conflict, etc.) for the will. It seems to occur to none of them that there is any evidence for the complete determination of any kind of voluntary behavior, or that, aside from their content that moral decisions, beliefs, etc., have no spe-cial status that sets them apart from political decisions, beliefs, or any other kind. Nor, is there in any of the three any penetrating psychobiological account of the nature of voluntary action, though to some degree a psychobiological understanding of the distinc-tion between involuntary and voluntary action was available to all three of them. It is to that distinction I now turn.

Reflexive and Voluntary Behavior

Common sense would lead one to expect that the topic of the reflex should have been part of chapter two, devoted as it is to scientific psychological determinism. However, the disappearance of the notion of the will in psychology and its replacement by notions like motives, drives, and social control makes, in a negative way the notion of the reflex important to psychological notions of freedom. To state my thesis forthrightly: The invention of the notion of the reflex forced thinkers about psychological matters and their biological bases to sharpen their conceptions of volition, if only to make it clear, by the application of the method of contrast, what they were talking about when they talked about reflexes.

There is a distinction in English, not so easily available to speakers of German, between voluntary behavior and willed behavior. The terms in German for will and volition are the same (*der Wille*). Any speaker of English with a head full of behavioristic theories would find the phrase "willed behavior" to be antique, if not downright suggestive of fascistic tendencies (*The Triumph of the Will*), but the phrase "voluntary behavior" falls easily from the lips of even the most dedicated behaviorist. That this is so is in no small measure the result of the history of the concept of the reflex.

The Origins of the Reflex

It is well known, not to say notorious, that Descartes invented the reflex.[12] The famous woodcut prepared for his *Traite de l'Homme* shows a full-fledged diagram of the reflex in which a person withdraws his foot from a fire when the flames become too hot. Descartes was not in the modern sense an experimental physiologist, and he had no notion how the reflex worked. His contemporary, the Dutch entomologist Jacob Swammerdam, did, however, and Swammerdam developed the prototype of the nerve-muscle preparation. If Swammerdam had invented the reflex it might have had a swifter history.

It was not until the early years of the nineteenth century, however, that the modern notion of the reflex establishes itself with some empirical authority in the developing science of physiology. I realize that such a statement ignores persons like Albrecht von Haller, whom Fearing describes as providing the dividing line between modern physiology and all that went before, and it even more pointedly ignores Robert Whytt. But it is in the nineteenth century, principally in Germany and England, that the great experiments establishing the validity of the concept of the reflex occur.

It is very hard to assign credit in the development of the notion of the reflex, for in the early years of the nineteenth century things happened so rapidly that priorities disappear. There were experiments, mainly with cold-blooded animals (the absence of anesthetics made experimentation with warm-blooded animals difficult). These established various kinds of preparations—nerve-muscle preparations, spinal preparations, decorticate preparations, etc. Fearing finds Marshall Hall (1790–1857) important enough to devote a whole chapter to him. With the era of Hall, the notion of the reflex comes into its own. Investigators could show that an isolated segment of the central nervous system could mediate a response to an external stimulus. The response did not occur in the absence of the stimulus, and it was an altogether reasonable inference that the stimulus was the distal *cause* of the reaction. It was, in the Cartesian sense, a mechanical process in which some physical event eventually, through the intervention of the physical action of the central nervous system,causes a contraction of a muscle. The characteristics of the response could be modified by all of the physical resources at the command of the experimenter. The experimental method, in all of its power, was exemplified by this work on the reflex in the early years of the nineteenth century.

Hall read a paper before the Royal Society in 1833 that is generally credited with being the first definitive account of the *physiological* difference between volitional and reflexive behavior. Hall anticipates but does not come close to the complexities introduced by the discovery of the autonomic nervous system in the early twentieth century. In his 1833 address he distinguishes among "four modes of muscular action." First is "that designated voluntary: volition, originating in the cerebrum, and spontaneous in its acts, extends its influence along the spinal marrow and the motor nerves in a *direct line* to the voluntary muscles."[13] The second is exemplified by respiration. It surely is voluntary on occasion, but it does not continuously demand conscious attentional control. The third type of action delineated by Hall is genuinely involuntary. It depends upon the principle of irritability, that foundation stone of the neurobiology of the nineteenth and early twentieth centuries. The fourth category is made of those actions that are purely spinal in origin. Hall's categorization is complex and wrong, but it does end up with a description that becomes basic to research that follows, research on the spinal reflex.

Hall's experiments were brilliant, simple, and impressive. They were mainly done on the frog, and they are the sort of thing that is (or was a generation ago) done in the introductory zoology laboratory with decerebrate frogs. They showed us that the lower centers (spinal centers) mediate behavior, but only upon the introduction of a stimulus; they depend upon the principle of irritability. Various studies, including some using anesthetic (opium) convinced Hall that reflex motions depended neither upon (conscious) sensation nor upon volition.

Hall's contributions to neurophysiology are profound, but, as he himself recognized, they are chiefly in the discovery of the automatic nature of reflex action. Reflex action is not dependent upon consciousness or the cerebrum. Volition does not appear in the reflex. Hall describes the concept of the reflex arc almost in its modern form (the notion of the synapse did not exist in Hall's time).

Johannes Müller parallels Hall's discoveries in Germany. But he is more conservative. He does not deny sensation to the reflex, and hence, one would suppose, he must have believed in a kind of consciousness available to the spinal cord. This question led to the famous Pflüger-Lotze controversy, but Hall and Müller engaged in controversy on other matters. Müller criticizes Hall for asserting that such reflex actions as sneezing and vomiting

do not involve sensations, while Hall points out that the sensations involved in these actions are the *results* of the "excito-
motory" system, not a part of its cause.

The midyears of the nineteenth century see vast advances in neurophysiology. The invention of good, controllable
anesthetics, chiefly ether, enabled such landmark discoveries as
those of the German physiologists Fritsch and Hitzig, who showed
that the cerebral cortex contained tissue uniquely assigned to the
control of particular muscles of the body.

One of the less glorious aspects of mid-nineteenth-
century neurophysiology was the controversy between Eduard
Pflüger and Rudolph Lotze. I mention it here to illustrate that not
all controversies that rage in the name of science are, in fact,
scientific. It concerned the alleged psychical powers of the spinal
cord. Pflüger asked whether the soul is a single, indivisible whole,
and if so what is the result of segregating the lower central nervous
system from the higher centers. Pflüger thought that he had found
evidence of consciousness in the control of movement by the
isolated spinal cord. Lotze merely noted the purposive character
of movements initiated within the isolated spinal segment. For
Lotze such actions were not due to sensation and consciousness
but were the result of the residual influence in the lower centers
which survived decapitation.

The controversy obscured and made more complicated
the fourfold distinction introduced by Hall. But one simplifying
result was to isolate the notion of the reflex. After the controversy
died down, the reflex was seen, as Descartes claimed, as a purely
mechanical kind of physical action, not at all influenced by mentality. The other questions, such as localization of action within
the spinal cord, are important but not in this context.

What happened during this period was that the notion
of voluntary behavior became an accepted category of neural action for physiologists. Not that physiologists were much concerned with voluntary behavior—they left that to their clinical
brethren. Almost without exception they were concerned with the
experimentally more tractable problem of reflexive behavior. But,

beyond any doubt, voluntary action got established as an important part of neurophysiology.

Sir Charles Sherrington could, in the 1900s,[14] resolve the Pflüger-Lotze controversy by pointing out that the spinal cord was incapable of associative memory.[15] It was a circuit in which an impulse, known to Sherrington to be electrochemical in nature, traversed a sensory nerve, got shunted about in the spinal cord, and emerged in the motor neurons to excite the muscle endplates.

Sherrington's great discoveries of the complexity of inhibitory action in reflexive behavior and in particular postural reflexes need only be mentioned, for they only lightly touch upon our main problem, that of the development of a scientifically acceptable notion of voluntary action—freedom of the will, if you like—in a hard science. That notion arises in the negative context provided by the great theoretical and empirical discoveries of reflex action. However peripheral Sherrington's notions of inhibitory and excitatory action may be, they need to be alluded to.

Given the present context, I can summarize Sherrington's discoveries only generally. The best way I can think to introduce them is to describe what students of neurophysiology in the 1930s and 1940s believed. According to the then current ideas, spinal reflexes, through the marvelous interaction of inhibitory and excitatory actions, produced the basic coordinative patterns for movements of the limbs, including locomotion. Furthermore, by then, inhibition and excitation had been divested of some of their mystery. Earlier in the century there had been an argument over the possibility of special inhibitory fibers or possible chemical inhibitors. But by the 1930s it had been pretty well decided that inhibition and summation of excitation was the result of timing at the synapse. We know differently now.

The important point was that such important functions as locomotion could be ascribed largely to the role of reflex action, action, to be sure, that could be overridden by voluntary decision. Generally, however, the higher centers had to intervene only to smooth things out and to alter rate, etc. The crossed-extension reflex provided the basic example. If the plantar area (the region between the pads of the feet of dogs) of an animal whose spinal cord had been disconnected was stimulated, the result was a sharp and clearly *caused* retraction of that leg. But the true marvel was the coordination, for the muscles that produced extension in the limb opposite contracted. Thus, as one limb retracts, the other extends, as if to provide in a purposeful way the basic coordination of walking. In fact, in a chronic spinal preparation, it is possible to induce an animal, paralyzed in its hind limbs from the spinal transection, to walk a distance of ten or twelve feet before it collapses.

This conception of motor action might be regarded as the high watermark of the incursion of the concept of the reflex into the functions of striped muscle. Reflex action, even of striped muscle, was viewed as under the control of the cord and the lower brain centers. When the higher brain centers enter, reflexive action of the limbs is masked by volition. The plantar reflex disappears in human infants as the cortex begins to function, and it reappears only as evidence of neurological damage. We now know that while striped muscle is subject to reflex action (the familiar knee jerk, a monosynaptic reflex), almost all of the important action of striped muscle is under the control of the higher brain centers and may be properly described as voluntary, *even when we are not conscious of the voluntary control*. The higher centers use the information apparent in both monosynaptic and polysynaptic reflex, but the reflexes themselves and the notion of kinesthetic feedback that persisted so long as an explanatory device in psychology long after it disappeared in physiology are not the *cause* of such coordinated movements as locomotion, they are only minor contributors to the *planned* action initiated by the cortex and other higher centers.

The early fascination with the spinal reflex, however, does highlight the aspect of bodily control that is involuntary, the action of smooth muscles and glands. They are under the control of the autonomic nervous system. The autonomic nervous system is the name for the peripheral nerves not subject to voluntary control which regulate the internal state of the body. The *central* control of the autonomic nervous system is not spinal. It is found in a complex of centers in the forebrain. Whatever the nature of the central action that induces autonomic activity, it is not subject to voluntary control, or if it is, as certain of the students of bio-feedback and yoga claim, it is control of a very different nature from the voluntary control available to anyone who does not suffer from some profound neurological disorder or trauma.

The Present Situation

Why is all of this on the history of the reflex relevant to a chapter devoted to freedom of action? Because the develop-ment of the concept of the reflex led to the notion that there is something called voluntary behavior, that is to say behavior *not* under the control of stimuli, chemical agents, and the other con-ditions which make reflex action such a splendid laboratory dis-play. By the growth of our understanding of the complexities of involuntary behavior, here exemplified by the concept of the reflex, there has come into the modern neurosciences, including psy-chology, an absolutely essential conception, that of voluntary be-havior.

Nowhere does this notion have a more central place than in the very heartland of behaviorism itself, the psychology of learning. Psychology had a very hard time absorbing Pavlov's no-tion of the conditioned reflex (despite the ground laid for it by association theory) for the simple reason that Pavlov's theories did not fit the kinds of examples of "elementary" learning that American investigators of the 1920s and 1930s studied—rats in mazes and cats in puzzle boxes. Watson and various others tried to make maze learning fit the description Pavlov offered for the conditioned reflex, and during his highly influential career as a behavioral theorist, a career that extended into the 1950s, Clark L. Hull almost convinced his fellow behaviorists that such a procrus-tean treatment would work.

The correct solution, however, was discovered in the early 1930s by B. F. Skinner and widely publicized in the celebrated textbook by Hilgard and Marquis, *Conditioning and Learning*.[16] Skin-ner's views received their authoritative statement in his 1938 book, *The Behavior of Organisms*,[17] though the basic idea was part of Skinner's Ph.D. dissertation at Harvard and was published in two papers some years earlier. Skinner's views have come to dominate the psychology of learning, though there is dissent here and there.[18] Though things are more complicated than they appeared to be in the 1930s, the distinction between involuntary and voluntary learning, though often under other names, is firmly established.

Skinner's solution was to assert that there were two kinds of learning. One kind, exemplified by Pavlov's conditioned reflex, applied to involuntary behavior, chiefly actions mediated by the autonomic nervous system. Skinner chose the word *respondent* to describe reflexive action. A respondent is any activity that can be *elicited* (Skinner's word) by a stimulating agent. Salivation is mediated by the autonomic nervous system, the integrative action of which is alleged to lie in the hypothalamus. Pavlovian learning occurs when a previously ineffective stimulus is paired with an effective stimulus. A weak acid solution will elicit salivation; the sound of a bell will not. However, as everyone must know by now, after the bell has been paired with the acid, it acquires the ability to elicit salivation. Voluntary learning, what Skinner called *operant* behavior requires a more subtle analysis, and I shall deal with it in a later chapter.

Skinner carefully avoided the terms involuntary and voluntary. But he does make it clear that operant behavior is not elicited, that is to say it is not *caused* by, or to use Skinner's preferred phrase, under the control of an eliciting stimulus. Operant behavior is emitted (once again, to use Skinner's carefully chosen vocabulary). That is to say, it is spontaneous. One brings, according to Skinner, such behavior "under control" by rewarding it. Once rewarded for "emitting" an operant, an organism is more likely to repeat the behavior than before, or at least until the motive that supports the behavior is exhausted (compare with the quote from James on willed behavior, p. 74).

I shall deal with the operant more thoroughly in a later chapter. I introduce the notion here to show that *in the most thoroughly deterministic system in contemporary psychology*, the notion of voluntary behavior, though not under that name, *not only survives but performs an essential function.* For, of course, operant behavior, even in the view of Skinner, is the very stuff out of which the actions of a complex organism like a human being is made.

Even those who have not fully accepted Skinner's analysis make use of the distinction, though most psychologists follow Skinner in carefully avoiding using the word voluntary. The distinction introduced by Hilgard and Marquis went by the labels *classical* (Pavlov) and *instrumental conditioning.* While neurological and physiological texts forthrightly use the contrast, voluntary-involuntary, psychological texts by and large do not, though I suspect many a teacher of introductory psychology helps explain the operant-respondent distinction by slipping in the word voluntary. For whatever reason, the notion of spontaneity is now enthroned at the very center of behavioral psychology.

The American Experiment in Freedom

To turn from the concerns of experimental physiologists and psychologists investigating the actions of dogs, rats, and pigeons to the foundations of the American republic would seem to be an exercise in the kind of old-fashioned Ph.D. examinations which featured such questions as: "What is the relation between the rise of the Dutch Republic and the comedies of Sheridan?" But it is precisely the purpose of this book to establish a connection between these concerns, a connection that is still in a state of turmoil.

The characterization of the American war for independence as something less than a revolution is now a familiar if not universally accepted idea. The American revolution brings a smile to the Marxists, who regard even the French revolution as a sham. Nevertheless, it is not far from the mark to say that the American war for independence began as a rebellion in 1774 and ended with the Bill of Rights as the beginning of a genuine revolution. Either as rebellion or revolution, that war was conceived in and suffused with the notion of freedom. It was freedom from the authority of the British crown and freedom for planters and merchants to prosper without what on this side of the Atlantic was regarded as the oppressive influence of London. This was certainly a rebellion, not a revolution. But it did spawn the Declaration of Independence and, in spirit at least, that was something new. To be sure, the notion of human beings assembling together in equal and voluntary agreement in order to draw up a social compact was not new, but in the Declaration of Independence a social compact in defiance of established authority did establish the beginning of a revolution.

Social compacts that provided precedent ranged from makeshift inheritance from colonial or proprietary sources all the way back to the Magna Carta. But despite the precedent, the Declaration of Independence and the American Constitution were something new. They came out of practical necessity, almost unenlightened by metaphysical, psychological, theological, or philosophical argument. The list of grievances addressed to King George include iniquities that appear to be almost petty after the grand language of the preamble to the Declaration. But it is in that preamble, of course, that the practical was transcended and a political philosophy expressed.

The philosophical ideas behind the American political enlightenment extend back, of course, to antiquity. But the seventeenth century, as in so many other things, provides the well springs of modernity in political philosophy. Locke is traditionally regarded as the godfather of the Declaration of Independence and the notions of government suffusing the American experiment, but Hobbes, that deep pessimist about human nature, that atheist, royalist, and determinist, can lay almost equal claim to the honor. So we have the paradox of the most important American testament to freedom and political responsibility coming from a pair of philosophers who were psychological and naturalistic determinists. Once again, however, I remind the reader that the seventeenth century and the eighteenth century were not the twentieth century. There did not exist then the claim to a vast empirical support, buttressed by the methods of science, for complete psychological determinism.

The Declaration of Independence

No document in the American heritage, not even the Constitution, nor the Bill of Rights, has the hallowed place in the secular faith of Americans that the Declaration of Independence does. Garry Wills, in his insightful book on the subject,[19] points out that this reverence is not only misplaced but a downright embarrassment to the document and its author. Thomas Jefferson had a practical eighteenth-century mind, and he wrote a document for existing conditions of a people who bore a peculiar and unique relation to another people. But that has not prevented the document from being a source of revelation for generations to come, no matter how much that revelation requires a great deal of free interpretation. The belief that it is a source of revelation has obscured the document itself.

Ever since Carl Becker wrote his little treatise[20] on the Declaration, we have been aware of the influence of Locke on that document. That it also owes much to Hobbes we have already acknowledged. That it owes more to the Scottish enlightenment than to the Continental enlightenment is a matter upon which most scholars agree. But there is a more general *Zeitgeist* to the eighteenth-century that spoke to Mr. Jefferson. He was a rationalist, but he was a practical man with a practical man's faith in the scientific method as a procedure for establishing useful knowledge.

Wills, in *Inventing America*, lays much stress on Jefferson's fascination with the eighteenth-century clockwork universe. Wills describes the Declaration as a revolutionary charter, *a scientific paper* (in the eighteenth-century sense), a moral paper, a sentimental paper, and a national symbol. Jefferson's fascination with scientific ways of doing things is evident in such different things as his admiration for David Rittenhouse's "orrery" and his enthusiasm for Sir William Petty's practical and (in spirit at least) "political arithmetic." It does not seem to have occurred to Wills how strange was the concern for freedom in such an intellectual context. He seizes on the word *necessary* in the preamble to the Declaration—"When in the course of human events it becomes necessary"—as an indication of a kind of Newtonian insistence on the inevitability of nature and nature's laws. One would have thought that a monarchical scheme based upon divine right, or the medieval notion of a chain of being, would have been more Newtonian than the disorderly and unpredictable effects of committees and congresses (Wills reminds us of Jefferson's annoyance with the editing of the Declaration accomplished by the Continental Congress).

I think rather than turning to Newtonian mechanics to search for the correct metaphor by which to interpret the Declaration, we must look elsewhere (apart from the pragmatic and immediate sources). I think we find it in the spirit of deism and even of forthright atheism with which the late eighteenth-century intellectuals toyed in the same spirit that the intellectuals of the mid- and later twentieth century toy with Marxism. Eighteenth-century intellectuals were, in a way in which neither Newton nor Descartes were, free from the tyrannies of a judging God. Ignoring the implications of clockwork men in a clockwork universe, eighteenth-century intellectuals could revel in the possibilities of mankind controlling its own destinies. There could be progress in the affairs of men just as there was progress in the affairs of science. Not many thinkers paused to consider the dark implications for the ethics of human actions.

We all know that it is the preamble to the Declaration that expresses these sentiments. Wills points to "necessary," the phrase, "the laws of nature and of nature's God," "truths," that are held to be "self-evident," "inalienable rights" (in Jefferson's original, "inherent and inalienable rights"), in fact to almost every word in the first two paragraphs of the Declaration. But at the same time, the importance of these phrases lies in a political theory that is inconsistent with the view of an orderly nature that they speak to. The notion of the need for revolution from time to time (an offhand notion of Jefferson's) belies the clockwork universe.

Then, there is a dark Hobbesian undercurrent.[21] It is not so much expressed in the preamble as it is in the long list of grievances. It is not against the institution of monarchy that the grievances fume, it is against a particular breach of constitutional rights by a particular monarch that they rage. As Wills points out, the deleted passages even more reinforce this aspect of the Declaration. So, despite its noble preamble, the Declaration is not quite a revolutionary document—a rebellious one but not revolutionary.

The Constitution and the Bill of Rights

In the ferment of pamphlets, commentaries, committee reports, and declarations that came out of revolutionary America, one can find most any point of view. My purposes might better have been served by grubbing among the more obscure documents, but rightly or wrongly, the educated man in the street regards his freedom as stemming from the Declaration of Independence, from the Constitution, and, if he is a liberal, from the Bill of Rights.

The Constitution is a more sober document than the Declaration. It is one that carefully interweaves a thought-out political philosophy with practical matters, matters that grew out of the history of the former colonies, their various governments, special interests, fears, and prejudices. But this is not the main point. The important characteristic of the constitution (including the Bill of Rights) is that it is intensely conservative in tone, indeed defensive. It was designed by eighteenth-century minds who wished to guard against all of the awful contingencies that might befall the newfound tradition of freedom in America. The sections that give permission to the federal authorities to establish taxes, duties, imposts, and excises are more out of the context of the times than are the sections that permit the raising and supporting of armies. In short, whether out of submission to Patrick Henry's views and the views of the others who orated against a federal establishment, the Constitution became a document which, given the historical context, can be read as a defense against the incursion of the governors upon the governed. It is a document that, above all, protects the governed, even though we know that the governed meant only white male property owners.

I know this is a vast oversimplification, but I make these simplistic assertions to point out that reading the Constitution with fresh eyes reveals it to be a document vastly grander in conception than the Declaration. The historical context provided by British neglect, the fears of the smaller states, the interests of the mercantile and plantation establishments aside, it is and was intended to be—current liberal dogma to the contrary— a document for the ages.

It is Hobbesian in its view of the venality of human nature to a degree vastly greater than the Declaration. No one, not in particular the governors, is to be trusted. Everything must be arranged so that each center of power can check every other center of power. No greater testimony to the sense of human freedom to make decisions and the need to check and control the consequences of those decisions could be imagined.

I make these points to contrast the meaning, intent, and uses of the Constitution with those documents which grow out of a boundless trust in human good intentions, scientific skills, and all of the certainty that we, in this later age, seem to be willing to grant to the social sciences. It is, of course, easier to point to Skinner's *Beyond Freedom and Dignity* in this matter (or his earlier *Walden Two*),[22] but such ready targets cause us to ignore the thousand practical and direct ways in which psychology and psychological theories intrude themselves into our affairs in a way which renders insipid the real and imagined tyrannies of King George. These intrusions, both in practice and in principle contravene the purposes which the founders wrote into our Constitution. We can congratulate our political fathers with anticipating the insidious intrusion of religion into the public schools, in the form of prayer, but we must also forgive them for not anticipating the proliferation of sex education courses and life-adjustment courses, which just as surely introduce ethical principles not only alien to but antithetical to an aggrieved portion of our citizenry, surely as numerous as those who object to prayers, but who are not provided with redress through the provision of separation of church and state.

In short, I mean to argue that the social sciences are at war with the specific eighteenth-century purposes of the Constitution, and through loopholes not anticipated by our founding fathers, they are able to impose upon all of us an ethical point of view antithetical to at least some of us. I deal with this problem, as well as the alarming problem of the narrowing of the base of the American consensus, in a later chapter.

The American Constitution, however, I say in its defense, is, as such documents go, mercifully general, and the ever more latitudinarian legal interpretations of it over the past two hundred years have made it even more so, but still it contains such quaintly antiquarian prohibitions as (in the Third Amendment) those against quartering soldiers in citizens' houses. It was silent on the subject of interning Americans whose forebears happened to come from a country at war with America, all's the pity. And its specific prohibition against religion influencing the state does not cover those who claim their ethics to descend not from God or Moses but from the social scientists, more's the pity. The Constitution is appropriately general. Its main thrust against trusting government, no matter how much Hamilton may have argued to the contrary, is something for which we should be thankful. But it does have holes.

The Eighteenth-Century and the Twentieth-Century Mind

I have already, at several places, pointed out that any eighteenth-century faith in material determinism differs from the twentieth-century faith in one important positive respect—the rise of the modern empirical social sciences. There is, however, also a difference that is a debit on the side of the twentieth century. Those eighteenth-century politicians who framed the documents of American freedom were rationalists. That is to say, they believed men were rational, that they could reason correctly, given the correct premises, to correct conclusions. The intellectuals of the twentieth century have not only adopted a naive faith in the validity of empirical social science, they have, in large numbers—perhaps the majority, rejected the notion that man is rational.

Thus eighteenth-century determinism differs from that of the late twentieth century by another important characteristic. Determinism, in the materialistic sense, was a new idea in the eighteenth century. It could be toyed with in a way so as to shock the religious reactionaries. It was part of throwing off the yoke not only of the tattered remains of medieval Christian philosophy but that of the Protestant rebels as well. In the eyes of eighteenth-century deists—Voltaire, Paine, Jefferson—Protestant and Catholic ideas alike were shackles of the past. Rationalism without faith was the order of the day. It is surprising that it has taken us nearly two centuries to catch up with the consequences of that notion.

I cannot resist one further comment on the difference between eighteenth and twentieth-century psychology—as a way of illustrating the retreat of rationalism. Twentieth-century determinists talk about the personalities of their sons and daughters as being shaped by their sexual relations with their parents as easily as eighteenth-century philosophers could discourse on pleasure and pain. One's attachment to a phase of childhood sexuality is irrational; the general search for pleasure and the avoidance of pain is not. Thus, the authors of the Declaration of Independence and the Bill of Rights may have pinned their allegiance to material determinism, but they were also rationalists. That is not to say that they were not guilty of the very human failing of inconsistency. They were, in a curious way, like the Western intellectuals of the 1920s who went to Russia and said "I've seen the future, and it works." There is, in the eighteenth century as well as in the twentieth century, the allegiance of unthinking rhetoric. The real faith of the eighteenth century was in the importance of human freedom in the social order and in the intense, indeed overriding need to defend that freedom. The faith of the twentieth-century psychologist, be he or she psychoanalyst or behaviorist, is in those external conditions that control the irrational follies of human behavior and mentality. There is all the difference in the world. The eighteenth century was real in its rationalism and academic (awful phrase to a professor!) in its determinism.

The twentieth century takes irrational determination of human actions for granted, at least as the twentieth century is represented in the mainstream of the social sciences.

The Will in Popular American Culture

In the last chapter, by way of providing illustration for the current of pessimism, materialism (in the philosophic sense), and determinism in American culture, I mentioned some of the figures from the naturalism movement in American literature—Dreiser, Norris, and London. I also alluded to Twain (both as a novelist and essayist) and to H. L. Mencken.

Is there any comparable body of writing on the side of the freedom of the individual to regulate his own life? The answer is yes, though that body of writing does not usually come to the attention of students of literature. I mention, by way of illustration, Horatio Alger, Ayn Rand, and the vast American addiction to self-help literature. To be sure, those who comment on Horatio Alger remind us that the climb to the top managed by his heroes is always initiated by some bit of luck. But such is often the case with individual effort. I reminded the reader at the beginning of this chapter that there is one overriding difference in assumptions between those who argue for determinism and those who argue for freedom. Determinism, almost by definition, is meant to be universally applied. It is the iron law of history, the omnipotent will of God, or the steel grip of heredity and environment. Those who argue for a modicum of individual human, or even more generally, animate freedom do so always with the disclaimer that to a certain degree actions are determined. They are, in the view of most who so argue, determined more by nature than by God, though scattered throughout the history of Christian theology are arguments to the effect that either God relinquishes some of His power to human beings or that He only occasionally intervenes in the affairs of His creation.

Thus, the initial luck achieved by Horatio Alger's heroes is not out of keeping with a faith in individual freedom and responsibility. Being at the right place at the right time is important. The self-help literature is less candid, however. The success of such figures as Dale Carnegie and Napoleon Hill depended upon their absolute resistance to any possibility of failure.[23] Everything was up to the individual. "Think positively," said Carnegie; "think and grow rich" said Hill. It is this unyielding, categorical faith in the ability of the individual to rule his own life that makes these writers so distasteful and trivial to anyone who thinks at all seriously about the human condition.

At the same time, the more sophisticated self-help literature, particularly that of more recent times, does admonish the reader to take advantage of opportunities. Seek them out, but be alert to identifying them when they happen along, then use them. Implicit in such advice is the fact that the individual cannot control everything. Furthermore, a considerable portion of the self-help literature is given over to advice about how to control others. That is to say, the theme is be master of your own destiny, but learn to prey upon the human weaknesses of others.

Most Americans, I suspect, hold to the commonsense view that certain things are determined for them, while they are free to a degree and in charge of themselves. However, the range of perceived freedom is narrowing, and that is the problem. Sociologists, particularly those with Marxist leanings, talk of alienation in this connection. However it is conceived and to whatever we attribute its causes, there is a developing sense of individual powerlessness. At the same time, the management of American politics, the distribution of criminal justice, and other official and institutional exemplifications of the balancing of our faith in freedom and determination all show a tilt against freedom. Criminal justice as well as the remedial steps taken by government and social agencies to reduce crime all appear to be on the side of the notion that moral and social deviancies are caused by the conditions of the lives of persons and not in any way the responsibility of those individuals. At the same time, political campaigns are managed, not in the interests of arguing the merits of one set of proposed actions or another, but in the interests of packaging attractive candidates and influencing voters by the techniques designed to sell one soap powder rather than another.

These things are the result of managerial, bureaucratic, and professional classes reared, so to speak, on the social and behavioral sciences. Those currently responsible for the management of politics, social policy, and criminal justice may be the first generation to have been educated in an ethos provided chiefly by the modern social and behavioral sciences. There is certainly no precedent in legal history for the now common practice of hiring sociologists and psychologists as consultants in jury selection.

Chapter Five

The Ethos
of Contemporary Psychology:
I. Behaviorism

In the next three chapters I examine three representative aspects of modern psychology: behaviorism,
experimental social psychology, and psychohistory. These by no
means exhaust the astounding range of psychology today, but they
are representative respectively of hardheadedness in psychology,
the experimental intrusion into "real life," and the detailed analysis of a single individual's personality. All three of these illustrations serve as examples of a misplaced faith in psychological
determinism. This chapter is devoted mainly to behaviorism and
specifically to the behaviorism of B. F. Skinner and his school.

Experimental Psychology

Both behaviorism and contemporary social psychology owe their
primary methodological allegiance to experimentation. I have, in
earlier chapters, commented on aspects of psychology's devotion

to experimentation as the method of choice, but before I can deal with these two representative aspects of modern psychology, I must make explicit certain views that I hold about the experimental method in psychology.

The nineteenth-century notion—that is to say Wilhelm Wundt's—of experimentation in psychology bears almost no resemblance to the late twentieth century's view of it. Brass instruments, the Hipp Chronoscope, and introspection have given way to animals, the computer, and the observance of behavior. What, however, has remained unchanged over the intervening century is the faith that psychology is a kind of natural science, that is to say the faith that all of the great tools of the physical sciences are at the service of psychology. Among these tools is experimentation. The ability to tease out physical variables, change them, and then observe what happens to other physical variables is the empirical basis for causative inference. And this is the essential message of any good textbook in experimental psychology, save for the fact that psychologists ignore and drop the adjective *physical*. For psychology, the supreme method of investigation is supposed to be provided by the ability to alter variables in the interests of observing changes that result in other variables. I believe the omission of the adjective physical to be a profound mistake, and it has resulted in the common abuse of the experimental method by psychologists.

I shall argue that experimentation can be properly interpreted only when both the independent and dependent variables are physical. When genuine *psychological* conditions intervene, experimentation becomes, to the degree of the intervention, uninterpretable. However, there are, as I pointed out earlier, various senses of the word physical. At the risk of being repetitious, I invoke that distinction again.

The Two Senses of Physical

I use the word physical in two ways. They are related, but they are different enough to require description. In particular they need to be contrasted with the psychological. The common meaning of physical is simply a way of pointing to the world of things and motions as·these are represented in experience. The other is a way of describing the totality of the theoretical foundations of the physical sciences. That description evokes the entire grand structure of physics and chemistry, those sciences which, at their very best, manage to portray the world as a set of abstractions, ultimately mathematical in nature.

That ultimate meaning of the nature of physical theory, however, is seldom achieved in practice. Physical theory exists in as many ways as there are people who understand it. We all comprehend the nature of molecules, atoms, quarks, pions, and the like in different ways. My comprehension is surely different from those of my colleagues who are molecular biologists, chemists, nuclear physicists, and particle physicists. And all of these persons surely comprehend the physical world in their different ways. We all, including mathematical physicists, share a dependence upon models. Models are really metaphors of a kind. Models or metaphors of abstractions in terms of the familiar help human beings understand the mathematics they embody by stating them in a form which lend themselves to human ways of thinking. Human ways of thinking are determined by experience—by learning—and the fundamental categories of human perception and learning.

But there is another sense in which the theoretical entities of physics have meaning. They enable us to do things—to build meters and scintillation counters, to do chromatography and electron microscopy. The psychobiologist who uses a scintillation counter has only a vague and impractical notion of how the thing works. He has faith, a faith in physical theory and in the physicists and engineers who design and build the thing.

By contrast, I use the word psychological to refer to our states of experience, the various ways of characterizing the abilities that lie behind our actions, and the various ways we have of characterizing our individualities. Words like emotion, seeing, motivation, and character have no physical description (though we often try to give accounts of physical processes that may accompany them). It is precisely this fact that gave rise to the attempt to make psychology a science of behavior, for behavior is physical in the simpler sense of that word. Along with that attempt went a vast interest among experimental psychologists in the philosophy of science.

In a more refined and philosophical vein the view of physical theory as the embodiment of ideas in things and actions is exemplified by the once popular philosophy of science known as operationalism. Operationalism was invented by the experimental physicist, Percy W. Bridgman and given voice in his 1927 book, *The Logic of Modern Physics*.[1] While Bridgman's methodological strictures have largely been forgotten by physicists, in the form of the notion of "converging operations" they are very much alive in psychology. Operationalism's twin, logical positivism, seems to have fallen on evil times in psychology; no one wants to own up to it nowadays. But the spirit of these ideas, particularly of operationalism, lives on in psychology. The reality of psychological concepts is to be found in the operations and results they produce, and, so experimental psychologists have argued lo these many years, operations upon psychological matters in the laboratory can produce theoretical entities that in the mental realm are the equivalent of those in physics.

However unsophisticated operationalism might appear to contemporary philosophers of science, many of whom have come to appreciate the deep role faith plays in science, it does describe an important aspect of the reality of scientific investigation. Physical theory *is* useful in dealing with things in the world. A great deal of classical experimental psychology, particularly as exemplified in the study of the special senses, reveals a comparable usefulness. The study of sensation and perception makes use of physical theory to provide control over and a rational means of describing the results of experiments. Students of sensation and perception have made notable contributions to the knowledge of how the body works. The reader may remember from his or her course in introductory psychology something called the duplicity theory of vision. It is a theory about the receptors in the eye, and it was originally based upon observations that could have been made in the psychological laboratory.

Thus, in both senses of the word physical, certain experiments in the psychological laboratory are physical. I have already alluded to the study of the special senses, ordinarily called psychophysics. The contemporary psychobiologist recording activity from cells in the geniculate body of the cat brain when light is shined on the retina of the cat's eye knows pretty much what he or she is doing in physical terms. The investigator may not fully understand the events that transform the photic energy into the electrochemical energy of the nerve impulse. But if he or she does not fully understand the physical process, it is totally unnecessary to suppose that some judgmental process on the part of the anesthetized cat intervenes. The psychobiologist works then on a purely physical system.

The psychophysicist who works with human beings on similar problems is only slightly less fortunate. He may, on the one hand, have to make do with a poorly understood electrical response of the cerebral hemispheres recorded in an inexact and awkward way from the scalp of his experimental subjects, or—worse—may have to work with the frank help of human judgment. That is to say, he may ask his experimental subjects to say when something—a light—is first detected. While the psychophysicist does depart in principle from the physical demands of experimental science, he or she does so in a minor way only. The judgmental process, however little it is understood, in practice produces reliable results. In a simple psychophysical experiment any deviation from instructions, either through failure to comprehend or through willful misbehavior, is easy to detect. Many years ago, in teaching experimental psychology I subjected students to an experiment on hue discrimination. The students tested themselves on a spectrophotometer. One student produced a perfect hue discrimination function—textbook quality. I was suspicious, and I administered the Ishihara test of color blindness to him. He failed the test. Indeed, his hue discrimination function was textbook perfect.

So while human psychophysical experiments have an inherent weakness, they are rooted enough in physical theory and psychobiology to be reliable. Occasionally they mislead, and occasionally we must use the results from them with great caution.

Psychophysical measurements are occasionally used to establish the time course of the action of some psychologically active drugs. The experiments employing such procedures are useful, though we do not know how they work; therefore, they must be used with care.

I now turn briefly to the more common interpretation of the word physical as it might apply in psychological experimentation. Biologists of the nineteenth century had few physical tools useful in experimentation, but to a remarkable degree they were able to do things without physical instrumentation or theory. And many of the things that they did were profoundly important. The most famous example is provided by Mendel and his experimental crossing of sweet peas. Mendel needed no appeal to physical principles. Unlike the psychophysical experiments of the nineteenth century, these experiments could have been done by someone totally ignorant of and uninfluenced by the whole of the physics of the time. Mendel simply did what plant breeders had been doing for a century or more. The difference was that he did his crossbreeding in the interests of establishing the validity of a theory of inheritance. Out of Mendel's work grew one of the two great triumphs of pure biology, the gene. In the last half of the twentieth century that purely biological concept has become assimilated to —become reduced to—physical theory, perhaps the most striking example of successful reductionism in the whole of science.

It was this kind of physicality—Mendel's—that the behaviorists have generally yearned for. Behavior was observable and hence, in the ordinary sense, physical. Very few behaviorists are or were committed reductionists.[2] Most were content to believe in vague slogans about the unity of science, but for the most part they sturdily defended the study of behavior as a science in its own right. Even so, they did not, as they claimed, really study "responses." Rather they studied the *consequences* of responses. It is of no concern to most owners of Skinner boxes how rats press levers in them; they are only interested in the fact that the levers are pressed. Whether the rats, on particular occasions, use teeth or tails is of no consequence. Hence the physicality of experiments on operant behavior is at best dubious.

This brings me to a major point. Much behavioral investigation, in the laboratory or out of it, is characterized by a feature that removes it even further from the canons of physical experimentation than were Mendel's observations. Many so-called experiments, including field experiments, deal with behavior that, in the previous chapter, we saw were characterized by physiologists as voluntary. I find it hard to deny that investigators can point to evidence for a degree of "control" over the voluntary behavior of animals and small children—and even over adults in strange circumstances, but it is, from the standpoint of the canons of science, a very strange kind of control. It is not control in which some *antecedent* event appears to influence some *subsequent* event, a state of affairs demanded of ordinary science save in the wildest flights of imagination. The operant is controlled by what happens afterwards.

The Fruits of Experimentation

Where behavioral experimentation has been at its weakest is where it is the servant of psychological theory. The thousands of experiments performed in the mid years of the twentieth century attempting to establish the validity of one or another theory of learning were, with few exceptions, a vast waste of time. Nothing was settled, and the experiments themselves uncovered almost nothing of intrinsic interest. The sterility of these experiments drove a sizable army of investigators into so-called cognitive psychology. Cognitive psychology timidly reintroduced the rhetoric of mind, but the methods, the ideas, and the problems were those of behaviorism wedded to what was once fashionable to call verbal learning.

It is true that current psychological theories of possible mental processes are concerned with more important matters than were earlier ones—the question of massed versus distributed practice seems mercifully to have disappeared. Some of the impetus for this development has come from outside of psychology—from the study of artificial intelligence and from linguistics. But theories or models of thought and memory remain deficient to a large and unknown degree. And, what is more important, we have few ways to apply theories of mental processing, studied by behavioral methods, to anything that might exist outside of the laboratory.

This lamentable state of affairs stems from two conditions. One is the devotion the behavioral sciences have paid to the *idea* of experimentation, and the other is to the belief that behavioral data will enable us to decide among one or another theory as to how the mind works. The larger part of data from cognitive psychology and in particular data gathered by the methods traditionally regarded as experimental has had as its chief if not sole function that of deciding among various psychological theories. Most data relevant to the testing of theories about how mental processes comprehend and produce language come from the use of artificial materials—bits and snippets of language especially invented for the purpose, and these materials are reacted to by human beings called, with a certain irony, subjects, under artificial and sometimes very odd circumstances. The reactions, furthermore, are seldom those required in ordinary life, or, if they are, they are supplemented by the need to perform additional, strange reactions. A person may be asked, for example, to try to locate the precise moment at which a click interrupted or was superimposed upon a sentence to which he or she was listening.[3] Or the person may be asked to push a button when a decision has been reached as to the correct interpretation of an ambiguous sentence. The sentences (and, more recently, discourses) are systematically varied with respect to certain features. Grammatical constructions, content, and even the way the sentences sound may be the objects of study. The point of such investigations is to inform us what goes on—presumably in the network of neurons that constitute the brain—when we comprehend and produce language.

The authors of such investigations do them because various theories, models, or fragments of theories are supposed to generate hypotheses about the way in which people will react under specified circumstances. If the results of an experiment resemble the results predicted by a theory or model, the theory or model is supposed to be made more plausible and perhaps even elevated above all of its rivals (rival theories are very important; the significance of a given theory can only be appreciated by contrast with its alternatives, often made of straw). Long experience has taught contemporary investigators not to expect any particular result to be crucial in this respect.[4] Nevertheless a particular result is supposed to establish at least the parochial superiority of some one notion, that is until some disbeliever demonstrates an artifact in the experiment or produces one that contradicts it. The superiority is parochial because another experiment, using different techniques with different materials, may establish the superiority of a rival theory, usually a new one, thought up by the experimenter.

      The process inherent in the generation of such experiments has, of course, the multiplying effect familiar to economists. New experiments proliferate. They are ever more complicated, subtle, and removed from the demands made by the ordinary use of language or intelligence. The process continues until the investigators lose interest and turn to some new method, theory, or line of experimentation.

      Sometimes the theories are highly developed and sophisticated. They make use of mathematical reasoning. More often than not, however, the prediction of some particular result entails a host of unwritten assumptions. Sometimes these assumptions are plausible. For example, most cognitive theorists of the past dozen years assume that some process requiring a large number of steps or stages to accomplish the end result takes longer than a process requiring few steps or stages. However, it doesn't really make any difference, for the issues at stake disappear with the next generation of theorists and experimenters. I suspect that we shall hear less and less about the click experiments in the future.

      The resources used in this enterprise are awe-inspiring, even by contemporary standards of megabuck science. I estimate, by counting the appropriate entries in the *Psychological Abstracts* for the years 1970, 1976, and 1979, that the decade of the 1970s has seen nearly 8,000 papers published, whose principal aim is the establishment of the correctness of some particular notion about how language is processed by the mind. This is a wild underestimation, for I eliminated from my count any paper which (1) examined some special group of people, such as four-year olds, persons afflicted with aphasia, or senior citizens; (2) made use of some physiological measure such as event-related potentials; (3) examined some special problem not arising from information processing or cognitive theory (thus I excluded any paper that purported to examine the differences between the functions of the right and left cerebral hemispheres); or (4) which studied a task that had some remote possibility of having practical application (reading, for example). These eliminations provide for underestimation because, as anyone knows who has ever tried to obtain funds to support research or get access to people to test, remote, very remote possible practical applications are used to justify experiments the real purpose of which is theoretical.

Again, on the absurdly conservative estimate that each of these experiments costs an average of $20,000 each,[5] the cost of all of this activity for the decade in question has been about $160 million. And I left out of my count dissertations not published, books, and chapters in books. Finally, there is no way to count the experiments performed and never published. It is my firm opinion that all of this activity has produced almost nothing of permanent value. This judgment is based upon the belief that we can neither understand how the mind works nor how the brain works by subjecting people to the kind of testing procedures that are the stock in trade of cognitive experimental psychology.

The result of a long history—stemming back to Ebbinghaus—of experimental cognitive psychology is a huge wastepile of experimental problems that have not been solved but which are now seen as irrelevant to any matter of importance. Who would be so bold nowadays as to offer for publication a paper aimed at testing the inhibitory-excitatory theory of the serial-position effect?[6] The serial-position effect is still with us. One sees occasional reference to the matter, and it always turns up if not as an artifact of some experimental arrangements at least as a side effect. And it still stubbornly resists explanation.[7]

I preface my account of the heartland of modern behaviorism by this recital of the melancholy business of modern cognitive psychology not because I am particularly disenchanted with cognitive psychology (or as it seems increasingly to be called, information processing) but because it has often been held up as the savior of mentalistic psychology out to slay the dragon of behaviorism. The truth of the matter is that it suffers from all of the faults of behaviorism—the devotion to experimentation, the belief that somehow psychological theory can pick itself up by its ears, and an imagined objectivity. Furthermore, it lacks some of the virtues of the most important brand of contemporary behaviorism, the experimental analysis of behavior. I refer to the important and widespread work that has followed from the writings of B. F. Skinner. The great virtue of this work is the steadfast faith— in which only a few waver—that psychological research cannot explicate mental processes nor (and here I disagree) should much concern itself with underlying biological processes.

The Prediction and Control of Behavior

The history of psychology is strewn with paradoxes, but none more ironic than the fact that the psychologist most responsible for introducing the distinction between voluntary and involuntary behavior into behavioral theory is the author of *Beyond Freedom and Dignity*. The distinction, which we touched on in the last chapter, is between operant and respondent behavior, and the psychologist is B. F. Skinner. That distinction, introduced in the early 1930s by Skinner, has been almost universally acknowledged. Although there are occasional attempts to ignore it or to reduce operant learning to respondent learning, it is hard to find a contemporary textbook on learning that does not accept the distinction as given.

The distinction is both important and puzzling. It is puzzling because Skinner is, as are most behavioral psychologists, a complete determinist. The distinction is important because the "control" over operant behavior is very different in nature from that exerted by stimuli in reflexes. I go back to Aristotle's distinction among causes to point to the significance of the distinction. However, I shall content myself with saying that the "control" of operant behavior by reinforcements violates the most fundamental canons of modern conceptions of scientific causation. To put it simply and bluntly, it operates backwards. I know that this interpretation (first suggested by critics of Thorndike) is smiled at by behaviorists. The operation of reinforcement is not backwards on the response just made but is forward on the probability of producing the same response in the future they say. But it is precisely this view that produces the problem. It requires that an organism, a rat or a human being, *interpret* the reinforcement and its probable future course. There is no way by using the tools of science that we can understand or trace that interpretation. What is more, it is certain to be different in rats and human beings. We understand reflexes in principle, even though we may not be able to trace all of the physical events from stimulus to response for every reflex in rats and people. But it is a sequence of physical events. There is no interpretation that intervenes (though, of course, autonomic, that is to say reflexive, actions may be elicited *indirectly* by mental events). We can do no better in trying to understand the gulf that separates operant from respondent than to examine Skinner's view of the problem.

Skinner's Operant and Respondent

The distinction between operants and respondents was first made in Skinner's Ph.D. dissertation submitted to the Harvard department of psychology. It was published as a paper in 1931.[8] It did not attract as much attention as it deserved until the basic argument reappeared in Skinner's 1938 book.[9] It is from this influential work that I take a description of the distinction.

First of all, Skinner distinguishes between narration and a reflex. Narration results from the methods of natural history —what we would now call ethology. It is descriptive, but it is not, in Skinner's view, scientific because one cannot study "functional relations" by the method. Skinner then goes on to tell us that one kind of functional relationship is established by the external forces acting upon the organism. He then goes into a very sophisticated *psychological* account of how the environment controls the respondent. He tells us that a part of the environment may be segmented out, and that that segment is correlated with a particular kind of behavior. The segmented part of the environment is the stimulus, and the correlated behavior is the response. The stimulus-response relationship is the reflex. The reflex provides an instance of "predictable uniformity" in behavior.

This account is far from the traditional physiological definition of the reflex, though it does hark back to Descartes, not surprisingly, because Descartes' ignorance of how the central nervous system operates is matched by a willful decision on Skinner's part to ignore, in so far as possible, the physiological aspects of behavior, reflex or operant.

Skinner then goes on to reject the "botanizing of reflexes."[10] He quotes Watson to the effect that psychology is the science of predicting responses given certain stimuli, but then he goes on to say that this is an "impracticable" program. The number of reflexes is simply too large. Skinner at the same time sees the reflex as of comparatively minor interest in the study of behavior, and it is in this dismissal of Watson that we see this view coming to the front. He does not deny that behavior is reflexive, he simply says that the study of what he calls the "topography" of reflexes is uninteresting.

A considerable section is then devoted[11] to a very traditional rephrasing of the dynamic characteristics of reflexes (the laws of the threshold, latency, facilitation, etc.). This section concludes with the statement of the "law of conditioning of type S and the law of extinction of type S." These "laws" are simply a restatement of some of the basic principles of conditioning discovered by Pavlov. Skinner here makes no mention of any special segregation of type S conditioning to involuntary behavior or to behavior of the autonomic nervous system. In the light of what he had said earlier we must be left with the simple conclusion that any identification of reflexes with involuntary or autonomic behavior is uninteresting, just as the topography of reflexes themselves is uninteresting.

But, in the very next section, Skinner backs down from the position that the reflex is *merely* uninteresting or unimportant. He tells us that there is a large body of behavior that *does not seem to be elicited*—by contrast, presumably with the large body of behavior that is elicited. He uses the example of a cinder in the eye as something that does elicit behavior, behavior that is presumably reflexive. He describes the alternative to reflexive behavior as "spontaneous" (the quotation marks are Skinner's, not mine). He quotes the anatomist Bethe to the effect that spontaneity is simply a term for describing behavior for which the stimuli are not known. Having so capitulated to the common deterministic idea of emitted behavior (to use Skinner's term) as simply a case of reflexive behavior to unknown stimuli, an article of faith to many of Skinner's rivals, he then goes on to treat spontaneous behavior is purely spontaneous—that is to say endogeneous. He tells us that spontaneous behavior is behavior for which the "originating forces" (Skinner's words) are not in the environment. It is behavior that is emitted. The word emitted is italicized in Skinner's text.

And so now there is elicited behavior, called respondent, and spontaneous or emitted behavior, called operant. But nothing more is said about the "originating forces" that produce operant behavior. Skinner goes on to tell us how operant behavior may be brought "under control" by reinforcement and how the rate of emission of that bahavior is governed both by "drive" and by conditions of reinforcement. Skinner has little to say about drive, both in his *magnum opus* and elsewhere. There is, in the *Behavior of Organisms*, a late chapter on drive,[12] but little is said about the concept except to illustrate it through variation in time of deprivation of food. He does tell us that drive is a hypothetical state meant to summarize relations between the "operations" of deprivation and behavior.

The operant that is to be brought under control by reinforcement must be produced spontaneously. There are, as every student of behavior modification knows, various stratagems for bringing a response that is not likely to occur when one wants it to into existence. Shaping is the principal of these stratagems. In shaping, a response that is likely to occur naturally is reinforced; the response is as close to the targeted response as the natural behavior of the organism in question allows. Then, by a process of discrimination (alternatively reinforcing responses closer to the targeted response and extinguishing responses distant from the targeted response), the desired response is shaped. Thus pigeons can play Ping-Pong and chickens perform on a toy piano.

All of this is perfectly tuned to the determinism-freedom dichotomy. I have not ever encountered any advocate of the notion of free will who argues that the will is totally free, or totally —to use Skinner's term—spontaneous. There is a lunatic fringe ranging from the Marquis de Sade to Ayn Rand which seems to argue that, as a matter of morality, the will *ought* to be totally free, but I know of few other writers who do not adopt something like the distinction between respondent and operant behavior, however named. However this may be, Skinner argues that the operant is under just as much control as the respondent, only the principle of control is different.

How the Operant Is Controlled

A response is selected, and it is reinforced by water for a thirsty animal or food for a hungry animal. The response is something that is perfectly clear to see, but more importantly it is something that can be recorded. The response must close a circuit, operate a solenoid, or whatever. For rats it is a lever which these animals, with their clever forefeet, push down. For pigeons it is a button which they press with their beaks. For very clever animals and animals with opposable thumbs it may be something as complicated as a joy stick.

The initial events in such experiments are not impressive, nor are they particularly orderly. It may take one animal only ten minutes to learn the connection between its response and the resulting delivery of food or whatever, while the next animal may take two hours, or may have to be removed from the experiment in order to make way for a more cooperative creature. But at some point, most animals will begin pushing levers or buttons with monotonous regularity, at least so long as they are hungry or thirsty. The response is now said to be under control. And to the naive it is impressive indeed, particularly if the response is not observed directly, so that all of the quirky variations in responding can be seen. It is very impressive when it is observed through that special device of Skinner's, the cumulative record. The graph of a cumulative recorder is difficult to visualize, and I intend to present no illustration of it. Suffice it to say that every time the animal responds, a line jogs upward on a piece of graph paper. The result is to show the *rate* at which an animal performs the response (about seven responses per minute for a rat pressing a lever). The line appears to be extraordinarily regular—smooth, that is to say. That part of its regularity is an illusion created by making the temporal units very small on the graph paper is well known, as is the fact that the cumulative nature of the curve itself produces a false sense of regularity.

All this aside, it is a fact that the animal generally goes about producing its appropriate operant in the Skinner box with great industry. Furthermore, we may observe "lawful" changes in behavior when (1) schedules of reinforcement are varied, and (2) drive or motive conditions altered, or (3) when drugs are given to the animals. The cumulative curves bend or take on scalloped shapes depending upon the variations in external conditions. It all looks very much like the regularities of genuine experimental science.

A closer inspection reveals that these regularities rely much more heavily upon the circumstantial context than any experimental results in the physical world. First of all, the results depend upon the geography of the Skinner box. To put it bluntly, the box must be as boring as possible for those marvelous regularities to exhibit themselves. There must be no companions, nothing interesting to do but push the lever or the button. In short, if there is nothing else to do and nothing to distract, the animal will press the lever. This is not, as we shall see, the same as the simplifications of physical science. Otherwise the behavior is unpredictable. There is in this situation nothing like the principles of inhibition and facilitation that so fascinated early students of the reflex. To be sure, any one reasonably familiar with the behavior of animals *of the particular species in question* could "predict" the effect of introducing, say, another animal of the same species into the box, but such a prediction would not be based upon a hard theory of the determination of animal behavior so much as upon careful observation of what animals do when they are free to behave naturally.

But all of this is more or less irrelevant, for the real problem comes in interpreting the control that is exerted by the reinforcement. It depends upon the animal seeing a connection between its behavior and the consequences of that behavior and thus altering its actions accordingly. Feedback devices do exist in reflexive behavior, but they are of a fixed and invariant sort. Thus, sweating is a useful device for lowering one's body temperature under ordinary circumstances, but it will not help save one in a burning room. Such a situation requires the potentially variable and intellect-driven character of voluntary behavior.

There are a number of theories as to how organisms see the connections between acts and their consequences, none of them having any basis in fact. Some theorists derive the relation from classical conditioning (or classical associationism). Others gabble about means-ends readiness. But almost no one among behavioral theorists is apparently even willing to contemplate the possibility that the relation may be achieved differently in different organisms and even differently in different members of the same species.

In order to have some scientific understanding of the relation between the operant and its consequences, we should have to possess knowledge of the physical mechanisms underlying the performance of the response. We should have to know how the brain organizes itself so as to emit the response in the first place, and then we should have to know how it puts together the complicated consequences of that response—the visual, auditory, olfactory, and gustatory consequences so as to mobilize that system for another attempt to produce roughly the same set of consequences again. Needless to say, we have nothing like the neurophysiological information that would enable us to give a satisfactory account of that relation. Furthermore, if and when we do—and there are dedicated and clever neuroscientists working on the problem—the solution will be stated in *neurophysical terms*. Concepts of reinforcement, response rate, etc., will disappear and be replaced by an account of the problem stated in terms that come out of an understanding of how the nervous system deals with information.

The Uses of the Study of Operant Behavior

All of this reads as though I disapprove of the Skinner box and the study of operant behavior. I do not. It has proven to be a useful tool in psychotechnology. Rate of responding in the Skinner box (or a comparable device for other organisms) provides a sensitive indicator for psychopharmacological studies. Furthermore, studies of schedules of reinforcements have served to remind us that we (and other creatures) react differently and to a degree predictably to various rates of reinforcement. I suspect that the study of operant behavior in devices like Skinner boxes has a less important role in the understanding of the natural history of organisms than do field studies in ethology, but they do have a role. My problem lies in any notion which views the reinforcement as the cause, in the physical sense, of the behavior. Thus what I object to is the notion that experiments in Skinner boxes reveal voluntary behavior to be rigidly controlled by the consequences of actions. Skinner tells us in *Beyond Freedom and Dignity*:

> Behavior which operates upon the environment to produce consequences ("operant" behavior) can be studied by arranging environments in which specific consequences are contingent upon it. The contingencies under investigation have become steadily more complex, and one by one they are taking over the explanatory functions previously assigned to personalities, states of mind, feelings, traits of character, purposes, and intentions.[13]

Such a statement goes far beyond the modest uses of the study of operant behavior in the laboratory, and I suspect that such statements do little to give modern behaviorism intellectual credibility beyond the narrow circle of its believers. One of my purposes in writing this book is to try to persuade my fellow psychologists that making extravagant claims about psychological knowledge does far more harm to our discipline than it does to bring prestige and acceptance to the psychological sciences.

I cannot resist one more quotation from Skinner's work, both because it reveals the depths of fatuity from which these ideas spring and also because it makes a claim that nearly all psychologists do and that is embarrassing in its error—namely that it is "ethically neutral." To wit: "A culture is like the experimental space used in the study of behavior. It is a set of contingencies of reinforcement, a concept which has only recently begun to be understood. The technology of behavior which emerges is ethically neutral, but when applied to the design of a culture, the survival of the culture functions as a value." [14]

That last phrase, "the survival of the culture functions as a value" could almost be attributed to Spengler. In any case, Skinner's claim to the truth of a determination of human fate is even less well grounded than Spengler's. And it demeans all of us who think of ourselves as trying to understand man's mind by whatever means are appropriate. The worst of it is that there are probably some true believers out there who are trying to design or, as the more usual phrase goes, "engineer" a culture in which we all may maximize our positive reinforcements.

Behavioral control, applied to a variety of problems, has achieved a modicum of success. Programed learning, which goes back at least to Sidney Pressey and more likely to E. L. Thorndike, has made some contribution to technological aids in learning, though the vastly larger part of such contributions have been made by computer engineers. In fact, all of the various notions that the psychologists have advanced—from "error-free programs" to "immediate feedback" are neither new nor demonstrable as being the royal path to immediate and tearless learning.

In short, behavioral technology has made some contributions to ways to studying the central nervous system; it has also adapted some old pedagogical techniques to the modern world, but it is by no means the wave of the future, despite the inflated claims by Skinner and others. A final quote from *Beyond Freedom and Dignity*: "An experimental analysis shifts the determination of behavior from autonomous man to the environment—an environment responsible both for the evolution of the species and for the repertoire acquired by each member." [15]

So much for an ethically neutral behavioral psychology. All of the ethical burden falls on the environment. As much as most psychologists regard Skinner as being hopelessly simplistic, almost all psychologists share a faith in the culpability of the environment. Even the Freudians do.

The Varieties of Behaviorism

I do not mean to say that Skinner and his followers are the only behaviorists about. It is true, however, that there is no one so completely in command of the self-conscious aspect of the behaviorist movement as to be almost identical with it. But behaviorism has permeated the whole of psychology. Mercifully, we hear less about stimulus-response psychology than we used to (and we have to thank Skinner's operant for that), but even contemporary cognitive psychology, which, though it is influenced by Chomsky and other linguists, is at the bottom behavioristic. It indulges in theories which are supposed to be justified by "behavioral" measures—reaction time and the like. Skinner is a convenient target not because he is so ingenuous but because he creates the very argument against a deterministic behaviorism. In his naive devotion to experimentation he is not very far from those who claim allegiance to cognitive psychology. Furthermore, Skinner is to be thanked because he refuses to indulge in the empty theorizing that so permeates experimental psychology. We no longer make our students learn about "reaction potential" and "habs" and "wats." Under the banner of cognitive psychology, however, we subject them to the absurdities of the new mental chronometry.

On these scores Skinner is to be applauded. It is only in his simplistic notions about the control of behavior that he endangers
the conceptual structure of psychology and our concepts of human
freedom.

Behavior Therapy

By now, those who deal with the complexities of the
varieties of psychotherapy know not only that there is something
called behavior therapy, but that such label covers a great diversity
of theories, techniques, and hortatory advice. Behavior modification seems to mean techniques of improving the human psyche
through the reinforcement methods more or less adapted from
Skinner's study of operant behavior. As such it falls in the mainstream of the vast American appetite for self-improvement programs.[16] To be sure, token economies lie outside of that
mainstream,[17] but even token economies, for all of their dependence on the repressive atmosphere of the Skinner box, have a
certain air of if not self-improvement then putting someone on
the road to self-improvement. Once again, I am astonished by the
contrast between Skinnerian rhetoric of determinism and the
sense of old-fashioned help-yourself-up-by-your-bootstraps that
comes out of behavior modification. The whole object of behavior
modification, when one reads the literature on the subject in an
objective way, appears to be to provide conditions under which
the *choice* of the right thing to do is made as easy as possible—see
no evil, hear no evil, etc.

On the other hand there is another vast wing to the
behavior therapy movement which relies not upon operant techniques but upon control of the environmental elicitors of respondent behavior (to remain with the terminology invented by
Skinner). The techniques described in this method are variously
labeled aversive therapy, implosive therapy, conditioning therapy,
etc. The whole point of the techniques advocated by these notions
is to provide for extinction of reflexive like (in the sense of involuntary) reactions to stimuli in the environment. The techniques so
advocated merge over into the myriad programs for bodily im-

provement described in such notions as biofeedback, yoga, etc. Despite the reliance on limited and not very convincing theories ("learned helplessness"),[18] these notions have a certain appeal, for they deal with the undeniable fact that there are certain actions of our bodies that are either beyond voluntary control, or, at the best, are very difficult to control and, in all probability, must be controlled indirectly through those aspects of our behavior that are normally under voluntary control.

By this brief description of some of the practical consequences of behaviorism I mean to show that it is, in practice, neither so mechanistic nor so effective as its propagandists might lead us to believe. The methods of behavioral therapy are often versions of those employed by simple folk uninformed by psychological theory, and where the theory is plausible, as in the application of classical (respondent) conditioning to autonomic activity, it has relatively little to do with the specific procedures for producing the therapeutic effects. These methods may take their place alongside physical therapy and the enormous variety of *ad hoc* techniques that are of help to us in coming to grips with our bodies.

At the same time, I wish to emphasize the dangers of taking the theoretical pretentions behind various practices of behavioral therapy seriously, for those theoretical pretentions, when they are part of a claim that modern psychology can, by its theories and experiments, control and determine human behavior, are dangerous both to the credibility of psychology and to our conceptions of ourselves.

Chapter Six

The Ethos
of Contemporary Psychology:
II. Social Psychology

William McDougall and E. A. Ross are the godfathers of social psychology. We may also suppose that the Frenchman Gustave Le Bon with his notion of a mass mind lurks in the background.[1] But it was McDougall and Ross who did the christening. They wrote the first books labeled social psychology. But it was only the name they provided, not the modern issues. Social psychology as we know it comes from scraps and odds and ends here and there, but it was really invented by Floyd H. Allport in his textbook of 1924.[2] The discipline grew slowly. It was only after World War II that the conception of an experimental social psychology really took hold. Since then it has mushroomed only slightly less than the various disciplines that deal with psychotherapy and counseling. The reason is easy to find.

Social psychology deals with commonsense, everyday problems. The real impetus behind it comes from the view that we can construct theories about human social interactions and then subject those theories to experimental tests. Theory in social psychology is primitive even by the standards of behavior theory of thirty years ago and certainly by the standards of contemporary cognitive theory. Therein lies its charm. It may consist of nothing more than the assertion that we make excuses for and come to like what we must endure (cognitive dissonance theory) or that we are forever trying to attribute motives to people for their actions (attribution theory). Such bits of folk wisdom do have their implications, and just as we see confirmations of all of those adages we cherish in our daily lives ("You get what you pay for," "You can't win 'em all"), social psychologists see confirmation for their theories also. The trouble is that they do so in experiments, experiments which have almost no generality and which bear only the loosest relation to the "theory"—no better than that found between adage and experience in folk wisdom.

Another endearing aspect of social psychology is that social psychologists are not the implacable determinists that Skinner and Freud are. Rather they seem to take things as they come. Nevertheless, a detailed treatment of aspects of their work belongs in this book, for they are enormously responsible for the widespread misconception that psychologists have explanations for everything. In short, the implications of their work are deterministic.

Another reason for providing a critical account of social psychology in this book is that social psychologists self-consciously and deliberately deal with moral choices. In fact, one could use a survey of experiments in social psychology simply to illustrate the consensus of moral values among psychologists. That social psychologists often disclaim any moral stance, or worse, argue that the moral values they represent are or should be the moral values of everyone is all the more reason for dealing with them critically.

In short, there are many reasons for examining the preconceptions and attitudes of social psychologists. I do this by example. I shall first discuss three well-known "experiments" that are supposed to be of great generality. Then I shall digress to talk about the statistical evidence for the reliability of effects reported in social psychological investigations. I do this to emphasize the utter lack of justification for the notion that the effects discovered in these investigations provide any evidence for the notion that human behavior is determined. Finally, I shall examine a contemporary textbook in social psychology. My purpose in so doing is to show how weak and statistically variable results are made out to be positive and definitive in accounts written for lay consumption.

Research in Social Psychology

Experimentation in Social Psychology

In the previous paragraph I put the word experiments in quotation marks. I did so to emphasize my conviction that for the most part these investigations bear almost no relation to experimentation in real science. Sigmund Koch described them as happenings,[3] and that is as good a description as any—though charades might be more accurate. They generally consist of little skits acted out for the benefit of the experimental subjects, whose reactions to the skits are recorded in various ways. Some of the skits are acted out on the street—literally—but most happen in the confines of the psychological laboratory.

The skits are intended to be representative of some broad and generally unspecified aspect of human experience, and they are supposed to embody the principle at issue—cognitive dissonance, attribution, etc. The reactions of the experimental subjects are behavioral. That is to say there is only an occasional attempt to probe for the beliefs, feelings, and rational processes that went on in the subjects' heads during the experiments. Furthermore, as two social psychologists have pointed out in a trenchant rediscovery of one of the main points of the Würzburg psychologists, many of those processes are unconscious and either not available at all for retrospective analysis or, if they are, subject to serious distortion.[4] The behavior examined may be physiological, or it may be the result of a pencil and paper rating scale, but it is generally not complicated.

The main reason I refuse to characterize these investigations as genuine experiments is that the persons tested must *interpret* the skits in order to react to them, and we have no idea save in a very few instances what that interpretation is like. In short, the results are filtered through a process about which we know little or nothing and about which we can make assumptions that have no hope of being made plausible. To be blunt, these are experiments in which the experimenters have no real idea about what they are doing. It is true that a biologist, using a scintillation counter, may have no idea about how the device works, but he has a well-founded faith in the theories and the techniques of the physicists and engineers who designed the device. Can the same be said about the social psychologists' faith in theories of cognition? (Cognitive social psychology is very big as I write.)

In brief, social psychology provides some of the worst examples of the trappings of a materialistic science grafted onto wildly inappropriate conditions. Perhaps this view can best be explained by turning to the examples. In the section that follows I examine first a laboratory experiment, then a field experiment, and finally an exercise in triviality.

Experiments in Social Psychology

The first two experiments I describe were inspired by the horror of the Kitty Genovese case. You will recall that some forty persons who allegedly witnessed the murder of this young woman did nothing to intervene, much less come to her aid. This gave rise to a concern among social psychologists about the number of people witnessing some event and the willingness of people to come to the aid of the victim. Social psychologists, as with experimental cognitive psychologists are fond of "variables" like number of bystanders, because number can be quantified.

The two experiments I report are representative. One was conducted in a laboratory and the other in the field.[5] Concocting a cover story for experiments in the psychological laboratory plagues investigators, for college sophomores have become wary and worldly-wise. They are apt to question what they are told about the ostensible purpose of an experiment in which they are to participate.

The cover in this particular experiment was provided by the information that the participants were to be part of a group discussion session. The experimenters told the students, who were the guinea pigs, that they would discuss with other students questions about the kind of personal problems college students face. The students were put in isolation booths, and their discussions were supposed to be carried out via intercom. (Has any reader been in a group discussion by intercom?) In fact, there was just one real live participant in each session—the experimental subject. The rest of the supposed-to-be-students were tape recorders. Given the limitations of tape recorders, the experimental subject had to be told that each participant would talk about his or her problems for only two minutes. The experimental variable was the number of participants that the one real participant thought was in the discussion group. The whole thing had to be repeated many times, because there were three conditions, and, of course, there had to be a number of experimental subjects in each condition. In one condition the victim was led to believe that there was only one other student present, while in the other two conditions, he or she was told that there were either two or five students present.

The first phony participant (via the tape recorder) mentioned that he or she was subject to epileptic seizures. Later in the skit, the presumed epileptic began to moan and make the other kinds of sounds that could be interpreted as the beginning of a seizure. Now all proper experiments have dependent variables as well as independent variables. The independent variable was the alleged size of the group (two, three, or six persons); the dependent variable was the percentage of experimental subjects who left their booths to seek help. The results were clear-cut. Eighty-five percent of the students who were told they were the only other person present went for help; 62 percent of those who were supposed to be with two other people did so; only 31 percent of the students who were conned into believing that they were in a six-person group so responded.

In the field experiment, four experimenters entered a subway train in New York City. Two of the experimenters recorded what happened, while the other two put on the show. When the train began to move forward, one of the actors staggered forward and fell. In some of the repetitions of the skit the person falling had a cane; in others he was doused with enough booze to lead any sensible onlooker to believe he was drunk. The man with the cane was helped by bystanders more often than the apparent drunk, *but it did not make any difference as to how many people were present*. Someone came forward in about the same time no matter whether the train was then crowded or nearly empty.

It isn't the apparent contradiction between the results of these two little charades I wish to comment upon (a contradiction noted by the authors of the field experiment, which came second, as well as by various apologists who must comment on the literature on this problem). What I wish to point to is the lack of concern about the context of these skits. To be sure, the field experimenters tried their results with black shills and white ones, and they did think of other obvious specificities. But was the train going uptown or downtown? (We do know that it took place on the 8th Avenue line between 59th and 125th.) To return to the first investigation: What if the poor epileptic had begun to have a seizure in a restaurant? In an apartment after a meeting in a singles bar? What if, in the second study, the boozer had been a woman? Was she/he young or old? Carrying books or a shopping bag? Was it 2 A.M. or 3 P.M.? All of these and a thousand other things could have influenced what happened. *The point is that there is no way, as there is in genuine science, to generalize the results of such a charade*. In physical and even biological experiments, the number of things that could conceivably influence the results can be specified physically. In these so-called experiments they cannot. And yet, introductory textbooks in psychology gabble on as if these kinds of investigations offered an "explanation" of the events surrounding Kitty Genovese, Patty Hearst, and Jim Jones.[6]

Of the two, the laboratory experiment, with its strange intercom system, is more likely to arouse skepticism in those not indoctrinated in the ways of social psychology. Contemporary college students are more wary about this kind of thing than were their predecessors who were the pioneer guinea pigs in such matters. But, social psychologists do something they call debriefing. That is, both by way of making a gesture toward the ethics of psychological investigation and by way of bolstering their interpretations of the results, they tell the participants about the true purpose of the experiment and quiz them about their reactions.

But one of the ironies is that modern social psychologists know to a fair certainty that retrospective ruminations about one's mental processes is at best incomplete and at the worst utterly unreliable.[7] Also, telling a vulnerable student who fails to come to the aid of an ersatz victim that everybody reacts that way cannot undo the self doubts. The variety of ideas that may flow through one's consciousness in a few seconds (or in the hours afterward) cannot easily be articulated. What surfaces in some such experience as that offered by an experiment in social psychology is subject to distortion and retrospective correction. If you now know you witnessed a fake, would your reaction be the same? And, if not, which reaction is the correct interpretation of your state of mind during the skit?

Both of these experiments were inspired by the Kitty Genovese case, and they are offered as attempts to explain failure of people to come to her aid. Social psychologists are as inventive as newspaper reporters, and they evoke such notions as "pluralistic ignorance" and "diffusion of responsibility" as explanations. Such may be interpretations, but they are not, in the scientific sense, explanations. There are a thousand other ideas that are just as plausible. The plain fact of the matter is that we do not know enough to establish an explanation for either a concrete situation like the two experiments or the Kitty Genovese case and for the actions and thoughts of a particular person participating in such situations. We shall never achieve such a degree of *psychological* explanation. If we are ever to understand the intervening processes, our understanding will be couched in terms which are not psychological in nature, nor will it be possible to "reduce" any psychological explanation to an explanation in terms of the activity of the central nervous system of a particular person.

However, another and simpler way to look at these experiments is not to evoke some psychological explanation but rather simply to regard the variables that are supposed to control the behavior of participants in experiments as the explanatory devices. I chose the two examples I did because in most respects they represent the most common features of social psychological experiments: They deal with problems of genuine human interest; they require elaborate scripts and deception; the principal independent variable is often something that can easily be counted— in the case of the laboratory experiment and to a lesser degree in the case of the field experiment, number. In both cases, the number of observers was supposed to be important. The notion that numbers of individuals present or otherwise active has pervaded social psychological thinking since the days of Le Bon. In contemporary work this notion pervades because number is as close as a social psychologist can get to physical variables. These experiments also illustrate that lamentable fact of social psychological experimentation—the need for "instructions to the subject" as the way of producing the essential variations in the experiment.

I am not unduly harsh upon these experiments. They have their value, if it is no more than a kind of academic exercise parallel to that exhibited in *Candid Camera*. They provide the major source of items for the columns in Sunday supplements dealing with such questions as: "Should women trust someone they meet in singles bars?" Fortunately, the mass of contradictions in the results of social psychological experimentation shows us that few of the ideas generated by these experiments have anything more to produce than a passing fad. I shall return to their merits near the end of the chapter, but before that I have one more experiment to describe.

This third experiment tells us that there is nothing so trivial that it escapes the attention of the social psychologist.[8] The skit in this charade required female college students to volunteer to take part in some meetings in which students would discuss their sexual problems. These students were told that they would exchange views about sexual standards with another woman, a person she did not know. Before the ostensible discussions were to take place, the experimental subjects were given two folders. These folders, the subjects were to understand, contained personality profiles of some of the other participants in the experiment. As nearly always in social psychological research, there were two groups of victims—often labeled an experimental and a control group. In this instance, however, that distinction doesn't really apply. For half of the subjects were told that they were going to have to talk about their sexual problems with the person described in the first folder, while the other half of the subjects were told that they were going to have to reveal all to the woman described in the second folder.

Now the subjects were asked to evaluate, in an elaborate manner characteristic of such investigations, the personalities of those persons whose evaluations they had just read. The catch is that the subjects were told which of the shills—the one described in the first folder or the second—they would be exchanging sexual confidences with. The results: If the subject thought she were going to have to deal with the person described in the first folder, she found that person more appealing than the person described in the second folder, whereas, *mirabile dictu*, those who thought they would have to deal with a woman described in the second folder found *her* more appealing. I spare the reader the kinds of questions I raised about the first two experiments.

Accounting for Variance

One of the graces of modern social psychology, as opposed to the magisterial but sometimes equally prejudiced statements coming from writers like McDougall and Le Bon is that experimental social psychologists subject themselves to a kind of hair-shirt treatment called statistical inference. It is true that the hair shirt is more often of cashmere, but nevertheless it does operate to restrain those who know from swallowing the results of social psychological experiments without reservation. That such reservations are often not passed on at the next level of informing the public at large about social psychology is the subject of the next section of this chapter. For now, however, I deal with the question of statistical inference in psychology, and I do so in order to exhibit the utter lack of justification for any principle of determinism arising out of empirical psychology.

While I deal with this question in the context of experimental social psychology, I do not mean to limit my remarks or their implications to that field. The problems of statistical inference in psychological experimentation permeates the whole. It is a particular problem in social psychology and in those fields that used to be called verbal learning (now psycholinguistics and cognitive psychology). Psychobiologists have as little truck as possible with the crutch of statistical inference; they are properly suspicious of results that are not so stable or repeatable as to be obvious to the merest dolt and hence which do not require some statistical validation of their truth. On the other side psychometricians (students of testing—the kind of people who design the Scholastic Aptitude Tests) commonly deal with such large numbers of people that they have only the smallest need for the arcane wisdom supplied by statistical inference (as opposed to descriptive statistics). Certainly, they do not have the need for so-called small sample statistics that students of experimental social psychology and cognition do. It is in these two branches of psychological knowledge that the high learning known as methodology is pushed to its farthest limits.

Because results in these fields are so variable and *unpredictable*, and because samples must be so small, special statistical techniques are needed to tell the investigator whether or not she has a result. The data in most experiments in social psychology are rather like hearing the phone ring while in the shower; the noise of the water makes it very difficult to tell whether there is a signal or not. In a similar way, the unpredictable reactions of human beings in psychological experiments make it very difficult to tell whether there is an effect in the results—whether some average calculated by combining the results from twenty or so persons can be counted upon. Hence the need for sophisticated methods of statistical inference in order to interpret the results of psychological experiments.

The most common approach is something called "testing the null hypothesis." It requires a line of reasoning so tortuous that merely understanding it, much less doing it, probably constitutes the most taxing course with which undergraduate majors in psychology must cope. In testing the null hypothesis you first do some calculations; these calculations enable you, with a mathematically specified degree of confidence to tell whether you have an effect at all. The calculations tell you nothing about your effect —how large it is, for example; they only tell you whether you have one or not. The reasoning is negative. That is to say, if your calculations work out right, you can *reject* the notion that there is no effect at all. That is why it is called the null hypothesis. But strictly speaking, according to the logic of statistical inference, your calculations tell you nothing about how large your effect is.

In practice, such a restriction is roundly ignored. Authors of papers discuss their results as if the exact findings were precisely correct. And, of course, textbooks follow suit. All of the textbooks which I consulted about the experiment on helping the presumed epileptic always either reported the actual obtained percentages or described those percentages in equivalent ways. They said nothing about the fact that on something called a Duncan multiple-range test, only two out of the three possible statistical comparisons among the groups were significant even at the usually modest 5 percent level.

In the experiment which purports to show that we are more likely to like someone if we know we must interact with that person in the future, the strongest statistical effect was granted to the finding that 36 out of the 43 persons tested preferred to be with the person they like most!

The fragility of these findings can be appreciated when they are contrasted with statistical results that come out of testing programs. Psychologists who invent tests and who study the relations among psychological tests—how tests correlate with one another—usually employ enough people as subjects to produce very stable results. Experimental social psychologists typically test twenty or thirty persons in a single experimental group. Thus an entire experiment may be based upon fewer than one hundred people. In test development hundreds or thousands of people are tested. And any given result is fairly stable. Thus year after year, the correlation between SAT scores and first-year grades for students entering the University of Virginia is such that the SAT scores account for about 13 percent of the variance among grade averages. To the layman this sounds like a small thing to boast about, but I assure the reader that if we could make the appropriate calculations for the results of social or cognitive experiments (we can't because the number of observations is too small) that the percentage of variance in performance, ratings, or whatever, accounted for by the independent variable would be, on the average, vastly more modest. In plain fact, the independent variables that are so confidently described in textbooks account for so very modest a portion of the variability in the reactions among subjects or even among different tests on the same subject as to be embarrassing. Thus it can only be said that the impression that social psychologists can account for human behavior in the kinds of situations they investigate is at best exaggerated.

The greatest precision in psychological experiments is achieved when the independent variables are physical in nature. Thus experiments on visual and auditory thresholds are generally very precise, so precise in fact that experimenters often dispense with statistical tests of significance altogether. The least precision is found when human beings must interpret what is being done to them in order to choose an action. But it is not simply a matter of experimental precision. Generally, the work of students of vision and hearing do not get into the Sunday supplements. They generally talk little about the prediction and control of behavior. They do not purport to show us how our most trivial actions are controlled by the circumstances surrounding those actions.

My point in including this section on statistical inference in psychological investigation is to illustrate that the claim that psychologists understand how behavior is controlled well enough to be able to bring it under experimental variation is largely empty. Even when we accept the limited lack of generality of social psychological experiments because of the inability of these experiments to provide a complete rational connection between the variables that are presumed to control behavior and that behavior itself, we seem to be left with the facts of the experiments themselves. But the experiments are frail foundations for the notion that the modern psychologist understands human behavior well enough to bring it under experimental control.

The Textbook

It would be very easy to demonstrate that those who write columns and prepare true-false quizzes for the Sunday supplements gloss over the difficulties in accepting the conclusions of experiments in social psychology, but it should be a harder job to make that demonstration by describing the contents of a good textbook in social psychology. While it is more difficult, I believe that I can demonstrate that the exaggeration, the hyperbole, and the glossing over difficulties embarrassing to the establishment in social psychology are there in the textbooks. Rather than survey the cascade of new textbooks in social psychology that issue from publishers every year, I shall treat in detail a single book. It is not representative. It is one of the best. It has been, as of this writing, through three editions. It has won awards. It is a big seller, and its author is one of the best-known social psychologists in the country.[9] In short, by all standards—those of the science of psychology as well as of the marketplace—it stands on its merits.

The Book

The author, Elliott Aronson, is a disarmingly good writer, even on an absolute basis (the level of competence in writing in social psychology is not very high). He tells us in the very first sentence that the book grew out of a year spent at the Center for Advanced Studies in the Behavioral Sciences at Stanford, California. He beguiles us with an aside to the effect that his favorite city, San Francisco, was only 30 miles away. But more than that, he tells us that with a whole year in which to do anything that he desired, he chose to write this book. He then goes on to point out that experimental social psychology is a "young science." But he does not, in his words, want this to be a "cop-out." Rather, he tells us that his purpose in writing the book is to show that social psychological research is *relevant* (italics mine).

There, from the outset, we learn that what we are dealing with is not science, but persuasion. He intends to tell us how the wisdom of social psychology will be relevant for solving the social problems of our time. I do not wish to be unduly harsh upon Aronson in this respect. The whole of modern social and scientific research is shot through with the need to justify basic research by its relevance. Geneticists have to argue, in order to be funded, that what they do will help in the cancer crusade. Physicists mutter about the need to find new sources of energy. But there is a peculiar difficulty in social scientists, particularly social psychologists, in so arguing, for their *work directly impinges upon the moral choices of society.* After all, physicists as physicists do not tell society that it ought to use nuclear power. Physics merely offers nuclear power as an alternative. But there is, even in the most objective of social psychologists, a vein of telling us what we *ought* to do about some social problem or another. Finally—before reminding us that he wrote the book for students, not colleagues—Aronson tells us that he believes that the experimental method is the best method to solve a complex problem.

The book then goes on to ask: "What is Social Psychology?" and to answer by dealing with such topics as conformity, mass communication, self-justification, aggression, prejudice, and attraction. The topics are not exhaustive, and the book is refreshing in that the main topics are not dictated by social psychological theory (cognitive dissonance and the like) but by questions that most of us would agree are of human importance.

The plan of the book is simple and effective. It mixes headline events from recent history (the Jonestown massacre, Patricia Hearst, the Vietnam War), with made-up anecdotes that have a certain flavor of academic humor, and with the results of social psychological experiments and field observations. From these it occasionally establishes general principles and adduces evidence for theories. But, as I pointed out earlier, this is an extraordinarily good book as books in social psychology go, and it is very modest in this respect. Some of the incidents (real and made up) are trivial and some are interesting and important. The same may be said about the experiments. The disturbing prison experiment by Zimbardo and his students,[10] and a study of getting children to like broccoli, are given equal weight.

However, the book does defend the verities of social psychological research. At the outset Aronson deals with the ethical issues involved in the notorious experiments by Milgram in which ordinary people are apparently induced to torture other people, the prison experiment, etc.[11] He defends these by saying: "For a social psychologist, the ethical issue is not a one-sided affair. In a real sense, he is obligated to use his skills as a researcher to advance our knowledge and understanding of human behavior for the ultimate aim of human betterment."[12] It does not seem to cross Aronson's mind that the experiments, which are the chief ethical issue, do not provide us with information that we might have achieved simply by being observant of the world around us. Aronson's faith that the experimental method, applied in these experiments in which people must puzzle over and adopt one or another belief about what is going on, contribute something to our understanding of the causes of human action that is not achieved through real incidents in the world at large is touching. Milgram tells us nothing about human nature that Hitler, Eichmann, and their countless equivalents among all peoples of the world have not already told us.

Then, in the chapter "Mass Communication, Propaganda, and Persuasion," there is a curiously naive and, in the context of social psychology, embarrassing discussion of the difference between education and propaganda. Here Aronson tells us that propaganda may even be introduced in the study of arithmetic, when the very capitalistic practice of lending money leads to illustrations about interest rates.[13] He seems to be totally unaware that his whole book is a propaganda piece for the ethical values Aronson cherishes and, naively, seems to believe are shared by all psychologists. He finds it even difficult (though he does clearly try) to disguise his political biases.

Though he is careful not to say so, he leads us to believe that experimentation in social psychology enables us to discover particular causes of human action. He suggests to us that experimentation may lead us to believe that compliance is some particular situation may be attributed to conformity, rewards and punishments, or internalization (to use his categories) by knowing the characteristics of the situations. He uses a lot of examples to illustrate the differences between his threefold scheme, and his statements are as plausible as any, though a very clever person might argue alternatively for the collective unconscious or E.S.P.

The author's faith in the efficacy of experimental social psychology is curiously intermixed with a realistic assessment of the problems of generalization. In his final chapter (titled "Social Psychology as Science"), he contrasts the Kitty Genovese case, in which thirty-eight witnesses did not come to the aid of the woman being murdered, with an incident in Yellowstone Park in which a number of people *did* come to the aid of a person in trouble. He tells us that he speculated at length at what might make the difference between these two outcomes. He admits that his speculation was in vain, for, he says, there are "literally dozens of differences." There are not "literally dozens of differences" but an uncountable number.

Furthermore, experimentation does not help (as the author tells us it does in the next paragraph), for experiments, no matter how carefully designed, are as context bound as uncontrolled incidents. One cannot generalize from an experiment to Yellowstone Park any more than to New York City. Each experiment is locked in the particulars of its procedures. Generalizations from it are speculations. Such experiments might occasionally be useful in revealing something that we didn't expect to happen, and hence for giving rise to some speculation that might otherwise not have occurred for us. But their results cannot be generalized with the sense of security that even a purely empirical generalization gives rise to in the physical world. Extrapolation, as physical scientists occasionally call such generalization, runs the risk of being wrong. But, because the physical world is vastly simpler than the psychological one, a good empirically based guess has a far better chance of being right than does a similar guess about psychological conditions.

The Ideology

We turn now from the relatively pleasant task of dealing with a readable and even likeable textbook in social psychology to an effort to grasp the ideology of social psychology. Here we need to broaden our coverage, for ideology rides only lightly on the author of *The Social Animal*. It is, along with social psychological theory, there, but it is unobtrusive.

When one reads broadly in social psychology [14] a sense of the ideology of social psychology emerges. First of all the ideology is based on the assumption that man's conduct is essentially irrational. Aronson cannot make himself quite say it that baldly. He does compare rational and irrational behavior,[15] and from what he says we are left to infer that, given the things that influence human behavior in foolish ways, we vote irrationally, we choose mates irrationally, we accept friends irrationally, and we arrive at moral decisions irrationally.

A second assumption in the ideology of social psychology is that behavior is externally caused. Hence there is an important role for experimentation, which is mainly a way of altering the external world for the object of study, that is to say, the subjects in the experiment. If such alterations are viewed as causative—and they are—then the power to produce behavior lies not with a rational mind but with the external world.

A third assumption is that some aspects of human actions are good and others bad. That is to say, social psychologists implicitly adopt a moral stance toward the material they study. The moral stance is not explicit, nor is it generally derived from some well-reasoned assumptions. Instead social psychologists simply assume that everyone possesses their values; to state them is unnecessary. It is true that it would be difficult for anyone who accepts the American consensus to object to certain of the values that govern social psychological research, but there are other values that are neglected by social psychologists and still others that show psychologists, in the main, to hold values at variance with a sizable if not major part of the American people. However, the really important thing is that social psychologists do take a moral stance toward their subject matter. This is something that even so soft a scientist as a naturalist or ethologist cannot do. The field observer may be unhappy at observing that male lions occasionally devour their own cubs, but he or she would not suppose that research on the matter was designed for the particular purpose of putting an end to so depraved a practice.

In the section that follows I propose to deal with each of these aspects of social psychology and to point out how the ideology of social psychology provides propaganda for the notion that psychologists, in principle if not in practice, can account for the causes of human action.

Rationality and Conduct

There are different senses of the conception of rationality. In one proper usage I may be said to reason correctly from some premises to a conclusion, even though I may know the premises to be false. Or, in a more inclusive sense of the word, I may suppose my premises to be true and correctly reason from them without examining why I believe the premises to be true. At the deepest level of the meaning of rationality, I may be said to derive my premises from the most general and fundamental assertions to which the process of reasoning itself leads me.

Given these variations in the conception of rationality, it may seem to be difficult to distinguish between rational and irrational acts without understanding the motives and processes of reasoning that led to the acts, but that is not the case. The essence of rationality is in the ability to reason correctly from premises to conclusions. Social psychology, despite its pretensions, does not understand either the motives behind the actions it studies, nor is it equipped to follow the process of reasoning that leads to a particular act in a particular person.

Aronson distinguishes between rational and irrational behavior in his discussion of dissonance theory, though we cannot be certain of what he means by rational, for he does not tell us. We cannot be encouraged, however, for he defines "irrational" as "maladaptive." [16] He then goes on to tell us that dissonance-reducing behavior is useful; it is ego-defensive. As with most social psychologists, Aronson ends up telling us that while people are capable of rational behavior, a good deal of our behavior is not rational.

Obviously such a discussion does little to tell us what "rational behavior" is, but it does tell us that social psychologists ignore the most fundamental sense of rationality—that of correct reasoning. They also ignore the tradition of rationalism from the seventeenth century on—the sense that we human beings have an inborn sense of how to reason, but that is perhaps less surprising.

External Causation

No one save the most dedicated Pavlovian would want to label a reflex as being rational. Nevertheless, by describing what the causes of actions are in social psychological experiments, social psychologists come close to so asserting. I am reminded of what one of the grand old men of the past generation of psychologists once said to me. He was a famous experimental psychologist, a member of the National Academy of Science, and he had a touching faith in the laboratory. He told me that every psychological laboratory should have a sign over the entrance reading "Stimulus-Response." And to the extent that such laboratories are dedicated to making causative inferences I suspect he was right. And external causation of voluntary behavior is certainly irrational. Whether adaptive or maladaptive, elicited behavior is irrational, and if the conditions of the social psychological laboratory are such that the independent variable is the "cause" of behavior, the behavior it controls is clearly irrational.

The faith in the external causation of social interaction is perhaps the most important reason why contemporary social psychology cannot in any sense be scientific. If social psychologists were content with being describers of action and chroniclers of social relations, they might deserve some modest claim to science, much as the nineteenth-century observers of the behavior of rabbits and badgers deserved such a claim. But laboring under the delusion that they are investigating the causes of social relations by working with them in the laboratory, they deprive themselves of such a claim as much as if they were to proclaim that they were scientific because they were Marxists or single-tax advocates.

To be sure, to use a Skinnerian term (though an Aristotelian one might have been better), other people doing things in our presence provide an *occasion* for our behavior, but that behavior, unless it is reflexive, is filtered through the activities of a mind, save when it is disordered, that has the capacity to be rational.

The Values of Social Psychology

Scientists do what they do because, among other things, they are motivated by values. They prize in varying ways information about our world and ourselves. And they often study problems because they have direct relevance for human affairs, even when the investigations are said to be in basic science. But they do not regard outcomes of their experiments as supporting their values or denigrating the values of other people. They may be unhappy with a particular outcome, and they may find out things that are distasteful to society at large, but they cannot show that it is scientifically valid to murder Jews or, on the other hand, that prejudice is evil. But social psychologists, along with social philosophers, theologians, and ethicists accept certain things as being good and others as being bad. There is nothing inherently wrong with this; in fact it is to be applauded, except for the fact that social psychologists masquerade as scientists, and they do not make explicit the assumptions behind the particular set of values they espouse. In this respect, they are probably the worst offenders among social scientists at large, though economists, sociologists, anthropologists, and political scientists, when they aspire to science, show the same overreaching ambition.

Precisely what the values are that social psychologists accept is difficult to say, for they go under the guise of being value free, and if one accuses them of accepting a certain value, they may indignantly ask one to cite chapter and verse. This is particularly the case because their values are often indicated only by what they choose to investigate and the results they achieve. They are much concerned about the effects of TV violence on children, but they show very little concern for the effects of eroticism in the various media. One is important, and the other is not. Whether one agrees or not, it still comes down to a judgment about the moral value of the problem under investigation.

One is even more struck by the values of social psychologists when one examines the conclusions they reach, and the recommendations they make. I can do no better in this respect than to quote from one of the two or three most widely used textbooks in introductory psychology:

> Criminologists believe that a number of crimes—particularly assaults and sometimes murders—are committed only under intense provocation by people who would not ordinarily dream of doing such a thing. It is the situation, rather than the disposition, that triggers the action. But jury members and judges are just as likely as anyone else to fall under the fundamental attribution error. They are likely to infer a criminal disposition from a criminal act, regardless of the circumstances. Attribution theory suggests a nagging question about the possibility that otherwise law-abiding citizens, trapped into an uncharacteristic criminal act by some quirk of events, may be treated too harshly by our legal system.[17]

In short, psychologists are quite willing, using attribution theory as the vehicle, to recommend sweeping changes in criminal justice, recommended changes that surely incorporate the values of the social psychologists as well as the assumption that they fully understand the causes of human behavior.

Once again, such a statement written by you or me

and published in the letters to the editor column in the local paper would hardly be the occasion for distress. But written with the magisterial authority of a textbook (with its ever-present threat of a true-false test) and invoking the presence of scientific research, it is quite another matter.

Some Conclusions

Speculation about human nature is an absorbing enterprise, and from time to time all of us must act upon our speculations and our beliefs. Social psychologists no less than the rest of us are entitled to their speculations and beliefs; in fact they may even be more entitled, for they spend more time than the rest of us in thinking about human behavior. But the pretense that social psychology is a science on a par with the experimental sciences of physics and biology is an insidious error. It is insidious because it gives the prestige and authority of real science to the view that we are victims of our circumstances, that we behave mindlessly and irrationally about things that matter, that we cannot arrive at decisions about politics, beliefs, friendships, and marriages without being the helpless victims of the external conditions that impinge upon us.

Once again, I remind the reader that the dichotomy between freedom and determinism is lopsided. Those of us who believe in human freedom are quite aware of the fact that we are influenced by circumstances and that human beings are capable of irrational actions. But by their very choice of method and their devotion to explanatory theories in psychology, social psychologists give shelter to the belief that we are in no way free, that our every action is, of necessity, irrational.

Chapter Seven

The Ethos
of Contemporary Psychology:
III. Psychohistory

Psychologists are not much given to the practice of psychohistory. Its adepts are drawn mainly from the ranks of psychoanalysts, historians, and social philosophers. One pioneering book of readings on the subject[1] brought together articles that had originally appeared in *The Journal of Religion*, *The American Journal of Sociology*, *The Partisan Review*, and the *International Journal of Psychoanalysis* among others. There was not a single article from a psychological journal in the narrow sense, and only one of the authors could give any claim to belonging to the fraternity of psychologists. Nevertheless, I have chosen to include a discussion of psychohistory under the general rubric of the ethos of contemporary psychology because it so clearly and perfectly illustrates the misplaced faith in psychological theory and determinism in accounting for the actions of human beings.

Psychohistorians rely almost exclusively on psychoanalytic theory in the main tradition. In some bibliographic comments to his collection of articles, Mazlish says of Fawn Brodie's *Thaddeus Stevens: Scourge of the South* that it "is a fascinating book, which like the Georges' book on Wilson is psychoanalytically informed but does not express this information in formal, technical terms."[2] Its commitment to so well-defined a psychological theory makes it an easier object to dissect than say, the case histories found in an eclectic text in clinical psychology. Because psychohistories are case histories, generally extended case histories of persons important to political, social, and cultural life, we should explore the notion of case history and the significance of the idea.

The Idea of the Case History

The notion of the case history is, in its origins, medical. But the beginnings of medicine itself are so vague that one must be very generous in interpreting the concept of medicine. And, nowadays, the term has been widely used in all of the helping professions, so that the term "case load" almost automatically brings the social worker to mind.

K. D. Keele, in his insightful little monograph, *The Evolution of Clinical Methods in Medicine*,[3] makes two simple but profound points about the origin of taking case histories. First of all, he tells us, the idea antedates literate civilization, for if the shaman is to cure the pain in your right abdomen, he must know whether you have, in the past month, crossed the path of your tribe's totem animal. The second point that Keele makes is that the clinical history takes the form of the theory of medicine underlying it. In ancient medicine, the allopaths and the homeopaths agreed upon one thing: The specific cure for a symptom depends upon the cause of the symptom, and in order to find that cause, one must take a case history.

The formalization of taking case histories is one of the great achievements of the anonymous authors whose works are generally ascribed to Hippocrates.[4] Detailed case histories are found in the *Epidemics*, case histories which in their form if not in their content seem surprisingly modern. Of course, contemporary case histories may take mainly the form of filling out a checklist which inquires into family history, childhood illnesses, chronic symptoms, etc. Such a checklist version of a case history (and the method of taking it) is seldom found in psychiatric practice, though diagnostic as well as therapeutic psychologists sometimes make use of such a practice and, in administering tests such as the *Minnesota Multiphasic Personality Inventory*, have occasionally reduced it to automated form. Rather, psychiatric case histories adjust themselves to psychological theories of the causation of psychological disturbances, and so they deal, in narrative fashion, with the nuances of interpersonal relations between the patient and members of his or her family, etc.

The eleventh-century Arab physician Avicenna is generally given credit for describing explicitly the first psychiatric or psychological case histories.[5] Such an attribution should be made with caution because not only in primitive medicine is it difficult to separate the psychological from the physical, but even in the writings of someone as sophisticated as Galen the separation is problematic.[6] It is only if we have a clear notion of mind and mental that it becomes possible to deal with psychological aberrations as such. Often this is, in the context of physical medicine, done negatively, as in the concept of a functional psychosis. Most textbook descriptions and definitions of the psychiatric term *functional* lead one to suppose that the writer really would have preferred the medical term *idiopathic*.

One of the reasons for bringing this whole matter up is that the psychiatric or psychological case history makes so explicit the notion of psychological causation, whether the psychological cause is described as the acquisition of bad habits or as the inevitable acting out of a universal human tragedy. The astonishing diversity of opinion in the psychological community as to what the "true" causes of psychological disturbance are leads one into the easy trap of supposing that psychological diagnosis and prognosis are as primitive as were these for physical medicine in the days of Galen. This is an insidious trap because it presupposes that there lies ahead a long history—truncated because of the rapidity of the advance of science—that will lead in psychiatry from the Galenic mixture of empirical observation, superstition, and ignorance to the relative precision of modern medical knowledge. There is no evidence that such a history awaits the understanding of psychological disorders.

First of all, we do not in any way know what we mean when we use the old "technical" terms neurosis and psychosis. Some symptoms of mental disorders strongly suggest physical causes, though unknown (idiopathic epilepsy readily comes to mind). Sometimes the symptoms associated with such psychological disturbances are so major and alarming that they receive the label schizophrenia. In so diagnosing, we do not know in the case of a particular individual if the nervous system (or its biochemical hormonal support system) has in some subtle way ceased functioning properly to the degree that can produce psychological symptoms.

Certain obvious cases associated with damage to the sensory windows or the motor capabilities of the cerebral cortex tell us that some psychological incapacity is the result of some (unknown in detail) damage to a part of the central nervous system (aphasia, for example). But in the general question of the causes of psychological disorders, such a diagnosis tells us scarcely more theoretically than does the fact that an unconscious person cannot answer questions.

Perhaps it is to the definition of psychological disorder that we need to attend in order to resolve this problem. I have deliberately used the term disorder, rather than disease, or problem. in order to be as neutral as possible. A person who is described as psychologically disordered or suffering from some psychological insufficiency is, in theory, a person who cannot manage the demands made upon him by the ordinary conditions of living. Whether these stem from an inadequacy of the individual or from a failure on his part to appreciate the values and conditions society has assigned him is a matter about which we can only speculate in individual cases. Deviant individuals, as Thomas Szasz has reminded us,[7] are often inconveniences to society. An elderly derelict who persistently interrupts the Sunday services in a downtown church was, at least at one time, much more likely to find herself dealing with the state mental health establishment rather than with the local police department. But whether with the embarrassing derelict or with the violent criminal, the notion that we can "explain" his actions pervades the modern social sciences and the notion of the psychological case history.

According to the *Washington Post*,[8] a man won a judgment of $40,000 against two poker clubs because they had failed to deny access of his wife to their gambling tables. Dr. Robert Custer, a psychiatrist with the Mental Health Division of the Veteran's Administration in Washington gloated over the verdict: "This decision recognizes the responsibility on the part of the gambling industry, an industry that is going to have to deal with people sick with this disease."

So we come full circle. Whether the causes are physical or psychological, or whether we pay attention to those subtle distinctions refined in the history of philosophy, medicine, and psychology, there are causes which the doctor can cure. It is a disease. Hence the psychological case history. It is probably the case that most psychologists, psychiatrists, and other therapists do not write formal case histories unless they are to produce a book or an article or must report at the staff conference, but they do take notes, and most of them dictate their notes. And the notes are the interpretations of the therapist about what the patient tells the therapist about him or herself, interpretations that are guided by the regnate theory of the therapist. The patient's problems, the view goes, are caused, in the same way that the trajectory of a bullet is caused by the chemical reaction in the cartridge. The bullet may be influenced by wind (and throughout—on earth at least—by gravity), and it may even ricochet. The ricochet is highly unpredictable and even dangerous, but it is understood in principle. Once one knew the nature of the surface and the angle with which the projectile struck, the ricochet is as predictable as the angle of reflected light. So it is with the subject of a case history.

Nowhere is this assumption that the course of an individual's life is completely predictable from the congruence of his life history and our psychological theory than in psychohistory, relying, as it does, upon a single deterministic theory of the nature of human mentality.

Four Psychohistorical Case Histories

I might well have discussed the two most famous psychohistorical studies made by the master himself, Freud's *Moses and Monotheism* (which also purports to explain important elements of Jewish and Christian theology as a form of neurosis) and his account of Leonardo da Vinci. However, these, as interesting as they may be, are sufficiently lacking in subtlety to make a discussion of them easy. Even the proponents of psychohistory seem to find them embarrassing. They were, after all, pioneering works that, however learned Freud was, lacked the full historical perspective which later works brought to the psychoanalytic interpretation of important figures. However, two other classical works, Ernest Jones' study of Hamlet and Erikson's analysis of Luther, have been so influential that they demand attention. Then I shall deal with a curious work, purportedly written by Freud in collaboration with William C. Bullitt, and I shall also deal with a representative work of the modern discipline of psychohistory, Bruce Mazlish's essay on Richard Nixon.

Jones, Hamlet, and Shakespeare

Ernest Jones, disciple and biographer of Freud, first wrote about Hamlet in an essay in the early years of the twentieth century: To put it in Jones's words, "as an exposition of a footnote in Freud's *Traumdeutung*."[9] It was published, inexplicably, in the *American Journal of Psychology* and later revised as a full-blown essay in the twenties. The final version, from which I quote, was published in 1949.

Psychological studies of Hamlet abound, of which Jones was much aware, because he quotes from the literature on Hamlet with a fullness that would have satisfied a German professor of a century ago. But, Jones implies, his psychological study is different because it is scientific. It is true that certain aspects of the diffidence of the early version in discussing mother-son sexual feelings survive in the latest version, but Jones is quite emphatic about the matter, the problematical character of Hamlet stems from his infancy.

With that notion in mind, Jones can make quite astonishing assertions. For example he says: "As a child Hamlet had experienced the warmest affection for his mother, and this, as is always so, had contained elements of a disguised erotic quality, still more so in infancy."[10] Jones is not the unsophisticated commentator that such a statement might imply. He knows that we only know of Hamlet what Shakespeare intends to tell us. The rest is fancy made possible by the rich ambiguity of Shakespeare's creation. Hence the profusion of interpretations of Hamlet, of which Jones is fully aware. But, fantasy to the side, Jones seeks to tell us that our intuitions that the situation of Hamlet and Oedipus are, at the bottom, the same is correct. This is not only a correct intuition, but, he tells us, it may be demonstrated as being right through the science of psychoanalysis. The relation of Hamlet to Gertrude, Jones admits, is far more ambiguous than that of Oedipus to Jocasta, but these both admit to the most basic of psychoanalytic interpretations—the dominance of adult character by the infant-mother relation.

Suppose that Gertrude had been a certain kind of mother well known to those psychologists who are convinced that early childhood experiences fix character in concrete, the kind of mother who is not only loving but overprotective. And suppose, furthermore, that Hamlet's father, the king, was a certain kind of character well known to those same psychologists, the cold and rejecting father. It is received opinion, of course, that a male child, reared by such a pair, would be homosexual. Now the exact interpretations put upon the homosexuality induced by such a condition varies from authority to authority, but it is not implausible to assume that homosexual longings represent a striving for the affection of the rejecting father (though, of course, the father as the rival is the more orthodox interpretation). If we follow the logic of Jones' analysis of Hamlet, we must assume that he had repressed homosexual tendencies. But Jones makes little of this matter, all the more surprising both because the master himself, Freud, interpreted those symptoms associated with paranoia as the outcome of repressed homosexuality and because the question of homo-sexuality has always lurked in the background of Shakespearean scholarship.

My point in this little diversion is not to argue that homosexuality does not arise in early experience (or one's ge-netics) or whatever but simply to point to the infinite variety of interpretations of Hamlet that are possible given psychoanalytic theory. Locked up in a room, having never heard of Hamlet, and then given the play to read, one hundred recently graduated ana-lysts asked to interpret Hamlet would produce one hundred inter-pretations.

Various psychological interpretations of Hamlet, of course, produce various readings, and this is a matter of the ac-tor's and the director's art. Recently I saw a version of Hamlet in which he was portrayed as simply being mad (in the old-fashioned sense). I suspect, given this performance, an audience of psychol-ogists and psychiatrists might have agreed that he was a paranoid schizophrenic.

In short, any interpretation of Hamlet can only be re-garded as an interpretation, one that leads to a particular nuance in the reading of the play. We can accept Hamlet's actions and ruminations as being psychologically plausible or implausible, de-pending upon our psychological point of view. But they are baf-fling and an enigma; that is the reason why the play attracts the dissectors, Jones included. The essence of the character invented (invented is the right word, despite the historical and dramatic precedents for Shakespeare's play) is in his contradictory nature. That, together with the ambiguities, leads to all of the manifold interpretations of the play.

There may well be deep and important connections between Hamlet and Oedipus (and Orestes, for that matter). It is not altogether implausible that there is, to use Ernest Jones' gen-teel language, "a disguised erotic quality" in Hamlet's relations with his mother. But it is an altogether fruitless exercise, when regarded as scientific in nature, to speculate upon whatever events in Hamlet's childhood led to the state in which we find him in the play.

Jones titles the crucial chapter in his book *Tragedy and the Mind of the Infant*. That dates the book. A later and vastly more sophisticated psychobiography, Erikson's *Young Man Luther*, might well have had the subtitle "Tragedy and the Mind of the Youth." Infancy, childhood, old age, whatever, have gone before whatever we are now. To pick elements and pieces out of our personal histories as causes in the scientific sense is to defy all of the principles of scientific inference.

Of course, all this talk about Hamlet is irrelevant, for, as Jones reminds us, it is really about the character of Shakespeare. Hamlet is Shakespeare, says Jones. The difficulties of maintaining this view occupy a most uncomfortable chapter (it should be said in Jones' defense that this is not an unknown idea among Shakespeare scholars). My literal mind causes me to niggle at the consequences. Surely Hamlet, in his exalted position, would have been reared by wet-nurses and attendants and thus have had a very different relation to his mother than that imagined by Jones. But then Shakespeare grew up among the middle classes, and so perhaps Jones may be right about Shakespeare and his mother. But who is to know?

The important research of Spitz, Bowlby, and Ainsworth[11] tells us much about the empirical facts of mother-child relations in early life, but it does not, I fear, establish the validity of any specific theory of child-mother relations. Infant-parent interactions, as with interactions among siblings, takes place in an infinitely variable context, and context determines the particular meaning that a particular relationship has. Once again, we are faced with the impotence of any psychological theory to be correct in particulars. The assumption of complete determinism fails not so much because any particular deterministic theory is wrong in general but because no theory can take into account the rich variety of circumstances that bear upon human existence. Psychology, as that wise commentator, Gordon Allport,[12] reminded us, is both a nomothetic science and an idiographic science. In its former aspect it is like biology and can, in certain instances, produce reliable generalizations about causes. In its latter sense it is like history, in which one can record in as meticulous detail as possible but for which any theory about causes remains beyond the reach of verification.

Erikson and Young Man Luther

Easily the most elegant and convincing of the psychoanalytic biographies of important people is Erikson's treatment of the youth of Luther.[13] The particulars of psychoanalytic theory ride very lightly upon this biography. Perhaps the most intrusive notion is Erikson's notion of an identity crisis, an idea that can be fitted to Luther only if one assumes, as Erikson does, that Luther's crisis was delayed far beyond the normal span of adolescence. Erikson makes much of Luther's stormy relations with his father, but because only speculation is available, Erikson has little to say about Luther's relation to his mother. The term *Oedipus complex* occurs only four times in the index (as opposed to thirteen for identity crisis). Erikson, being a psychoanalyst, of course assumes an Oedipal situation. But his allusions to it in Luther are tentative and, as I have noted, sparse. At one point he says, "most certainly we would ascribe to Luther an Oedipus complex, and not a trivial one at that."[14] It is almost as if a moment of doubt crossed Erikson's mind. Later he does say: "The father's prohibitory presence and the anticipation of his punishment seem to have pervaded the family milieu, which thus became an ideal breeding ground for the most pervasive form of the Oedipus complex—the ambivalent interplay of rivalry with the father, admiration of him, and fear of him which puts such a heavy burden of guilt and inferiority on all spontaneous initiative and phantasy."[15] That quotation is about as heavy-handed as Erikson gets in this book. In short, the speculation, the attribution of particular patterns of relations are scarcely more than might be found in a biography uninformed by theory. There is little of the magisterial sense of absolute rigor that one gets in reading the pages of Jones' account of Hamlet.

Even Erikson's interpretation of Luther's well-known scatology, his constipation, and his preoccupation with bodily functions is for the most part light. He says: "We have no information concerning little Martin's cleanliness training."[16] Erikson does speculate about the occupation of Luther's father (a miner) and the symbolic identification of the earth with the body's interior and of dirt with feces. But we are left to judge for ourselves; we are not treated to an account of the conditions that determined Luther's life, his relation to his God and his theology as if they were rigorously derivable from a theory that commands all the authority of physical science. Erikson does tell us that *ideology* comes from unconscious tendencies and that these tendencies are such as "to create a world image convincing enough to support the collective and the individual sense of identity."[17] But he does not tell us or even imply that all systems of thought are irrational in that they are determined by the iron hand of psychosexual development. Luther was free to reason about God unhampered about his relation to his father. Erikson even gently hints that the rebelliousness and stubborness that characterized the adult Luther may have owed something to an original nature.

Freud and Bullitt on Wilson

Thomas Woodrow Wilson: A Psychological Study[18] is a curious work. First published in 1966, it purports to be a collaborative effort between Freud and William C. Bullitt, the American diplomat who was, at one time, a patient of Freud's. The copyright statement reads: "1966 by Sigmund Freud copyrights LTD and William C. Bullitt." There is a foreword by Bullitt describing how the collaboration grew out of a chance meeting in Berlin between Freud and Bullitt. Bullitt had planned a volume on the Treaty of Versailles, with separate chapters on Clemenceau, Orlando, Lloyd George, Lenin, and Wilson. Freud, according to Bullitt, expressed a strong interest in collaborating on the chapter on Wilson, an interest, Bullitt says, which partly grew out of the fact that Wilson and Freud were born in the same year, 1856.

The collaboration lasted for ten years. Midway, Freud and Bullitt were convinced that they needed access to private, unpublished papers from Wilson's intimates. This information Bullitt set out to collect. The notes Bullitt gathered proved to be so extensive that they eventually had to be cut back to only those that dealt with Wilson's childhood and youth. A difference of opinion led to an abandonment of the project in 1932. According to Bullitt, he and Freud agreed that the first publication would be in the United States and that Bullitt would control the publication date. Both signed the chapters for which each was responsible. On Freud's exile, says Bullitt, they agreed to certain changes, and the text we find is the result of that agreement. The book was not published until 1966, to save embarrassment to surviving members of Wilson's immediate family.

This brief account, corroborated by a brief statement in Jones' life of Freud (quoted on the jacket of the Freud-Bullitt work) leaves a plethora of mysteries. Did Freud write in German and Bullitt in English, or both in German, or both (unlikely) in English? There is no mention of translation. Beyond the aforementioned foreword ascribed to Bullitt and a seven-page introduction ascribed to Freud there is no indication of which author was responsible or chiefly responsible for which chapter. A fascinating bit of detective work, on the order of that required for the authorship of the *Federalist Papers* but infinitely more difficult, awaits some dedicated scholar. My amateur sleuthing leaves me satisfied that Freud drafted the introduction attributed to him (with perhaps heavy editing at Bullitt's hand) but there is little in the rest of the book to suggest Freud's pen.

The first chapter is a clumsy biographical sketch of Wilson, full of misinformed judgment (e.g., "Yet no passion for the lost cause ever burned in him. In his heart he was not a Southerner but a Scotch Presbyterian who by accident was born in Virginia").[19] This brief biographical sketch is signed by Bullitt, and it is fair to say that it seethes with the venom that suffuses the rest of the book. Clearly Bullitt did not like Wilson. Perhaps Freud did not either (he lumped Wilson with the German Kaiser as both being men of God), but the venom of this first chapter gives the whole key to the study. It is not too much to say that it is an essay in character assassination under the guise of psychological science. It is that characteristic, together with the opinionated certainty of the work that makes it perhaps the least attractive of the well-known psychobiographies.

The authors tell us that they cannot give a full analysis of Wilson, but they say that they know enough to trace the main path of his psychic development. "To the facts we know about him as an individual we shall add the facts which psychoanalysis has found to be true with regard to all human beings. Wilson was, after all, a human being, subject to the same laws of psychic development as other men; and the universality of those laws has been proved by the psychoanalysis of innumerable individuals."[20] There follows the obligatory paragraph of modesty. Psychoanalysis can not explain everything about human beings, but Newton was not rendered obsolete by Einstein, we are told, only expanded upon. There is talk of "theorems" and all the other appurtenances of the philosophy of science of the twenties and thirties.

There follows a fairly orthodox account of the essentials of the psychoanalytic theory of development. In addition to the well-known entities, we are given dogmatic statement unsupported by any hint of derivation from the underlying entities: "Hostility to the father is unavoidable for any boy who has the slightest claim to masculinity."[21] Wilson's "large" libido "flows" toward his father, though later it is deflected to a young man, Francis J. Brooke, with whom Wilson "fell in love." But his libido is also expressed in a love for speech making. Finally, we are assured that the great "accumulator" of the charge of his libido causes Wilson to identify himself with Christ. That identification led to the many betrayals Wilson suffered, for every Christ must have His Judas. In a few pages, we are told that Wilson had a passion for writing and rewriting constitutions; that passion, needless to say, arose from the various fortunes of his libido.

I spare the reader details of this lamentable biographical study, except to inform him or her that the birth of Wilson's firstborn, unhappily a girl, further dammed the libido which flowed toward his father. In so doing, I pass over the interpretation given to the famous conflict between Dean West and Wilson as president of Princeton, the relation between Wilson and his familiar, Colonel House, and other things well known to freshmen students of American history. I do so because to repeat such fantasies would be as tedious as it is wrong. Suffice it to say that no important aspect of Wilson's life, either public or private, is left to a reasoned decision. Everything stems out of the misguided libido (the authors, it is fair to note, do not speculate upon how much better the world would have been if Wilson had undergone a psychoanalysis, say, in his Wesleyan or Princeton years). In this respect, I cannot resist one final quote: "Wilson's trip to the West in September of 1919 was the supreme expression of the neurosis which controlled his life."[22] For the authors of this book every action has an explanation to which they are privy, and their animus is so great that throughout the book they refer to their subject, even in his old age and illness, as "Tommy Wilson," or even "little Tommy Wilson."[23]

Mazlish and Richard Nixon

For the first time we turn to the work of a professional historian, Bruce Mazlish, and his study of Richard Nixon.[24] It is curiously superficial; its style suggests the National Enquirer more than anything else. The author is given to asking unanswered (and mainly unanswerable) rhetorical questions; "Did he, wishing to affirm his manhood, go to the other extreme of hating girls?"[25] ". . . He dreamed of being 'a railroad man.' Was this a heightened and successful version of his father's experience as a motorman?"[26] The result is a certain porous quality to the text, and no clear picture of Nixon emerges in the book.

There is a great deal of psychological interpretation of various actions by Nixon but, until the last chapter, very little in the way of psychoanalytic theory. The psychological interpretation leaves the reader with the impression, probably correct, that the author regards no action or no decision as uncaused by motives growing out of childhood experience. In fact, the author must use the word *cognitive* in a very curious way. He uses it to describe those instances in which some information was used to make a decision in a way *not* swayed by the personal fires that are presumed to rage in his subject. "Cognitively, he remembers that appeasement led to World War II."[27] That strange adverb, cognitively, is meant to convey the fact that the particular memory was not the result of some traumatic experience but a rational use of a bit of information.

The theory is relegated to the last chapter, titled "The Psychohistorical Approach." In it we find the familiar phrases. Psychoanalysis is a science; the "Oedipal phase" is universal, etc. We also learn that "psychohistory is not *merely* the application of psychoanalysis to history but a true fusion of the two, creating a new vision."[28] "Nor can psychohistory rest content with pseudostatements, or snap judgments, such as 'Nixon is a depressive type.' "[29] (I leave to logicians and the philosophers of language the difficult task of determining what a pseudostatement is.) In any event, the whole wearisome business of trying to "account for" the particular actions of particular persons must remain at best an interesting game and at worst the province of charlatans.

Psychology, History, and Character

By way of passing from Mazlish's trivial and tendentious study of Richard Nixon to the question of the relations between psychology and history, I comment upon a vastly superior study of the same subject, Garry Wills' *Nixon Agonistes*.[30] Perhaps the best thing about Mazlish's treatment is his recognition of the merits of Wills' book (though, of course, he quarrels with what he regards Wills conclusions to be). Wills, like Mazlish, clearly does not like Nixon, and he is both more cutting in his treatment and less given to apologies. He does not assert that, for example, Nixon is a man of peace.

The superiority of Wills' treatment lies in two things: One, he probes the character of the man without the prejudices of a theory, and two, he studies the milieu of Nixon. He actually visits Whittier, California, and though he brings all of the exquisite contempt of the Eastern intellectual to the setting, he does see it and, in his way, understand it. Wills does not describe Nixon's Orthogonian Society as a fraternity (there are no fraternities in Quaker schools), nor does he repeat the Mazo and Hess statement that it was Albert Upton who taught Nixon to cry (if anyone did that it was Charles W. Cooper). But all of this is minor. It is important that despite his superior attitude towards Nixon and his milieu, he lets actions speak for themselves. He accepts as given that beliefs, attitudes, and values must be accepted on their own merits and not as tokens of something universal and at the same time mysterious. If that assumption is occasionally wrong, it is not so monstrously wrong as the assumption that these stem from some magical "accumulator."

History, like the study of individual persons, whether incarnate in case histories or biographies, is idiographic. That is to say, no two events, no two individuals are alike, and there are no repetitions of things in a way to make experimentation possible. To be sure, we find common themes in history and common traits in human character, but there are so dependent upon their interactions with other circumstances and other traits that any degree of "prediction" based upon our knowledge of those themes or traits is pitifully imprecise. Historians, until quite recently, have not been burdened with interpreting Pearsonian correlation coefficients, largely because of the tradition in which historians work. But the principle applies to history as well as to individual human beings. To say that there is a correlation of .5 (a quite respectable number) between a given trait and some accomplishment (say, success in law school) and to know a particular score on that trait for a particular individual takes us a little way out of our night of ignorance as to how well that person will do in law school but not very far. The grand theories, be they Marxism applied to history, or psychoanalysis applied to individuals, do worse, for there is no way to assess whether or not their "predictions" are correct or not anymore than it is possible to assess the success of reading chicken entrails as a way of divining history.

History and Individual Psychology as Interpretation

There is another aspect of history and the psychological study of individuals that removes them from nomothetic science. Science deals with abstractions. That is to say, the unessentials are stripped away—"let us assume a frictionless surface." History and individual psychology do not deal with abstractions, they deal with concrete events, but these concrete events are always interpreted, for even the on-the-scene observer cannot grasp the totality of what he or she sees. This not the same thing as the abstraction of science (which knows of what it neglects), it is the action of the human mind *interpreting in the very act of perceiving what it comprehends.*

Thus, while in a sense the biographer and the historian abstract, they do not abstract in the way physical scientists prefer to do. The physical scientist deliberately chooses to neglect certain things or to make certain assumptions when recording data. The historian and the biographer must neglect some things because of the limitations of human perception and cognition, but the choice cannot always be deliberate nor can we always be aware of our choice, for it is determined by the way in which we perceive and understand events.

Then too, of course, the biographer and the historian are limited by the fact that their "data" have already been filtered through someone else's observations. The biographer (and the historian) may in a sense improve his or her perception of the subject of study by visiting some place associated with the subject. That is what Wills did in visiting Whittier, California, and that visit is in no small way responsible for the superiority of Wills' book to Mazlish's. But even so, the biographer seldom has the chance to be the direct observer of much of what he writes about (so remarkable a case as Boswell and his subject is surely unusual). In short, biography, whether in the adulatory biography or in the clinical case history, is subjective, and like the writing of history it generally is the result of the pooling of a number of subjective impressions.

To be sure, certain facts may be said to be objective—the date at which something happened or the place at which someone was born. But the kind of exposition of character that moves biography out of the category of, say, an entry in Who's Who is inevitably subjective. Recently, there has been a movement in social history to make use of statistical data, and while such a use may be said to be reasonably objective, interpretation of those data is controversial and subjective.[31]

It does not help to have the interpretation of biographical data or historical data informed by a theory. The interpretation is not more objective, as psychoanalytic biographers and Marxian historians seem to assume, only further removed from the original subject, for the theory interposes itself in such a way as to make it even more subjective (in the sense of removed from the reality being described). Facts are distorted through the lens of theory.

Psychology and Character

There is a recognition among certain critics, generally of an older generation, that good novelists are the real psychologists. James G. Huneker frequently so characterized Flaubert, and Mencken so described Cather and Dreiser. There is a genuine sense in which this characterization is correct. Novelists who are good psychologists create characters who are not only plausible but intimate. By that I mean that we can understand them in the way that we understand our friends and members of our families. That is not to say that they are not creations, for they are. They are not real people, but inventions. But they have the character of real people. No better way to illustrate that is by reference to Henry James and his splendid young American women.

They are, a clod might judge, all alike. Of course they are not, but common features characterize them all well enough to suppose that James, consciously and unconsciously, was creating something that was fundamental to his nature. What that something was is one of the mysteries no one can ever solve. To ask what *caused* that characterization is to fall into the mire of psychohistory, for not only does no one know what that cause was, but, we must assume, it must have been as multiply and complexly determined as any even trivial event in everyday life.

Consider one of James' American women: Isabel Archer, heroine of *The Portrait of a Lady*. Like all of James' young American women, she was more assertive (to use a current psychological cliché), more poised, and at the same time more naive than her European counterparts. We do not have much chance to see that, for though the setting is English, Parisian, and Italian, almost all of the principal characters are American.

But the main thing is how James tells us about Isabel. He does not do so by introducing her family—her father and her mother—her childhood and adolescence, he does so simply by introducing us to her, her presence and her interior life. During the course of the novel she "matures" (I put that in quotes because James surely would have hated its contemporary implications). She makes vast personal mistakes (though some things she does, as with everyone, are right). She changes but she is, we know, when we leave the last page, the same person we met when she first appeared.

When we are introduced to Isabel it is mainly by a description of the house in which she grew up in Albany. "Isabel of course knew nothing about bills; but even as a child she thought her grandmother's home romantic. There was a covered piazza behind it, furnished with a swing which was a source of tremulous interest; and beyond this was a long garden, sloping down to the stable and containing peach-trees of barely credible familiarity." [32] We are not meant to conjure what events led to Isabel's adult character, only those things which her imagination would know and reflect upon in such a way as to influence in ever so subtle a way those decisions that make up the framework of James's story.

The method employed by the great psychological novelists is one of description. A description, to be sure, that comes from the inventions of their minds, but a description nonetheless. Ever so tentatively we might see those descriptions move into structures, for the very commonality in the traits exhibited by James' heroines urges a structure upon us. But only rarely do great psychological novelists urge *causes* upon us (or if they do, it may be in the interests of parody). A contrast between Cather and Nabokov illustrates this point.

An American short story that turns up in almost every anthology is Cather's *Paul's Case*. It even turns up in the kinds of anthologies of fiction that are meant for supplementary reading in courses in personality, abnormal psychology, and juvenile delinquency, as well it should. The title gives the stance of the author away, for it is, given all of its pristine and luminous prose, the report of a caseworker, but it is such a report written before psychologists, caseworkers, social workers, and the myriads of other titles that grace those in the helping professions were bound and determined to seek out the cause of individual delinquency (as opposed to its statistical correlates) with a view of reforming the individual by banishing the cause.

Cather, once again, simply describes. She does not point to a broken home, nor does she evoke the tyranny imposed upon a dyslexic child of great intelligence by the ordinary public school system (which she might have). She simply gives us one of the most appealing and appalling accounts of an adolescent in literature. She describes Paul from the point of view of those who must deal with him: "His teachers felt this afternoon that his whole attitude was symbolized by his shrug and his flippantly red carnation flower, and they fell upon him without mercy."[33] But she also knows his interior. Paul, as much to escape his dreary working-class home as much as anything else, is an usher at Carnegie Hall, then the home of the Pittsburgh Symphony. One of the privileges, at least as great as that of mingling with the rich and the perfumed grand women of the city, was in hearing the concert. But: "It was not that symphonies, as such, meant anything in particular to Paul, but the first sigh of the instruments seemed to free some hilarious spirit within him; something that struggled there like the Genius in the bottle found by the Arab fisherman."[34] No speculation: Only the unfathomable account of a youth caught between the prosaic realities of hard-working lower-middle-class milieu and an ungovernable love of luxury and aesthetic sensibility.

Nabokov goes further, but given his attitude to what he describes as the "Freudian quackery" (by which he means all attempts at psychological explanation of character) and given his notorious chimerical sense of humor, we do not know whether to take him seriously or not. In any event, a sober psychologist might well read a good (and sensible) cause of Humbert Humbert's pedophilia into an early chapter of *Lolita*.[35] It is a cause based upon the intense emotional aspect of a first experience in sexual relations. We know, of course, that there is good reason to suppose that the involuntary conditioning of intense negative experience does occur in experimental animals, and there is no reason to suppose that it does not occur in human beings. Because of the difficulty of the problem (and I suspect, a lack of interest in the matter), we know less about the immediate conditioning to circumstances of intensely pleasurable emotions. Humbert, in his narrative, describes the delirious encounter at age thirteen with a pubescent girl, Annabel (by which Nabokov in his characteristic way means to evoke *Annabel Lee* and Poe's bride of thirteen). But Nabokov does not insist; indeed, given his literary methods, one could make a strong case of the episode meant as a decoy for the Freudian detectives. In any event, he simply describes. The episode is there, and the reader may make out of it what he or she wants. But it does, in its suggestion of a cause go far beyond anything that Henry James or Willa Cather would have said.

I write this to make the point that of all the psychologists in the world, novelists would or should be the freest to manufacture causes, for, after all, their characters are but puppets of their creation. And I suspect inferior novelists do just that. But James, Cather, Flaubert, Faulkner, and even Nabokov are content to describe and not to invent situations that fit current psychological fads as to the causes of the human condition. To a degree that is striking, good novelists do not project in the way that psychologists, psychiatrists, and others, ever in a search for evidence of their pet theories in case histories, do.

Chapter Eight

Objectivity and Subjectivity in Social Science

N o aspect of the human intellectual enterprise is free from the values of those who practice it. To be sure, a scientist investigating changes in the acidity of lakes in the northeastern part of the North American continent does not read into her measurements her values. If she does, the fraud is far more easily unmasked than most such claims in other intellectual enterprises. But looking at a problem like acid pollution almost certainly derives from some set of values. Such values may lead the investigator to believe, in a way not entirely dispassionate, that the effluvia from industrial sources in the midwestern heartland of the United States are major sources of pollution in regions to the east and north. There is nothing unscientific about so committed a view, providing the investigator is not blind to evidence against it. And those of us who have a certain faith in the objectivity of science suppose that even if the investigator were so committed as to ignore important evidence, or, even worse, alter such evidence, the scientific community would eventually unmask the pretense.[1]

The dedication to particular values is not uncommon in the physical sciences. Whether one works on nuclear power, particle physics, laser beams, and, yes, even computers, is a matter

among other things of ethical choice and decision. But, unless
there is unconscious or deliberate deception, the outcome of the
investigation, even in the study of so complex a system as the
atmosphere, is not dependent upon the ethical assumptions that
motivated the investigation in the first place.

But such is not the case in the social sciences. Here it
is almost inevitable that preconceptions about what ought to be
govern, to some degree, the outcome. The degree may be considerable or it may be negligible, but it is always there. The reason is
not hard to find. The very data that social sciences employ *are*
composed of the kinds of ethical choices that go into the reasons for investigating
scientific problems in the first place. Nowhere is this better illustrated
than in anthropology and political science.

Anthropology and the Objectivity
of Cultural Relativism

The reader who has worked through the earlier chapters of this
book might suppose that I would look with a kindly eye upon the
methods of cultural anthropology, and, indeed, I do. The methods
anthropologists employ, refined as they have been over the past
century, inform us in deep and profound ways about human nature
and culture. The methods of anthropology are designed to produce a descriptive science, not one obsessed with making inferences about the causes of things. Sometimes, in an effort to fit
data to some notion of cause, anthropologists will use some borrowed magic, such as time-path analysis, but in the main hand-
books on how to do anthropology stick pretty well to the ways of
getting accurate information from informants and how to construct systematic descriptions of cultures. Author after author in
the volume edited by Naroll and Cohen stress *doing* anthropology
in order to do it.[2] In short, making good and accurate field observations is an art as well as a science.

Given the impressionistic nature of much of the data

in cultural anthropology and given that many of those data are arrived at by conversations between two people—an anthropologist and a field informant, it is hardly surprising that the beliefs, attitudes, and feelings of anthropologists are often reflected in their data. Students of anthropology are warned against letting their cultural biases obscure their vision. In order to develop a science of anthropology "it was necessary first to arrive at that degree of sophistication where we no longer set our own belief over against our neighbor's superstition." [3] However, it is harder to find comparable warnings in the writings of anthropologists against letting the anthropologist's conceptions of human nature influence the collection and treatment of data. That such happens is the basic theme of Derek Freeman's analysis of Margaret Mead's *Coming of Age in Samoa.*[4] Freeman's treatment and the defensive reactions of the anthropological establishment toward it make the best possible case for the subjectivity of objectivity in anthropology.

The Case of Margaret Mead

Many anthropologists confess to embarrassment over the popularity of Margaret Mead's writings. Some years ago I was a member of a committee that sported some well-known anthropologists. At one point in our deliberations I made a favorable reference to something of Mead's. I quickly found out that the anthropologists among my fellow committee members regarded her as an amateur and a publicity seeker. Therefore, I was not particularly surprised to read Freeman's careful, sober, and balanced demolition of her work in Samoa, nor was I surprised to see an equally sober, careful, and balanced discussion of it by a distinguished senior anthropologist, Ward H. Goodenough.[5] In the pages that follow I deal first with Freeman's case, Goodenough's reactions to it, and then to my own reaction to the controversy and the implications it has for anthropology in particular and the social sciences in general.

Freeman's thesis is that Mead wanted to please her mentor, Franz Boas, by producing data that vindicated Boas' view of human nature. Such actions by graduate students are not un-known, even in the harder sciences, and so Freeman's thesis is not implausible on the face of it. Boas was one of the strongest pro-ponents in his time of the notion of complete cultural determin-ism. He argued that the characteristics of people entirely reflected their cultural milieus, and that they in no way revealed the exis-tence of instincts or inborn tendencies in human beings.

A popular method in anthropology of Mead's day, par-ticularly when demonstrating the absence of some particular in-stinct in human beings, was to find in some remote culture an absence of the influence of the supposed instinct. If you could find some people who never fought, then fighting was not necessarily and instinctively human. Mead saw her task of demonstrating the one negative instance that would counter the notion that the stresses of adolescence are part of the natural human condition. And, for whatever reason, she chose to demonstrate her thesis in American Samoa.

Mead reported after extensive interviews with twenty-five Samoan girls that adolescence, so difficult for Western youngsters, was a period of idyllic calm for Samoans. This Mead associated with the "fact" that there was no suppression of casual sex, either heterosexual or homosexual, among Samoan adoles-cents. Conclusion: The problems of Western adolescents are the result of the repressive attitude in Euro-American civilization to-wards sex, particularly sex in adolescence.

This specific "finding" was embedded in an account of Samoan culture that gave to it the hues of a golden age, unfortu-nately a golden age swiftly being destroyed by the Westernization of Samoa (in fact, Mead's informants were all pupils in a mission-ary school). Not only did Mead, in Freeman's words, present Boas with an absolute answer, she managed to depict an ideal world free from sexual repression, a portrayal that fulfilled the best vi-sions of a liberated young woman of the twenties.

Unfortunately, that portrayal is flawed beyond redemp-tion. In Goodenough's kindest words: "Margaret Mead does not and never has exemplified for anthropologists the highest stan-dards of ethnographic field research."[6] Even by the comparatively loose ethnographic standards of a half a century ago, her work can only be described as shoddy. Mead had only the most rudimentary acquaintance with the language of her informants, and she had only a superficial understanding of Samoan history (and earlier ethnographic work on the islands). She did not live with Samoans at any time (she spent her entire stay on Manu'a with an American naval family). Her informants were all Christians and from Christian families of long standing (though they did not, in Mead's view, have any conviction of sin, particularly with respect to casual sex). She saw little of adults and nothing, of course, of male ritual meetings, from which she would have been barred. Despite all these deficiencies she did not hesitate to pronounce Samoan culture to be free of competition and especially rich in cooperative behavior. In short, she simply capped off a myth about the South Seas that had been in the making in the fantasies of Europeans for two centuries.

I spare the reader Freeman's sober, detailed refutation of Mead's transparently imaginative portrayal. Suffice it to say that Samoan culture was not then, nor apparently never had been any more tolerant of casual heterosexual or homosexual relations than was the Philadelphia of Mead's childhood. Freeman attributes Mead's account to a blind desire to confirm Boas' notions of cultural determinism. It is more complicated than that.

Mead and her close friend, Ruth Benedict, despised, as did many if not most young intellectuals of the time, the mores, attitudes, behavior, and values of the American bourgeoisie. They were of a generation that saw all of the problems of civilized society as stemming from repression of the naturally good proclivities of human beings. It was particularly important to let children be natural. Mead read into the undoubtedly concocted or exaggerated stories produced by her informants (who were scarcely younger than she) her advanced ideas about the moral deficiencies of her own society.

And so *Coming of Age in Samoa* arose from a rich background of anthropological theory, imaginative (in the worst sense) ethnography, liberal social uplift of the twenties, and the Rousseau-inspired view that Westerners had of Polynesian cultures. We cannot single out any one of these, nor indeed the sum of them, as the cause of the picture Mead draws in *Coming of Age in Samoa*, but they are all part of the primordial matrix whence the picture comes.

Goodenough does a responsible job of placing a certain distance between modern anthropology, good ethnography, and the work of Mead. At the same time he apologizes for Mead, and he does so in a way that leads me to believe that he still does not comprehend the enormity of the pose taken both by Mead and by modern anthropology. He writes as though he believes it were truly possible to examine cultures *from an ethically neutral point of view*. After telling us that Mead's work has never anything like even a mediocre model for good field work he says: "Her contributions to science lie elsewhere. She raised important questions about things both scientists and the lay public were taking for granted about human behavior."[7] That the propaganda offered by Mead has anything to do with science is an assertion that is astounding. It says that anthropologists have a lot to learn about their self-proclaimed cultural and ethical neutrality. To suppose that any enterprise that depends so heavily upon the interactions between two people—an anthropologist and his or her informant—can be objective goes in the face of the very assumptions behind anthropology, social psychology, and all of those disciplines that see the human condition as essentially irrational.

Anthropologists are good visitors, and it is hard to find a monograph reporting ethnographic field work that does not thank, in addition to fellow anthropologists, governing officials in host countries, granting agencies, and the like, the anthropologist's informants. The thanking of the informants is often effusive and touching. Many anthropologists *like* the peoples they study. Very occasionally one finds a report in which the anthropologist describes his people as being quarrelsome, glum, and even nasty, but it is almost impossible to find examples of an attitude of total neutrality either toward the host culture, or the anthropologist's own. All of this unmasks the pretense of objectivity for what it is: the selective preference for those features of an alien culture that one finds attractive, a preference justified by the objectivity of science.

Anthropological Theories: The Plethora of Alternatives

Anthropology has escaped the domination by a single theory. So it is not so sorely burdened, as is the psychology of personality, by a single point of view, and, at the same time, it has escaped the bland homilies that often pass for theory in social psychology. Anthropological theories abound and, as Goodenough's comments amply illustrate, they are for the most part advanced in the guise of science. That is to say, they are in some manner or way supposed to be subject to empirical test. To be sure, most modern anthropologists have abandoned the older positivistic view of science common among social scientists of a generation ago for Popper's notion that scientific advancement consists of disconfirmation. Nevertheless, there is an expectation that anthropological theories should conform to the canons of science. Hence anthropology, whether it leans to the extremes of Boas' cultural determinism or to the more centerist views of Goodenough, is deterministic in its conception of human actions.

Benedict, Boas, Wissler, and, more recently, Evans-Pritchard and Firth could argue that anthropology was a science essentially the same in principle as the other sciences—that is to say, it discovered its truths by pitting hypotheses against hard empirical evidence. Things have changed. Goodenough, in his apology (though he does not admit it) must cope with the likes of C. G. Jung and the embarrassing presence of Carlos Casteñeda. In a more sober vein, there is the ascendence of the French structuralists, exemplified by Lévi-Strauss. These all disdain the canons of the philosophy of science, old or new, as social scientists in the mainstream understand them.

Nevertheless, one must have respect for serious ethnographers. Beset as they are by the subjective nature of anthropological reporting, by the embarrassments occasioned by shoddy field work, by outright fiction in the guise of anthropology, and by the proliferation of points of view, some of which cross the line into mysticism, good field workers give us a view of the human condition.

But anthropological theories, unless they are concerned with such particulars as the semantics of color or with kinship systems, are so grand and so encompassing that they can lay no claim to anything other than being learned expressions of faith and opinion—expressions that entail moral judgments. I am no stranger to the notion that faith suffuses the real sciences. I have pointed out that there is no clearly defined line between myth and scientific explanation (because they both are based upon belief and reason).[8] However, the practical results of science make science a dominant force in the physical governance of our lives. Such practical and physical consequences separate scientific knowledge in its effects upon human life from the kind of knowledge that arises from cultural anthropology. This is not to say that anthropological knowledge is not knowledge. It is, but it is not the kind of knowledge that can subject itself to the fires of disinterested observation without being consumed. The grand theories of anthropology serve to illustrate that anthropology, no more than psychohistory, nor social psychology, nor behaviorism, has any of the characteristics of the hard sciences.

Structuralism. Structuralism is concerned with the meaning of cultural things and, most importantly, with the relations among the various senses of meaning. I have labeled this enterprise in anthropology structuralism, though I mean to transcend the boundaries of particular schools, either of the older ideas embodied in structural linguistics or the school better known to contemporary intellectuals as French structuralism.

Among the first to call themselves structuralists were linguists, and since some of the early structuralists were Americans, it is not surprising to find the influence of behaviorism lurking in the background. A better term would have been descriptive, for many of the early structuralists were little concerned with the *relations* among things. It is an almost mystical concern with those relations that mark the later, anthropological and largely French structuralists. Here the idea of finding patterns by tracing the complexities of the relations among each and every aspect of particular cultures (as well as in the comparison among cultures) found its fullest flower. I have even heard it called symbology.

To the notion of structural relations anthropologists added the importance of understanding symbols. Symbols, we all know now, stand for deep and unconscious currents in human nature. Our generation associates this idea more than anything else with the ideas of C. G. Jung. That association has more than casual significance.

The early structuralists busied themselves with empirical problems. Some who worked in kinship tried to find, by combining a strictly objective empirical method with theory, some general principles about the nature of structures. Kinship itself was (and is) a matter of central concern, but semantic systems in general became important. The method for studying semantics was largely empirical, though a special issue of the *American Anthropologist*, issued at the high watermark of structural linguistics in anthropology, bore the title *Formal Semantic Analysis*.[9] It was not what the semanticists or generative linguists would mean by formal.

When Lévi-Strauss began to dominate the study of structural analysis (about the time that structural linguistics was being replaced by generative linguistics), there was a significant shift away from empirical evidence to ideas about general systems or structures that transcended particular cultures. This movement owed much to C. G. Jung and his search for universal symbols. Like Jung, the French structuralists disdained the prevailing clichés about science in anthropology, and, together with their allies among English anthropologists, the French were ready to develop a method unique to the mental sciences. As several of their critics have pointed out,[10] Lévi-Strauss and the other structuralists were in a tradition that easily made a distinction between natural sciences, capable of establishing lawful generalizations, and the human sciences, which largely were idiographic and structural.

Thus, to a degree, we are less obliged to say whether

these latter-day structuralists are right or not and more obliged to see if their views, often fantastic, help our understanding of human nature and the relations of human beings to the world. Most important of all, we must understand their moral posture. The influence of both the structuralists in anthropology and the writings of Jung tell us that there is not only an implicit moral posture there, but it is often an explicit one.

Jung and Anthropology. Jung's work began in psychoanalysis, and he both used and vastly extended Freud's notion of the unconscious. At the same time he divested himself of the need to follow Freud's theory of psychosexual development and the pretense that psychoanalysis is a science. He made overt gestures towards the arcane and to mystical knowledge, and he accepted such things as thought transference and genetic (or, as he put it, the collective) determinants of the unconscious. He brought into psychology, anthropology, and literature the notion of the archetype.

The richness and variety of interpretations of well-known symbols and myths that he invents are fascinating and instructive. These partly come from his early work in word associations. His earliest publications on the subject are not distinguished;[11] in fact they are dull and prosaic. Nevertheless, they are important, for if you read the later Jung, with all of its fantastic interpretation and evocation of symbols and myths, you can easily see how his ideas about the process of free association showed him the way.

While Jung is not an anthropologist, he has influenced a range of anthropologists from the neostructuralists to those whom most anthropologists label obscurantists (e.g., Carlos Casteñeda). The more prosaic early anthropological structuralism (hinted at in Malinowski and actively practiced by the linguistically oriented anthropologists—Murdock, Lounsbury, and others) is good descriptive science. It, by and large, does qualify as science even by those who demand theories, but the work of the later structuralists and such radicals as Casteñeda is avowedly not science. Whatever the defects of this movement, it has the merit of not offering as science intuitive and subjective explanations of human actions, institutions, and beliefs.

Cultural Materialism. An older generation of anthropologists put their faith in a philosophy of science that is now largely rejected. But one of the things in which all social scientists seem never to lose their faith is the need for a philosophy of science to explain and justify what they do. Working physical scientists go about their toil in a kind of innocent way, and though some, particularly among the popularizers, express their admiration for the ideas of Thomas Kuhn or Karl Popper, they seldom let such admiration influence the way in which they work. But social scientists must follow each turn that the philosophy of science takes. Thus, it is no surprise that the first chapter of Marvin Harris' *Cultural Materialism: The Struggle for a Science of Culture*[12] is titled "Research Strategies and the Structure of Science."

Harris finds his scientific ancestor in Marx, though he is very careful to tell us that his book is post-Marxian (my term). He rejects the dialectical treatment that Marx derived from the idealist Hegel, as he rejects all vestiges of idealism in Marx. Thus, he gives us a materialism unencumbered by the need to make the study of culture conform to the dialectic principle and all other such holdovers from nineteenth-century German idealism.

His book is interesting and worth commenting upon for several reasons. Harris is, both as an anthropologist and a neo-Marxist, an implacable enemy of the mentalism of the structuralists. At the same time he deals with history and prehistory in so sweeping a way as to make Spengler a miniaturist by comparison. Harris is a materialist in the Marxian sense, but he ranges far more widely than Marx (or Marx and Engels for that matter).

There are five behavioral categories that organize all culture: mode of production, mode of reproduction (mating rules, etc.), domestic economy, political economy, and behavioral superstructures (art, ritual, sports, etc.). Harris goes beyond Marx by making modes of reproduction as well as modes of production basic. These he calls the infrastructure. The domestic and political economies become the structure, and things like art, science, and

sports are the superstructure. The infrastructure determines everything. The production of children is as important as the mode of
production of things. The determination is through behavioral
rather than mental entities. Such things as the rate of growth of a
population is determined by the environment and mode of production, but it may also be limited by the level of female infanti-
cide just necessary to keep production at an adequate level. Such
is the case he tells us in a primitive, subsistence economy. But
even in a developed economy, Harris argues, "procreative ideology" is determined by the mode of production and reproduction
(as in the shift from a farm economy to an urban economy in the
early twentieth-century in the United States).

Harris then goes on to show how family organizations
change with the shift from hunter-gatherer economies to village
societies. He deals with the rise of chiefdoms and the emergence
of the modern state. Much of his account is drawn from Marx and
Engels, but Harris is able to elaborate by drawing upon the great
store of information in modern cultural anthropology. He deals
with historical cultures in a detailed way. He ranges so widely over
the historical and anthropological landscape that it would take a
very learned person indeed to find all the error of fact, much less
the misinterpretations. Perhaps, however, this is less important
than his avowed dogmatism in the matter of the material causes
of cultural change. In this he is more Marxist than Marx. At the
same time I remind the reader that any deterministic theory of
culture (sociobiology, for example) must share this quality of dogmatism, for there is no way of telling whether any particular causal
connection is correct or not.

Harris' materialism leads him to think of culture as
something driven by some fundamental conditions of human existence. He does not see culture as a finely woven network of
conditions, human, environmental, and material, the interaction
of which makes any particular notion of what causes what inevitably inadequate. The appreciation of the vastness of the problem
the structuralists grasp, though they forego in so doing the power
of causal explanation.

Speculations like Harris' are impossible of evaluation.

He says: "the credibility of the entire strategy rests upon the empirical status of the interpenetrating theories."[13] But there is no way to tell what that "empirical status" is. How, for example can we test the notion that one particular feature is responsible for the differences between say, feudal Japan and feudal Europe? There are an indefinite number of ways in which these cultures differ. The fact that we label them both feudal tells us that we think there are things in common, but precisely how many features they share and the causes of those features elude us. Any attempt to enumerate them would surely lead to argument. The rise of feudalism in Japan was a unique event. It was conditioned by the precise context of the time and place. And so with the development of feudalism in Europe. Demography, sociology, and even anthropology may contribute to our understanding of such unique events, but in the end historical explanation is idiographic and not nomothetic.

Thus, though I have chosen to single out Harris' cultural determinism, by so doing I only mean to show that any deterministic theory of the nature of human social organizations must be misleading in some respect or another. We have neither a knowledge of the things that cause the actions of particular human beings, nor do we have a sufficient understanding of the important features of cultures sufficient to allow us to predict the course of history.

The Convictions of Anthropologists

I find it hard to suppose that there are any anthropologists who regard their work as really being free from the influence of certain values, but there must be. I have chosen the examples of the work of anthropologists that I have because each of them illustrates the intrusion of particular personal social, or political values into anthropological studies in strikingly different ways.

Margaret Mead illustrates that results of ethnography reveal personal values both in the problem studied and in the outcome. Precisely why Mead said what she did, using the medium of her interviews with the young women of Manu'a is beyond our ability to recover. Freeman's interpretation is that she wished to please Boas. I suspect that it is more complicated than that. She (and Ruth Benedict) prized a free and easy approach to adolescent sexuality. By implication she led her readers to the view that the personal and social trauma of American adolescence was the re-sult of the repression of the natural expression of normal (what-ever that meant in this context) adolescent sex. That such an implication was made about American society on the basis of the observations of a handful of young Samoan women is astounding. No physical scientist would accept such a leap of faith.

I pointed out at the beginning of this chapter that the problems that social scientists choose to address reveal their val-ues. Sometimes these are values accepted by their society, or in any event those segments of society sensitive to social injustice and inequity. This is as it should be, for we cannot cease making observations of our and other societies simply because our obser-vations inevitably reflect, consciously or unconsciously, our own values, politics, and ethical presuppositions. But such observa-tions, if they are to be honestly accepted for what they are, cannot be evaluated in the reflected glory of the physical sciences. They are observations tainted with (or graced with, depending upon your point of view) value.

I was once a student of the late Alfred C. Kinsey. It was in a seminar in which we were supposed to be studying systemat-ics. Though we did treat issues in that difficult science (mainly in the guise of Kinsey's investigations of gall wasps), it was mainly a course in Kinsey himself. He was then working on the proofs of *Sexual Behavior in the Human Male*, and he was so full of it that inevitably it found its way into so irrelevant a topic as geographic isolation as a cause of speciation. He argued that he approached his study of sexual behavior in the same way that he approached his study of gall wasps—that is, as an objective biologist. Perhaps, but he let slip the circumstance that led him to the study of human sexual behavior. In the course of teaching elementary biology to freshman at Indiana University he had found both the ignorance of human sexual behavior and *the prevailing mores governing it* so appalling that he vowed to change them through the scientific study of sex. Even so great a skeptic as myself in the matter of determining the causes of historical changes must admit that Kinsey was at the very least an instrument of the expression of the change in our attitudes and beliefs about sex. That his interest in so doing was, in his own view, the result of a conviction of the evil of current sexual mores was apparent to those who knew him, his later protestations to the contrary notwithstanding.

The more general aspect of the inevitability of values intruding themselves into the social sciences is illustrated by Harris. His great general theory is scientific, he tells us. Marxists have been proclaiming the scientific validity of the historical views of Marx and Engels to an increasingly skeptical world for a long time now, but the faith in economic or material determinism (depending upon whether or not you accept Harris' revisionism) is still there. Harris fulminates against the moralistic obscurantism he sees as incarnated in a breath-takingly wide variety of forms (radicalism, positivism, phenomenology, etc.), but that does not prevent him from having his own vision of what society *ought to be*. It is inevitable that he sees his oughts as coming from an objective anthropology.

Finally, a brief word on values and the structuralists. They provide an ironic comment, for one of their central beliefs is that everything is connected to everything else in the world of human affairs. Therefore it is not surprising to see many of them say that it is impossible to separate one's views of the nature of human society from one's preconceptions about the oughts governing society. Perhaps it is this realization that allows the structuralists to be singularly modest in their claims for scientific validity. On the other hand, it makes them fallible moralists.

Political Science and the Practical

I chose anthropology and political science to illustrate, by way of contrast, the inevitability of the subjective in the social sciences because anthropology and political science are so different. The basic commitment in anthropology is to pure knowledge and theory. Political scientists, being mainly professors, harbor theorists among their ranks also, but the main enterprise in political science is the empirical description of the process of government. Theorists in political science are more likely to turn to traditional philosophy for guidance rather than to the philosophy of science. Hence, there is an air of earnest honesty about political science.

Political scientists, more often than anthropologists, are practical. They go about their work with the aim not only of studying government but with the avowed aim of improving it. One of the more interesting books in political science published in the months prior to this writing is called *Approval Voting*.[14] The authors propose a reform in election procedures and then, by invoking data and a computer model, they defend their proposal. Their ideas clearly come from what they value in the American political system, but they are honest about the matter. They do not hide under the cloak of scientific objectivity, though their data are often as objective as data can be in the social sciences. They want the voter to be able to express his or her opinion no matter who the specific candidates are and how many of them there are. If there are two candidates of a given persuasion and one of a different persuasion, it is certain that the two will divide the voters who prefer their position. It is to this problem that the proposal is addressed. In making their case, the authors use borrowed magic of various sorts; they devise models to predict the consequences of their scheme, and they even trot out the fad of social scientists of the fifties and earlier, "theorems." However, they do make explicit their interests in serving participatory democracy. One difficulty with which they do not deal is the conceivable side effects that would result if their scheme were to be put into practice.

On Understanding Political Science

The best way to get a feel for some intellectual discipline is to see what it offers freshmen and sophomores. On that score political science is most reassuring. It is mainly descriptive.

There is, of course, a palpable bias in most texts for the tradition of free governments, and though the authors may on occasion flirt with alternative forms, there is a bias towards the tripartite American system. The bias is honest and not, as critics have from time to time darkly hinted, born of a desire to please or placate reactionary trustees. There is a certain evenhandedness, not to say blandness, in dealing with other governments. There are very few texts that choose to damn Communists or Third World dictators on scientific grounds. Rather these miscreants are disputed on their political merits.

Political scientists deal with personalities, but rarely do they deal with personality. While they occasionally interpret political history by reference to the quirks of senators, chief justices, and presidents, they do not attempt to account for these quirks by resort to psychological theory. More importantly, they do not attempt to spread the view that all politics is at the bottom an irrational consequence of childhood experiences.

Political and ethical positions are often transparent. One popular text has as its subtitle: "To Keep the Republic in its Third Century." [15] This book, as with its numerous competitors, is mainly devoted to describing how government works. In the section on "election behavior and voting" it draws upon psychological theory, but like others of its kind, it does so gently and without dogmatism. It describes the technology of public opinion polling, and it presents the various theories about how opinion is molded. It even describes a model of public opinion, but it does so within the view that political decisions are, at the bottom, rational and not the victims of every irrelevant conditioned reaction that could be brought to bear upon them.

In short, while the mainstream of political science is alert to and concerned with the human determination of human events, it does not suppose that we have a complete understanding of the way in which human actions are determined. Political scientists, no more than the rest of us, cannot escape their own views, nor, by and large, do they pretend to do so (unless they are Marxists or something similar). In short, there is a great deal of common sense in political science.

One problem with political science is its reliance on empirical extrapolation. It "predicts" political decisions based upon elaborate statistical analysis of earlier decisions. Political scientists occasionally get carried away in this respect. An otherwise excellent study, *The Changing American Voter*,[16] is marred by the implication that such studies can also reveal the changeless. The authors borrow an analogy from Donald Campbell: The British chemists Nicholson and Carlisle, in discovering the electrolytic properties of water, perforce used a particular sample of water. However, their generalizations were to all water for all time. We are, by the analogy, led to believe that studies of the American voter lead to something equally changeless. However, having said what they say, the authors by and large ignore it. They tell us how the American voter changed between 1950 and 1970. They even, in their excellent though tentative last chapter, decline to extrapolate to the near future.

Public Opinion Polling

The branch of political science that has most interested itself in the prediction and control of behavior is public opinion polling, and public opinion polling is a major refuge for those who believe the political process to be irrational. Some social scientists believe that public opinion polls can reveal the *real* reasons why people vote for certain issues and candidates rather than others. There is a pervasive and often articulated assumption that people prefer certain issues and candidates for the wrong reasons, that is to say, reasons irrelevant to the issues and to the views of the candidates.

The enterprise of trying to determine the real reasons for patterns of voting begins, as Rossi points out,[17] with the series of investigations by S. A. Rice, published in 1928.[18] Rossi praises Rice as the pioneer in the field, and, indeed, Rice does appear to invent many of the tools used in the study of the politics of voting. Rossi finds him naive for accepting a single dimension of political attitudes (from liberal through moderate to conservative).[19] Rice's work is, however, more than just naive. It is a vast oversimplification. There is no way to assert that *any* dimension reveals the subjective nature of attitudes. Rather, any dimension is a subjective choice of the investigator which inevitably contaminates data with the investigator's own views. The choice of dimensions, whether arrived at intuitively as with Rice or through factor analysis, multidimensional scaling, or some other method for reducing data, depends upon the opinions of the researcher as much as it does upon some aseptic mathematical analysis. In order to frame his questions, the opinion poller must make some assumptions about what people believe, assumptions that come from his own intuitions.

The modern technology of public opinion polling, developed after World War II by Lazersfeld, Berelson, and others, is distinguished by sophisticated techniques of sampling, interviewing, and methods of tabulation. This technology provides the livelihood for all of those polling consultants, nowadays without whom no candidate for high office would even think of venturing into a campaign. This technology is also the source of those early evening projections that have received so much critical attention in recent presidential elections.

But polling itself remains merely a technology which exploits demographic "predictors" of voting. It adds to the determinism of the social sciences only to the extent that its successes are used to develop "theories" of voting based upon the irrational and the irrelevant. Such theories, fortunately, always self-destruct on some particular candidate or issue.

Politics, Psychology, and Morality

One of the most interesting books in political theory in recent years is Roberto Mangabeira Unger's *Knowledge and Politics*.[20] Unger criticizes what he calls the tradition of "liberal psychology" (unfortunate choice of adjective). He means the tradition of Hobbes, Locke, and Hume (as well as that of modern "scientific" psychology). The words he uses to describe the psychology advocated in this tradition are reason and desire (or will). I think he is right in his thesis that moral and psychological descriptions cannot be the same, but he is wrong in his choice of the word *reason* to describe what are theories of the intellect in the tradition of British empiricism and modern cognitive psychology. Both British empiricism and much of modern cognitive psychology can be described as attempts to escape from the notion that the human mind is rational.

I reserve the term reason for the process of reaching correct conclusions given certain premises. So defined, given any set of human desires, it would be possible for the human mind to reason correctly to any action that would achieve the goals of those desires. However, the process of reasoning from desires to actions is not the basis upon which one can construct a moral and hence political philosophy. One can easily imagine a psychological theory that would be both rational and morally unsatisfactory. Various troublemakers, such as the Marquis de Sade, have provided difficulties precisely of this sort for what Unger calls the liberal political tradition.

But matters are worse than Unger acknowledges (except in his brief remark to the effect that in Freudian psychology reason is completely subservient to desire). Modern psychological theory that has penetrated such mundane and ordinary things as public-opinion polling with the aim of "manipulating" (a favorite word in the psychological jargon) human action is far more radical. Opinions as conditioned responses not only provide no basis for moral choice but, if believed, must necessarily diminish any faith in the possibility of moral choice. Moral choice, by such a view, must be reduced to a belief in the consensus of ends. In short, when we are led to a belief in psychological determinism, no moral choice is possible. Either we can reason so as to achieve moral ends as well as psychological ends, or morality is not possible.

Whatever our views on morality, the notion that psychological choices and moral choices are one is both incorrect and devastating to our views of ourselves and our views of human freedom. In the first chapter of this book I said that a complete determinism makes the notion of freedom a black joke. And so it does.

The Subjectivity of Objectivity

The separation of the subjective and the objective has been made vastly more difficult and subtle by the philosophers of the seventeenth and eighteenth centuries. As no philosophers before them did, the thinkers of these centuries struggled with the question of what belongs to the mind and what belongs to the world. The great synthesis achieved by Kant near the end of the eighteenth century has forever altered the course of philosophy. It established that human knowledge was that—human, made into what it was by the universal characteristics of the human mind. At the same time it established the necessity for an external world, while showing that the true nature of that external world was only to be seen through the universal categories of human understanding.

As a consequence in the twentieth century, telling what is subjective and what is objective in human experience and knowledge is difficult beyond measure. I shall not attempt to explain the subtleties that twentieth-century philosophy faces. Rather I shall assume the naive realism of the man in the street. I am not a naive realist, but even as Hume himself so declared, so assuming is on occasion a useful way to get on with the solution of a problem.

Earlier I made a distinction between two kinds of physical knowledge, a distinction that was made within this pose of naive realism. One kind of physical knowledge is of the ordinary, atheoretical sort. It is descriptive and only lightly draws upon abstract theory (except to the extent that it may draw upon those Kantian categories). We may even declare a truce in that other great conflict in epistemology, the war between nominalism and Aristotelian realism. The names of things, neurons, chairs, and chasms, may or may not refer to universal essences, but the man in the street knows what they are and is seldom troubled with the subtleties of how he knows what they are.

The second meaning of physical refers to a much more complicated matter. It is the whole of physical theory, whether or not that theory is interpreted within the limits of the categories of human experience. If it is incorporated within the limits of the categories of human understanding, then we must surely acknowledge that Kant's list of those categories (even if the notions of space and time which Kant does not list among the categories) is inadequate. Theoretical physics in its most abstract and advanced forms relies on mathematics rather than on the categories of human understanding. In short, reason can transcend the categories, however one conceives them to be, and the theoretical notion of the physical does.

Whatever the philosophical subtleties, we recognize that these two senses of the physical are different from our sense of the subjective. Post-Kantian epistemology may take it as an article of faith that there is matter, but such a faith is beyond any doubt a different kind of faith than my belief in the rectitude of democracy. In short, however difficult the philosophical problem may be, it is not hard, taking the stance of the realist, to maintain a line between the subjective and the objective in daily life.

It is one thing to have a faith in democracy or in communism as the solution to all human ills and another to have a faith that bodies under the influence of gravity accelerate independently of their mass. Confirmation or disconfirmation of the latter depends upon the world of physical things. Confirmation or disconfirmation of one or another of the former depends upon one's assumptions about man and his place in the world. There is no way in which social science can confirm or deny that democracy is the best system of government, for any such confirmation or denial will depend upon the assumptions one makes about the nature of human beings and their place in the world.

Elitists may argue, for example, against democracy by saying that a free choice given to the masses is wasted, for they are not intelligent or informed enough to make choices.[21] On the one hand, the choice of the masses may be dictated only by a selfish instinct, or on the other hand by their easily swayed (and illogical) opinions. Both the arguments and these alternatives stem from a confusion between intellect and reason. Ignorance is not at issue, for in fact, all of us, including those wisest members of the intellectual elite, are ignorant of the ultimate consequences of any choice we make. That choice is embedded in the immense context of things. However certain we may be about some particular outcome, we have surely overlooked the possibility of some others.

There is no such thing as the objective study of man save as man as a physical entity. Anthropologists and political scientists, however firm their faith in physical reductionism, do not study human beings as physical entities, they study their values, social relations, beliefs, and ways of organizing themselves into governments. What aspects of these things they choose to study and what they conclude from their studies depend upon their assessment of their worth. Political scientists are rather honest about this issue, anthropologists, in company with psychologists and sociologists, are not.

What has this inevitable intrusion of values into the social sciences to do with the issue of freedom and determinism? It is at the core of the matter, for the claim of scientific determinism is that the social sciences can be value free in the way that the physical sciences are. It is only a matter of discovering the inexorable laws. A scientific determinism is not simply an objective kind of fatalism, as those American novelists I mentioned in chapter 3 appeared to think. It is, to use the language of dynamic psychology, a wish imposed upon the world. It is a way of saying "you must obey the rules we discover, for there is no other way." It is, in short, a tyranny of the mind.

Social science revealed as a way of looking at the world from the perspective provided by the viewer's values and beliefs is a rich and significant enterprise. It is not deterministic; it is structural. It describes without making the fatal assumption that we can uncover, by the use of the traditional tools of science, the causes of human action. Social science as the objective source of knowledge about the causes of human action is at best an intellectual embarrassment and at worst a fraud.

Chapter Nine

Our Conceptions
of Ourselves

A ny notion of human nature compatible with the
ideals and practice of democracy requires two
assumptions: that human beings are capable of arriving at decisions by a rational process, and that human beings have the freedom of choice to act upon those decisions.

The first assumption should not be hard to accept,
save among those readers who might be lost in the behaviorism
of the thirties or forties, or those who are so committed to the
psychoanalytic view of human nature as to rule out any possibility
of rational action, or those whose enthusiasm for sociobiology
knows no bounds. It should be patently obvious to all of the rest
of us that we can reason correctly from premise to conclusion.
Empirical demonstration of that fact would only be one of those
exercises in redundancy all too common in the social sciences.

It is true that we falter, and psychologists have, for a
long time now, looked into the kinds of errors we make in syllogistic reasoning.[1] The errors, more often than not, turn out to be
some abortion of the reasoning process brought about by the
wording or content of the propositions. These demonstrations tell
us nothing more than that the exercise of rationality requires intellectual vigilance.

More importantly, we also falter in reaching *correct* conclusions because we often reason from false assumptions. Sometimes it is hard to tell if we are rational, because often we do not articulate the assumptions from which we argue. But once again, such failures do not mean we are not rational beings; it means that the price of rationality is hard work. Furthermore, the evidence is overwhelming that we are the *only* rational beings about which we have concrete empirical knowledge.

The more difficult question is: Can scientific psychology and the social sciences in general tolerate the notion of freedom of action? Or, to put it more specifically, can any conception of human nature rooted in the social sciences as the study of the causes of human action tolerate the notion of human freedom? The earlier chapters of this book argued that the social sciences are not causative sciences precisely because accounting for human action eludes them. The attempts to bluff through causative notions condemn the social sciences to the foot of the table of the sciences. But the matter must be more squarely put: Are we *really* free? That is the subject of this final chapter.

The Free and the Constrained

Controlled and Uncontrolled Behavior

In several places I have acknowledged what every champion of human freedom must concede. Aspects of all living action, including the behavior of human beings, are both predictable and controllable. The distinction between reflexive actions and voluntary actions is a testimony to the fact that some actions are free and others are not. Reflexive actions are elicited by stimuli; voluntary action is not. The distinction between reflexive and voluntary behavior, however, is complicated by the existence of two loosely defined classes of action not properly describable as reflexes and yet not quite describable as voluntary actions. In their almost limitless speculations about human actions and society, the sociobiologists have made much of these classes. One of them is what ethologists call fixed-action patterns, and the other is a looser class of actions that I shall call compulsions. I must say something about both before I can deal with the question of human freedom.

Fixed-Action Patterns and Compulsions

Ethologists have revived the notion of instinct, but in part because they are embarrassed by the history of the notion of instinct, they have substituted several terms of which the most common is fixed-action patterns.[2] Such actions appear to be caused in the sense that they can be elicited in the same way that reflexes can. There are differences between reflexes and fixed-action patterns, however. For one thing the aspects of stimuli that appear to elicit fixed-action patterns are not easily characterizable by physical properties. Rather it is some configurational character of the stimulus that appears to do the eliciting. Secondly, they are much more variable in their execution and often more complex than reflexes. In fact, it is more accurate to say that they are released rather than elicited by stimuli.

Examples abound. Consider the frantic behavior of parental birds in the presence of the gaping movements of their young. The gaping itself, curiously, is more like a reflex. It has a simple and easily producible stimulus—the jarring of the nest ordinarily caused by an adult bird lighting to one side. But it can also be produced by simply tapping the nest lightly with a pencil. The behavior of the parents in feeding those yawning mouths is less easily described as reflexive. It is variable and appears to be under the control of a configuration of events, not simple stimuli. Both the compelling nature of the appropriate stimulus and the variation in reactions to it can be illustrated by birds who do not care for their own offspring. As the cuckoo and the American cowbird well know, any gaping mouth is likely to be responded to by other birds. And so these birds deposit their eggs in the nests of other species. The intruding offspring are likely to be fed by the parents, but there is often confusion and uncertainty. The unwilling hosts will sometimes try to bury the alien egg under a new layer of twigs, or will even attempt to dispose of them.[3]

Despite their variable character, their fragility in the presence of unusual conditions, and their released rather than elicited property, fixed-action patterns are clearly not voluntary. They reflect information stored in genes rather than information free to adjust to the infinite lability of the environment, but at the same time they hint at the intrusion of aspects of voluntary behavior.

Do human beings show fixed-action patterns? Yes, but the extent is a matter of great dispute. Most authorities (only the tight little group of Skinnerian behaviorists aside) accept evidence for their existence in human infancy, and indeed, the current regnant theory of the development of human attachment appears to require their existence. However, evidence for genuine fixed-action patterns in the actions of older children and adults is less easy to come by.

Compulsions are another matter. These are actions that are not released by specific stimuli but which seem to have some overwhelming cause. In certain cases that cause is rooted in the biochemistry of the organism. Despite the claims of the sociobiologists, however, the causes of many of them are unknown. The best examples of biochemical control come from the splendid research on specific hungers spanning the past half century. That research tells us, among other things, that strange and unusual patterns of eating can be often traced to deficiencies in specific minerals and other nutrients. But the existence of these well-known cases of the body's imperative to action in order to provide for its well-being does not in any way advance the claim that territoriality or the specific human sexual mores derive from similar conditions. Such arguments about human behavior have been advanced at least since the writing of McDougall's *Social Psychology* and in the incarnation of sociobiology are still with us. Nevertheless, the case of compulsive behavior deserves our attention, for it helps us understand the case for human freedom.

Compulsions take two forms. First of all, there are the inexplicable and illogical things we human beings do. I must, for example, make sure that the center headings in my manuscripts are reasonably centered, even in a rough draft. There is no logic behind it, and when I am in a hurry to get my ideas on paper it is a positive hindrance. Such instances, of course, are the standard fare of theorists in dynamic psychology; any issue of the *International Journal of Psychoanalysis* is sure to find one or more of the believers munching on a problem like this. More to the point, such actions appear to occur in animals that, like ourselves, are capable of voluntary action. In old-fashioned zoos in which animals were confined to narrow cages, compulsive actions ranging from relatively benign pacing to the more obviously pathological self-mutilation were the rule. All of this suggests that such actions are caused in some way (that is to say they are not dictated by reason), but their causes are obscure enough so that, once again, the various claims of sociobiologists and psychoanalysts to explain them are empty. I remind my reader that causal explanation requires not a presumed but a demonstrated physical basis.

Sociobiology. The term sociobiology is the invention of a biologist who was, until that invention, mainly known as a student of ants.[4] Sociobiology takes its place along with the popularizations of Robert Ardrey and Desmond Morris as a late-twentieth-century revival of the arguments made by Ernst Haeckel and others about the implications of Darwinian evolution for human life. Haeckel, as I remarked in an earlier chapter, was influential among those American writers in the tradition of naturalism. The sociobiologists and their allies have made no such literary converts (or, if they have, they are more obscure in our time than London and Norris were in theirs). However, they have been taken quite seriously by some biologists, by some psychologists, and by a scattering of other social scientists and philosophers. That their ideas have not engulfed the social sciences is probably the result of the fact that their strong hereditarian views are currently out of fashion in the social sciences and even regarded as politically dangerous.[5] Sociobiologists are complete determinists, and by contemporary standards they are forthright about the matter. They argue that genes are destiny. Most contemporary determinists, even among those who are forthright about the matter, are environmentalists, and many environmental determinists regard hereditarian determinism as a revival of Nazism. That all determinists are of a stripe seems not to have occurred to the participants on both sides of this argument.

As I write, the most recent book by the leaders of the sociobiology movement, Promethean Fire, is given over to a considerable degree to the refutation of the charges of racism.[6] The defense mainly consists of wrapping the robes of science about the position of the sociobiologists on the issue. That the issue is an embarrassment to sober ethologists and their allies is unfortunate; good observational science becomes besmirched with fantastic speculation.

In brief, the sociobiologists argue that human mentality has been shaped entirely by evolution. Genes provide the rules whereby the individual mind develops. The mind grows by its genetically determined capacity to absorb culture. Culture is created anew each generation. The more successful members of a culture survive and reproduce better in a given culture than others. The successful genes thus spread through a culture.[7] Genes and culture are locked in an ever-recurring circle that refines both the genes and the culture under the pressure of a particular ecological niche.

Culture includes moral decisions; thus human morality is a matter of genes and evolution. The authors of Promethean Fire deal with such questions as altruism (currently a fashionable topic among respectable ethologists) and aggression. But they reserve their most detailed treatment for an easy target, the (they say) universal prohibition against incest. Such a prohibition occurs, they say, because exogamous mating is genetically better than endogamous mating, and the genes know this. Hence the genes devise cultural systems forbidding incest.

Much of this book is given over to statements of this sort, statements that would have been heavily underlined if a copy of the book by some miracle had fallen into the hands of Jack London. Free will is nonexistent. People are guided by the biologically determined norms of their culture. And even if these norms are challenged, the challengers are still not free, for they "are skillfully led by the deep impulses and feelings prescribed by their genes."[8] Or, "ethical precepts are based on the predispositions, and they too can be altered in a precise manner."[9]

This is heady stuff, and one can imagine a naive reader regarding this as the very essence of the science of human nature.[10] That nearly all of the assertions made by sociobiologists have been made before does seem to take the bloom off a bit, but the believer is going to believe. This is not science any more than Marxism, psychoanalysis, or the vast bulk of experimental social psychology is science. What is more, as all determinism does, it ignores the nature of ethics. Ethics has not to do with whether or not we perform certain actions. It has to do with a systematic relation among beliefs, reason, and actions. Our beliefs reasoned through might lead us to regard incest as a moral act. The rulers of both ancient Peru and ancient Egypt so regarded brother-sister incest among the regnant classes.

The development of sociobiology serves a purpose. By setting up a competing booth in the marketplace where psychoanalysts, environmental behaviorists, and Marxists shout their wares, the sociobiologists show us the emptiness of the claims of complete determinism when made in the name of science.

The Concept of Motivation

I borrow the heading of this section from an engaging little book written by the philosopher of psychology R. S. Peters.[11] I owe the inspiration for much of what is written here to Peters. However, there are certain issues with which Peters does not concern himself. He is altogether too firmly convinced that a theory of human motivation is possible.

Any notion of motivation applies only to voluntary behavior. No one would be so quixotic as to propose a motivational theory of reflexes. Reflexes are explained by the relations among neurons. It is less obvious that we do not need a motivational theory of fixed-action patterns. In fact, some psychologists base such human motives as love and attachment upon generalizations

of fixed-action patterns in childhood. In so doing they are following in the explanatory footsteps of Freud and McDougall. However,
I shall argue that the only component of human action that requires the notion of motivation is voluntary behavior. Furthermore, I shall argue that any theory that supposes a small number
of motives to be the springs of all human action is doomed to
failure. There are as many motives as there are relations among
plans, actions, and goals. In short, motives provide us with descriptive categories of great value in human commerce, even in
the foundation of the law, but they are not explanatory devices.
For the most part, the really interesting study of human motives
falls within the provenience of mystery writers and psychological
novelists.

Fixed-action patterns do not need the kind of motivational explanations described by Peters, for they are, in the end,
caused. Even though they are complex neural events, they are
released by external stimuli. They are clearly caused by those stimuli. Explanations of most other kinds of behavior (the biochemi-
cally based compulsions perhaps excepted) are a matter of one's
choice of myths.

Because compulsions are of such a mixed character
they provide the key to understanding the structural or descriptive
status of notions of motivation. Withdrawal symptoms, genetic
predispositions toward the metabolism (or failure of metabolism)
of certain substances is reflected in altered states of the body.
These in turn can, without much difficulty, be shown to be experimentally related to actions designed to correct the state of the
body. At the same time the causative relations are complex, and
physical control often subtly slides over to the psychological. What
may begin as a rational decision to ingest alcohol or inject heroin
may end with a physical dependence upon the substance based
upon the drastic changes induced in the body's metabolism. As
every student of addiction knows, ingestion of substances is in a
subtle way related to social climate. And, as at least students of
AA know, it is *possible* to end the addiction to the substance by
moral means.

Thus in certain compulsions the physical and the psychological meet. Social relations, beliefs about drugs, people, and interpretations of experiences, all influence the course of substance-driven compulsions in human beings. None of these can be described as physical in the two senses described in earlier chapters. And there is an even more subtle relation between the physical and the psychological. It is provided by the possibility of something that is usually described as Pavlovian conditioning (for lack of better understanding of the matter). Involuntary autonomic reactions may be conditioned to environmental and indeed even mental events, thus subtly shifting the experience gained from some physical substance to something interpreted, that is to say, mental. This in no way eliminates the line between voluntary and involuntary actions. It simply reminds us of the fact that particular actions of real people are often complex mixtures of physically determined components, involuntary conditioning, and voluntary choice. The mixtures may be so intertwined in some specific instance that it is all but impossible to sort them out.

I return to the question of motives—that is to say, attempts to account for human actions on the one hand or descriptions of the relations among plans, reason, and action on the other. All *explanations* of motivation reduce the nature of actions to something else. Peters goes on about a certain person who crosses the street in order to buy some tobacco. Most of us, buried in our Egyptian night of ignorance, might suppose that such an action is motivated by the desire to smoke. But psychoanalytic theory (and even common sense, as Peters points out) suggest other possibilities. That is to say, such an action may reveal something more general and deeper at work. This possibility leads psychological theorists of motivation to reduce such action to a list of motives much smaller than the potential list of human actions (in the case of psychoanalytic theory to one or two motives). Such reductions are the basis for the various attempts to see relations among various actions, and to a degree such attempts are useful. We might hazard the guess that the seeker of tobacco is reluctant to return to what is perhaps a lonely and dreary apartment and thus seizes upon the excuse to pass the time of day with the tobacconist. Other of his actions, such as frequent trips to the grocer's, might then be encompassed by the same explanation.

Such explanations, however, are not scientific. They lack the potential for scientific verification. They are explanations of the sort we all offer for one another's conduct, explanations that are based directly upon our psychological interpretations of one another. Those psychological interpretations are subjective transformations of our own experience with ourselves and with one another. It would be a poor psychotherapist indeed, in dispensing the wisdom of whatever theory or school of psychotherapy to which he subscribes, who would utterly neglect his own experience with his own life and with the interpretations of the lives of others achieved through experience. In short, the psychology of personality as well as motivation are instances of *verstehende Psychologie*—that is to say, psychology as art.[12]

Both the psychologist and the man in the street know that ostensible motives are not always the real ones. Such a proposition is the cornerstone for the notion of motivation, for if there would be no need to interpret the plans to action from one's own experience, the circumstances, and the action in question, there would be no problem of motivation. Explanations for the behavior of Peters' tobacco purchaser are psychological (that is to say, belonging to the psychology of understanding). One or more of the infinite possibilities may be said to be more plausible than others, though surely not in any genuine scientific sense. Some people are simply better psychologists than others—whether they are M.D., Ph.D., and product of a school for training analysts, or simply the shrewd high school graduate who must judge for a small town savings and loan association whether a couple is a good risk for a mortgage or not. But as scientific explanation all general theories of motivation fail.

The Will

That wise and unjustly neglected psychologist, F. Rauch, brought a notion to the American continent first put forward by Thomas Aquinas.[13] He argued for two springs to human action. One he described as desires, inclinations, emotions, and passions. The other he described as law, moral obligation, duties, and rights. The basis for his distinction is not convincing, but he does remind us of the need to separate willed behavior from ordinary voluntary behavior. The difference between these is crucial to any conception of the human being in which the notion of personal freedom and its concomitant responsibilities play a role.

Rauch's mistake is psychological, rather than moral, theological, or philosophic, though I suspect he made his distinction for theological reasons. He says that will, as such, applies only to law, morality, etc. This mistake is a reasonable one, both given the history of the idea of the will and the context in which Rauch writes. My quarrel is not with ascribing will to moral, legal, and obligatory decisions but with the limitation. I may behave with free will—that is to say, willfully and with reason to guide my will—on so trivial a matter as a preference in toothpaste. Of course, such a choice may be a moral one—that is to say, based upon the investments a manufacturer makes in South Africa, but as it happens, I simply prefer the cheapest commercial toothpaste.

But Rauch is right on a more important point: Political decisions, moral decisions, legal decisions, duties, and the exercise of rights *ought to be guided by will*—that is to say, reason in the command of voluntary actions. This is not to say that the right will in every case prevail, for, as I have reminded the reader in several places now, reason may be misguided by information or faith. To reason correctly from wrong premises is no guarantee of ultimate moral rectitude. Nor is faith in the wrong assumptions going to lead to the right conclusions. Nevertheless, the assumption that reason can command voluntary behavior is essential to any notion of human freedom, however that freedom may be abused by the assaults of passion, inclinations, and emotions. Nor does the action of these things excuse any abuse of freedom, for they do not wipe out the beliefs from which we are to reason. Reason and volition, when operating together produce something which psychologists, anthropologists, sociologists, and even economists (who should know better) ignore at the peril of reducing their sciences to the pratfalls and rattling bladders that too often seem to characterize them.

Where Psychological Explanation Ends

The distinction between voluntary and involuntary behavior arose not in psychology but in neurology and physiology. Despite the now almost universal acceptance of the distinction, the cause of most voluntary behavior remains a mystery. Voluntary behavior, to use Skinner's felicitous term, is emitted. That is to say, it arises from some process endogenous to the organism. We may, in various ways, intrude into the process by physical intervention. We can convert a laboratory rat into a compulsive lever presser by producing an electric current in several portions of its brain following the press of a lever. Or, destruction of certain regions of the central nervous system produces in various animals, cats, for example, the most appalling kinds of compulsive actions. This is no more than to say that the process that normally regulates voluntary behavior owes its existence to various parts of the brain.

Psychobiologists have devised theories about the origin of voluntary action (arousal theory, for example), and the theories, accompanied by the relevant experimental evidence, are impressive. It is very possible that we may eventually come to know how such a self-organizing system as the brain of a rat retrieves information stored in molecules, cells, and cell networks in order to decide to preen itself rather than drink. Such knowledge might also, by extrapolation, provide a model for the way in which any voluntary action is organized by a complex central nervous system. Whatever the mystery of voluntary behavior, it is a mystery that may be, in principle, solved. To say, however, that we have already solved it is to indulge in the kind of hyperbole that all too often characterizes not only the social sciences but psychobiology.

The will itself admits of no new explanation, for we already have an explanation, one that is no mystery. The will is based upon one basic condition that we have already declared not to be mysterious, namely reason. Rationality is its own explanation, as mathematicians know when they argue for the purity of mathematics. Mathematics depends only upon the rules of logic and its assumptions. The will, in turn, depends only upon the rational processes which relate belief to action. Reason combined with choice makes human freedom possible. We need to examine one more aspect of the problem. however, before we can declare the human mind to be saved from the black fate of absolute determinism. The problem lies in the matter of the beliefs whence our actions arise.

The Rational and the Irrational

It may be objected that the irrational lies not in the process of reasoning from belief to action but in the beliefs themselves. After all, Freud tried to explain Judaism and Christianity in terms of that universal family tragedy that is the foundation of psychoanalytic theory. He regarded religions as well as everything else as expressions of the irrational. On a less elevated level, the student of "election behavior" (to use the phrase lamentably to be found in political science texts) may argue that our preference for describing ourselves as Democrats rather than Republicans lies in our self-image, in conditioned avoidance, in being duped by propaganda, or by any of a hundred other plausible causes.

None of these explanations can be taken seriously in the context of genuine science, for they are all psychological explanations. Psychological explanations, as we have already seen in this chapter, do not admit of causation in the scientific sense, for there is no way to apply to them the canon of scientific inference about causes. They are beyond experimentation, and either directly or indirectly, scientific explanation depends upon the causative inferences inherent in the experimental method. Even cosmology, that most remote of the physical sciences, depends for the ultimate plausibility of its arguments upon experimental evidence and theory tested by experimental evidence.

Any psychological explanation of beliefs is as valid or invalid as any other, and the explanations offered by psychologists, political scientists, sociologists, and anthropologists are neither more or less valid than the explanations offered by barbers, dentists, and others whose occupations permit them to muse on the conditions of human life while offering their services. To be sure, psychologists and political scientists may offer more nearly correct *descriptions* than barbers, for they do have the tools for making sophisticated observations. Their notions of sampling and their techniques for eliciting information from people have been refined by long use. The barber, in gathering his information, may be unduly influenced by those of his clients who choose to discuss such matters with him. But the prejudices of the barber are no less obvious than are those of the psychologists. In any event, description is not explanation.

Descriptions are not explanations even when they lead to actuarial predictions, unless those descriptions are part of a network of physical causes. Thus to suppose that I am a Republican *because* my income is above average, *because* I am a white male beyond the years of discretion, *because* I do not occupy a blue-collar job is to make the kind of mistake favored by newspaper columnists. To be sure, it might be correct to suppose that I contracted tuberculosis because I lived in the kind of environment in which I did, or that I am suffering from a physical disorder of the brain because I have been ingesting flakes of lead-based paint. While these inferences are very uncertain, they are uncertain *only* because all of the physical links have not been clearly established.

Sociological and psychological explanations of beliefs, where they have any evidential status whatever, are based upon correlations. That is to say, the structural description of my condition is like that for many people who are Republicans. However high the correlations, however sophisticated the description, however nicely the intricacies of the relations are described by factor analysis, etc., there is no basis for a causative inference. So much, of course, was said early in the last century by J. S. Mill. Mill might have said (if Republicanism then existed) that someone is white collar because he or she is a Republican, or white collarism and

Republicanism are both to be attributed to devotion to causes like the prevention of cruelty to animals.

This is by way of once again pointing out that the overwhelming force of theory in the social sciences is towards the irrational. It could not be otherwise, given the commitment of those sciences towards a vain emulation of causal explanations in the physical mode. Reason does not conform to physical causes, for reason is free to follow and only follow the rules of inference, not those of causation. To the extent that we are rational beings, causative explanations are irrelevant. But in nearly every aspect of the social sciences today there is a hunger after the fruits of causative inference.

I count among the irrational rules the notion that we are entirely controlled by our reinforcements, primary or secondary. Our beliefs, actions, nay our veriest slips of the tongue and our dreams are to be attributed to an overwhelming impulse that channels itself hither and yon according to our experiences in childhood. Any theory is irrational that attempts to provide a causative account in psychological terms of any human action. All such attempts are doomed to failure on principled grounds. Where Hobbes, Freud, and Skinner failed, some unknown of the twenty-first century will not succeed, for the failure stems from the paradox of applying rational methods and arguments to a view of human beings as irrational. The paradox is evident. If we are irrational, then our science must be irrational also.

If the notions of psychological causation fail in the general, do they not fail in the particular? By asking that question I mean to challenge the notion that any particular human choice can be accounted for by anything. It is impossible to separate those actions of human beings that are reasoned choices from those that are not. Reasoned choices are available to nearly all human beings at one time or another. No psychoanalyst nor behavior modifier nor student of need for achievement can tell why I wrote this book in the way in which a student of the cell can explain why there is an exchange of electrolytes across the cell membrane. Psychologists and sociobiologists and the like all chew upon their theories and thus masticate into shape something that resembles in its structure an explanation, but such an explanation is entirely based upon belief, not upon the mixture of belief and experimentally derived information that is the hallmark of science. In the social sciences, any explanation is as valid as any other.

Because human beings are not entirely free, either in the sense of being free from the laws of physical causation or being free from those influences (benign as in positive reinforcement in the classroom or not so benign as in the threat of incarceration in a mental institution in a totalitarian state), statistical evidence adduced by social scientists has a certain validity. To that statistical validity (which, among other things, says we *can* be influenced by reinforcement) is added the wisdom of those social scientists (e.g., Bruno Bettelheim) who choose to regard what they do as an art rather than a science. We can increase our understanding of one another and our actions both by attending to the structural science of society and human behavior as well as to the wise observations of sages who lend their intuitions to our grasp of the human parade. So much has been the case since the dawn of the intellectual enterprise. It is only in very recent times that concessions to human wisdom about human beings have ballooned into a science of human conduct *in which the very act of designing such a science is itself subject to implacable irrational laws.*

This is the historical condition that makes our age the age of irrationality. The fathers of the American experiment in freedom dallied with the ideas of determinism. They were influenced by that grandest of seventeenth-century materialists, Hobbes, and not a few of them were proud of their allegiance to the notion that human beings were simply a part of nature and were to be understood by nature's laws (which in the seventeenth century meant the laws of mechanics). But that flirtation with determinism in the guise of a scientific account of human nature was already by the late eighteenth century a palpable fraud. It could only be indulged in by the delicious play with the newfound freedom given to reason. Reason can toy with any idea it chooses, however self-contradictory may be the assumptions of the iron law of determinism and those of rationalism. But playing with contradictory, self-contradictory ideas was but an expression of that sense of reason that perfused the enlightenment. The obvious character of the contradictions provides one of the leitmotivs of the romantic era that followed. The major figures of the enlightenment, whether in Europe or America, regarded the sciences as the ultimate expression of the intellect. They could ask: Why not apply those processes that led to the great generalities of science to human action itself? The positive sciences (to use the heady phrase of Comte) were that application.

The authors of our freedom could regard persons as mechanical devices, but they could not be serious about the matter in the way that twentieth-century intellectuals are committed to a remarkable degree to the notion that our beliefs and actions are to be explicated by the methods of the physical sciences now applied to the social sciences—that is to say, by methods that, when applied to our own actions must, by the assumption of scientific causality, deny the role of reason.

Freedom and the Social Sciences

Psychology sits at the nexus between the natural sciences and the social sciences. It is on one side unquestionably physical (in both senses used in this book), and on the other there is the devotion to psychological explanations, the kind of explanations that abound in economics, sociology, and anthropology, explanations that are at the bottom psychological, because these disciplines must resort to psychological arguments (lacking the physical ones) to make their explanations plausible.

Sometimes, particularly in the heartland of psychology, someone says that the psychological explanations are only temporary. They will eventually be supplanted by physical ones. However, a few, most notably B. F. Skinner and J. R. Kantor, have insisted that psychological explanations cannot be reduced to physical ones. The irony of that belief seems to escape all who espouse it. Not only are Skinner and Kantor the most thorough-going determinists, but they are insistently monists (certainly material monism in the case of Skinner—Kantor is harder to characterize). Yet they have unwittingly held high the banner of dualism by their insistence upon the irreducible nature of psychological explanations.

Reduction of psychology to biology is, at the present, programmatic, to give the politest term to the matter. The reduction of everything to psychology is not. There is no aspect of human life to which intellectuals of the late twentieth century have not applied psychological reductionism. Ask the intelligent and educated man in the street about anything that tickles your fancy —martyrdom, for example. Almost always you will get psychological explanations (for martyrdom), even from those with strong religious convictions. One person may murmur about masochism (as if that were an explanation), another may use the word *thanatos*, while most will be content to say that the martyr has a crazy urge to die. Almost no one will mention the possibility that the decision to accept or seek martyrdom was something arrived at rationally on the basis of some well-defined premises.

If we cannot reduce the actions of free persons to the biological we try to reduce them to the psychological, that is to say, the irrational. Psychological explanations are irrational. In the end they reduce all actions to compulsions. That there are compulsions is one of the things I have tried to say in this chapter, but to ascribe everything to them as psychological theories of causes inevitably due is to resort to nihilism, or worse to self-contradiction. By such a view, even the economist's rational being is irrational, for though such a being may compute out a complicated kind of hedonic calculus, she is *compelled* to accept the outcome of the computations.

Social scientists talk about "accounting for" the behavior of persons by certain demographic facts. Thus, the sociologist tells us who is and who is not going to become a criminal by giving us statistical descriptions of neighborhoods, families, and even frequency of childhood diseases. Such "variables" however are the correlates of criminal actions, not their causes. Sociologists, psychologists, political scientists, economists, and even anthropologists are forever using the correlates of some psychological condition to "predict" that condition. Growing largely in sociology and economics is a movement to make causal inferences from temporal patterns among correlations. However sophisticated the various techniques invented in this movement may be, they still cannot have the power of explanation inherent in the physical experiment. In the physical experiment, every step in some causative chain is specified by a well-developed theory. Explanations from path analysis or time-lagged correlations demand great leaps over unspecified voids. Economic stress, say, may be said to be the cause of changes in divorce pattern, but just exactly how that process takes place cannot be described in anything other than fantasy. Furthermore, such explanations are statistical in nature, and they are not the statistical explanations of the physicist concerned with things like momentum and direction. They are concerned with possible relations among complex and poorly defined things like income, and empirically they are based upon samples often too small to bear the burden of inference required by the method.

Social sciences are successful at describing aggregates, but that very success leads to the fallacious view that human behavior is predictable by and hence controlled by the descriptions that enter into the aggregates. Psychology, because of its foothold in two realms and because it must perforce deal with actions that are manifestly not free, has the most difficult time with the notion of predictability and control. There are actions that are elicited, and through classical conditioning or something like it, mental events come to control the internal economy of the body to a surprising degree. The reality of such problems and the modest success psychologists and others have in understanding them leads readily to the notion that all human actions are under the control of the external world and thus, in principle, subject to a deterministic science.

Reason and Psychology

The study of human reasoning underwent an astounding revolution under the twin assaults of behaviorism and psychoanalysis. Particularly in America but elsewhere as well the attempts to reduce thinking to the irrational are almost unbelievable. The famous Yale behaviorist of the thirties and forties, C. L. Hull, derived reasoning (in rats!) from conditioned responses.[14] Fortunately, this kind of psychological reductionism has abated in recent years. It has, in fact, almost been taken over by what may be described as the rational investigation of human problem solving.

To more than anyone else this movement belongs to Herbert A. Simon, who from his earliest concerns with the matter declared human problem solving to be rational. He said in 1944: "The behavior of a rational person can be controlled, therefore, if the value and factual premises upon which he bases his decision are specified for him."[15] That says it all. What controls rational actions are the values that motivate them and the premises upon which such actions are based. The rationality comes in the application of the rules of inference as these have been made explicit at least since the days of Aristotle.

That the values that enter into human decisions are often explicit and do not need to be snuffled out by reference to some arcane theory of motivation is about the only thing I should want to add to that statement. When I say that someone prizes human freedom, I expect that statement to be accepted as a value in its own right; I do not expect that we need look for some imagined and imaginary path from the pre-Oedipal libido or from a set of early conditioned reflexes for an explanation.

Principles of logical reasoning have been stated since Aristotle. That the ultimate reaches of such triumphs of human rationality as mathematics are unprovable is one of the great intellectual discoveries of the twentieth century. But that discovery does not vitiate rationality itself. One always begins to reason from some accepted premises, whether those premises themselves can be logically derived from something else or not.

Nor does the existence of a variety of forms of logical reasoning reduce rationality. It is sometimes said that Aristotelian logic is only of historical interest.[16] Whether this is so or not probably depends upon the purposes to which one puts logic. However, Aristotelian logic, no less than any of the varieties of notational variations on propositional logic, makes explicit the rules for the governance of rational thinking. There is a certain psychological validity to the forms of the syllogism, for those forms make it easier for us to evaluate the truth or falsity of the premises from which we reason.

The rules of logic or their exemplification in something like arithmetic can be embodied in artificial devices. Computing devices and their relations to logic are important enough to invite some comment. Their existence has occasionally been used by social scientists to demean the human capacity for rational thought. In principle Aristotle or anyone since could have invented modern computers though the actual invention of one hinged on the discovery of two-valued propositional logic by George Boole in the middle of the nineteenth century. Aristotle did not make axiomatic his notions of the "laws of thought" though he might well have. And we may recognize the difficulties of applying the rules of syllogistic reasoning to mathematical inferences, though it would not be impossible. The ancients, after all, managed to do arithmetic with Ptolemaic or Roman numerals.

In mathematics and logic, notation is almost everything, and it was surely the invention of zero as a place marker, attributed to the Hindus about A.D. 800,[17] that made possible a computing machine based on the principle first realized by Charles Babbage, another nineteenth-century Englishman. It is really the convenience of notation that suggests the possibility of mechanical computing devices and artificial intelligence in general. These machines, which may be said to exemplify human rationality relieve human beings from tedious computation rather than supplant the human being as a rational creature. But artificial intelligence is often seen as a challenge to the uniqueness of human rationality.

Indeed, we have produced machines that are vastly

more capable than we are in certain ways. These machines do not suffer from the kinds of failures of memory that we do. They do not allow belief in propositions to influence and degrade the logical arguments made about those propositions. In short, they are only rational, not both rational and irrational. But their rationality is entirely derived from human beings. They cannot themselves invent devices that are capable of discovering the principles of rational thought. These machines are not testimonies to the failure of the unique position of the human being in nature but rather triumphant reminders of that unique position.

That we are both rational and irrational beings has been known since Aristotle, but it is only in the wake of the explosion of psychological theories about human nature that we have come to the view that we are entirely irrational. The whole weight of a third of a millennium has been to try to make us believe that we are subject only to the laws that govern the hills and the birds in the trees. It is no matter that those same centuries have shown us that we cannot model ourselves after some mechanical principle. But that has not prevented those of us who live in the late twentieth century from supposing that our character and nature can entirely be understood as being derived from the features of certain protein molecules. Such a notion may or may not go the way of the mechanical metaphors of the eighteenth-century materialists, but it is not more correct in our century than the human being as a machine was correct in the eighteenth century.

In short, there is no reason to deny that we are rational beings and that we are free to act upon the results of our reasons. Neither the social sciences, nor the existence of artificial intelligence, nor biological reductionism can deny that. Nor will any of these ever be able to deny our rationality, for their very existence (science is rational if it is anything) is testimony to the contrary.

Values and Freedom

There has been nothing like the revolution in psychological conceptions of values comparable to the shift from problem solving as conditioned responses to problem solving as reasoning. The psychologist's conceptions of values are still mired in the murky depths of theories of motivation.

Theories of motivation arose in the early years of the twentieth century. They came first from the application of the study of instincts in animals to human beings. Then they surfaced in psychoanalysis, the main thrust of which is to reduce all human action to a few (one or two) basic instincts. The critics of this movement were almost instantaneous and in the main correct.[18] They pointed out that it is easy to invent an instinct for every human action (or to reduce every human action to a single instinct). Human beings, like other social primates, are from time to time quarrelsome, and so there is an instinct of pugnacity. Or, in the case of Freud, quarrelsomeness can be reduced to some perversion of the libido, the result of childhood experiences. In either case, the reduction is empty, for counterexamples are explained by the same principles. They explain everything and nothing.

In the twenties and thirties there developed, through the important and pioneering experimental work of people like C. P. Richter and P. T. Young,[19] a respectable account of the biological conditions associated with what animals ate and drank. Specific hungers and their relations to deprivation of essential substances like vitamins were discovered. Furthermore, the things appeared to be universal. The notion of specific hungers applies equally well to rats and children.

The behavioral theorists of the time seized upon these respectable discoveries and converted them into monstrous exaggerations. The notion that all behavior was motivated by a few "biological drives" supplemented by secondary drives (arrived at through association with satisfactions of the biological drives) came to dominate theories of motivation among American psychologists of the thirties and forties. A well-known and popular behavioristic textbook of the 1950s explains the development of the infant's attachment to its mother to be the result of secondary reinforcement associated with feeding.[20]

Such simplistic reduction of motives has all but disappeared. Various psychoanalytic reductions have fared better, particularly because they are admired by certain humanists and students of literature. But they are not less simple, even though they have acquired an odor of profoundity through the metaphor of tragedy. Psychoanalytic explanations, however, are no less reductionistic than those of the biological-drive behaviorists. There was some sense, after all, to the efforts of those psychologists at Yale in the thirties who tried to synthesize behaviorism and psychoanalysis.

What is more insidious than the explanations of human motives is the assumption that they also presume to account for human values. In the eyes of the psychological reductionists (of whatever stripe) values arise out of motives. Thomas Huxley, the social Darwinists, and the sociobiologists assume that values can be explained by the utility of various inborn traits of survival. In a similar way, psychoanalytic theorists explain values, and so do most psychologists. That indefatigable developer of personality inventories, R. B. Cattell, titles a book A *New Morality from Science: Beyondism*.[21] One almost despairs that it has occurred to any psychologist that morals and values come from a different realm of discourse than fact and theory. Morals and values are not to be accounted for. When we attempt to account for them, they become something else; they become psychological theories. A value explained becomes something not to be attacked or defended by moral presuppositions, but only something to be declared true or false by some theory of the nature of things. As such it is no longer a value; it is a result or consequence of some condition of nature. Nature is free of values. Human beings possessed of beliefs and reason can entertain values. Whether or not those values are "explained" by one or another theory of motivation is irrelevant to the content of the values and the beliefs and reasoning behind them. Whether or not animals show altruism or incest taboos has no bearing on the question as to whether or not these values are correct.

The Assumptions of Freedom and Its Undermining

The assumptions behind the acceptance of the notion that we have the potential for free and rational choice are necessary to a faith in democracy. That faith cannot help but be eroded by the irrational theories of social scientists. As with most such matters, it is hard to point to each and every specific instance, for the erosion is so pervasive that one stumbles across examples without realizing their significance. We are often uncomfortable with our political, moral, and legal options. We find it easy to take refuge in the notion that it really doesn't matter because all such things are determined for us. Whether we accept that notion in a fit of Spenglarian gloom or because we have just read the new-age generalities of the latest textbook in social psychology is a matter of indifference.

There is, as I have argued at length in this book, no reason to accept the premise that our actions are determined by some implacable concatenation of the physical world masquerading as our environments and our genes. The need of the social scientist to explain is at one with the need of the witch doctor and the soothsayer to display their wisdom. As describers of the human condition, social scientists have much to offer. As witch doctors they are no better than their primitive brethren. The context of human actions is so manifoldly various that no explanation of a unique action is possible. The single action never obliges to yield what is necessary for scientific explanation, repetition. It is no accident that history is the queen of the social sciences, for historians above all others are forced to the recognition of the uniqueness of each event in history. History does not repeat itself, nor do the events studied in statistical aggregates by psychologists and sociologists. Along with the commonality that permits psychologists and sociologists to invent their statistical aggregates is the uniqueness of each event counted in such aggregates. A sociologist or an insurance actuary may determine that drinking is the major cause of death among men between the ages of seventeen and twenty-five. That fact, however, does not make each and every automobile accident out of which such a generalization is extracted the same. The consumption of alcohol and driving are surely physical causes for such an unfortunate statistic, but they do not provide psychological reasons for the statistics, nor do they provide evidence for some necessary cause at work in human affairs.

The notion that freedom has disappeared into the nightmare of determinism is nothing more than that—a nightmare to be dispelled by reality. The notion that morals and values can be derived from and explained by theories in the social sciences is but another empty claim, devoid of sense.

Notes

1. A Collision Course

1. D. N. Robinson, *Psychology and Law: Can Justice Survive the Social Sciences?*
2. The phrase "prediction and control of behavior" has been for more than a half century the rallying cry for objectivity in psychology. It originates with John B. Watson. See J. B. Watson, *Psychology From the Stand-point of a Behaviorist.*
3. As does my colleague, Larry Sabato. More significantly for my thesis, however, is that he is the author of a book on political consultants: Sabato, *The Rise of Political Consultants.*
4. William James, *Principles of Psychology* 2:576.
5. I use the term psychological community to refer to psychiatrists, psychologists, marriage counselors, and all of those other so-called helping professionals.
6. G. Wills, *Inventing America: Jefferson's Declaration of Independence,* p. 109.
7. J. Deese, *Psychology as Science and Art.*

2. The Rise of Scientific Determinism

1. The best-known biography of John B. Watson claims (incorrectly) that Watson was brought up a Calvinist. Behaviorism was supposed to find its roots in that faith. See D. Cohen, J. B. *Watson, The Founder of Behaviorism: A Biography.*
2. E. A. Esper, *A History of Psychology,* p. 155ff.
3. J. R. Kantor, *The Scientific Evolution of Psychology.* vol. 1.

4. In matters of translation I follow the Student's Oxford Aristotle, translated under the editorship of W. D. Ross. The term soul leads many casual readers to misinterpret Aristotle.

5. I put it this way to indicate that, unlike his medieval commentators, Aristotle did not hold human beings in any special awe.

6. David Hartley's important and surprisingly readable book is called Observations on Man.

7. p. 335. All references to Brett are to the abridged edition: R. S. Peters, ed. Brett's History of Psychology.

8. Kantor, Scientific Evolution, argues that dualism was imported into Western psychology and philosophy by the Neoplatonists. D. N. Robinson (personal communication), on the other hand, argues strongly for mind-body dualism in Aristotle. In any event, it is Leibnitz and Descartes who give dualism its modern form.

9. F. Fearing, Reflex Action: A Study in the History of Physiological Psychology.

10. See, for example, T. Szasz, Law, Liberty, and Psychiatry.

11. See Brett's History, p. 382.

12. E. G. Boring, A History of Experimental Psychology, 2nd ed., p. 506.

13. A term invented by J. R. Kantor.

14. A well-known psychologist and government official offered as a defense against charges of pandering and pornography that he suffered from a disease the principal symptom of which was ungovernable sexual compulsion.

15. Once again I remind the reader of the eloquent arguments of Thomas Szasz on this subject.

16. Published as: J. B. Watson, Psychology as the behaviorist views it. Psychological Review (1913), 20:158–177.

17. I was so informed by the late sociologist, J. H. Mueller, who had been an undergraduate student under Meyer at the University of Missouri before World War I.

18. J. B. Watson, Behaviorism.

3. The Varieties of Determinism

1. S. E. Hyman, The Tangled Bank: Darwin, Marx, Frazer, and Freud as Imaginative Writers.

2. The best account in English of the work of the Würzburg school is to be found in G. Humphrey, Thinking: An Introduction to Its Experimental Psychology.

3. While this is so, I should caution the reader that some investigators have revived the method of reflexion parlée in studies of problem solving. In this method, the person trying to solve a problem introspects about his choices and reasoning as he goes. See K. A. Ericcson and H. A. Simon, Verbal reports as data. Psychological Review (1980), 87:215–251.

4. S. Freud, The Complete Psychological Works, vol. 6 (1901): The Psychopathology of Everyday Life.

5. Hyman, Tangled Bank, p. 313 ff.

6. All quotations from Marx are from: K. Marx, *Capital*, *The Communist Manifesto*, *and Other Writings*.

7. G. C. Brenkert, Freedom and private property in Marx. In M. Cohen, T. Nagel, and T. Scanlon, eds. *Marx, Justice, and History*.

8. O. Spengler, *The Decline of the West*, 2:507.

9. H. Küng, *On Being a Christian*, p. 395.

10. Most of the material that follows is the result of my reading in: H. Bettenson, *Documents of the Christian Church*, 2nd ed.

11. Despite the recent interest in the history of Islam, I find the older account by G. F. Moore to be sensible and reliable. Much of what follows owes itself to my reading of G. F. Moore, *History of Religions, vol. 2: Judaism, Christianity, Mohammedanism*.

12. J. Deese, *Psychology as Science and Art*.

13. H. S. Commager, *The American Mind: An Interpretation of American Thought and Character Since the 1880s*, p. 108.

14. I. Stone, *Jack London: His Life, Sailor on Horseback*.

15. My reference is to the earlier bowdlerized version commonly published as a children's book, not the radically different "authentic" version reconstructed and published out of the University of California. In the reconstructed version Satan is called No. 44. See M. Twain, *No. 44, The Mysterious Stranger*.

16. M. Twain, *The Mysterious Stranger*, p. 253. The quotation is the same in the two versions.

17. I refer, of course, to the author of the horatory address *Acres of Diamonds*.

18. The only full-scale biography of Jeffers is M. B. Bennett, *The Stone Mason of Tor House: The Life and Work of Robinson Jeffers*.

19. A. N. Ridgeway, ed. *The Selected Letters of Robinson Jeffers*.

20. T. W. Adorno, E. Frenkel-Brunswik, D. J. Levinson, and R. N. Sanford, *The Authoritarian Personality*.

21. Erich Jaensch, the best-known psychologist to embrace the Nazis, did devise a test based on eidetic imagery for distinguishing between a personality type he, during the Nazi era, identified as being Jewish and one that was predominantly Nordic. His best-known publication available in English is E. R. Jaensch, *Eidetic Imagery and Typological Methods of Investigation*.

22. M. Rokeach, *The Open and Closed Mind: Investigations into the Nature of Belief Systems and Personality Systems*.

4. Free Will, Voluntary Action, and Freedom

1. H. H. Williams, The Will. In *The Encyclopedia Britannica*, 11th ed., 28:648.

2. W. James, *Principles of Psychology*, vol. 2, chapter 26. But also see James, *The Will To Believe and Other Essays in Popular Philosophy*.

3. W. James, *Pragmatism and Other Essays*.

4. The information summarized here comes from an entry in D. Malone, *Dictionary of American Biography*, vol. 8.

5. F. A. Rauch, *Psychology, or a View of the Human Soul Including Anthropology,* p. 293.

6. *Ibid.,* pp. 293–294.

7. W. McDougall, *An Introduction to Social Psychology,* 14th ed.

8. E. A. Ross, *Social Psychology: An Outline and Source Book.*

9. McDougall, *Social Psychology,* pp. 236–237.

10. *Ibid.,* p. 241.

11. *Ibid.*

12. Once again, I acknowledge my indebtedness to that splendid essay in the history of science: F. Fearing, *Reflex Action: A Study in the History of Physiological Psychology.*

13. Hall, as quoted by Fearing, *Reflex Action,* p. 129.

14. C. S. Sherrington, *The Integrative Action of the Nervous System.*

15. Whether this resolution is correct or not is still a matter of debate. See M. M. Patterson, C. F. Cagavske, and R. F. Thompson, Effects of classical conditioning in hind-limb flexor nerve response in immobilized spinal cats. *Journal of Comparative and Physiological Psychology* (1973), 84:88–97.

16. E. R. Hilgard and D. G. Marquis, *Conditioning and Learning.*

17. B. F. Skinner, *The Behavior of Organisms.*

18. For a dissenting view see A. G. Greenwald, Sensory feedback mechanisms in performance control. *Psychological Review* (1970), 77:73–99.

19. G. Wills, *Inventing America: Jefferson's Declaration of Independence.*

20. C. Becker, *The Declaration of Independence: A Study in the History of Political Ideas.*

21. Coleman finds influence of Hobbes both upon the Declaration and the Constitution, but particularly the Constitution. See F. M. Coleman, *Hobbes and America: Exploring the Constitutional Foundations.*

22. B. F. Skinner, *Beyond Freedom and Dignity.*

23. Carnegie was the author of the most successful self-help book of all time. Hill is less well remembered, but he was, in his time, almost as popular as Carnegie. The references are: D. Carnegie, *How To Win Friends and Influence People,* and N. Hill, *Think and Grow Rich.*

5. The Ethos of Contemporary Psychology: I. Behaviorism

1. P. W. Bridgman, *The Logic of Modern Physics.* The reaction to this book among experimental psychologists was enormous. It undoubtedly was responsible for the title of the thoroughly muddled attempt to combine an older introspective experimentalism with behaviorism by C. C. Pratt. See C. C. Pratt, *The Logic of Modern Psychology.*

2. Albert Paul Weiss, student of Max Meyer, survives in the history books precisely because he was the only thoroughgoing physical reductionist among the first generation of behaviorists. See A. P. Weiss, *The Theoretical Basis of Human Behavior.*

3. The original experiment but by no means the best known on the location

of clicks in sentences is: P. Ladefoged and D. E. Broadbent, Perception of sequences in auditory events. *Quarterly Journal of Experimental Psychology* (1960), 13:162–170.

4. Given the great influence of the philosophy of science upon experimental psychologists in the thirties and forties it is not surprising that there was a lot of talk about crucial experiments. A few investigators even immodestly offered some.

5. If one counts such things as reasonable compensation for the time of the experimental subjects (who are usually "volunteers" taken from introductory courses), overhead, and such things, the total could easily be twice or treble my modest figure.

6. My nomination for the most stupifyingly dull and unimportant book ever written was devoted to this topic. It is: C. L. Hull et al., *Mathematico-Deductive Theory of Rote Learning*.

7. See E. R. Harcum, *Serial Learning and Paralearning*.

8. B. F. Skinner, The concept of the reflex in the description of behavior. *Journal of General Psychology* (1931), 5:427–458.

9. B. F. Skinner, *The Behavior of Organisms*.

10. *Ibid.*, p. 10.

11. *Ibid.*, pp. 12–19.

12. *Ibid.*, chapter 10.

13. B. F. Skinner, *Beyond Freedom and Dignity*, p. 16.

14. *Ibid.*, pp. 173–174.

15. *Ibid.*, p. 205.

16. The wisest comment I know on the subject of this quirk of the American character is from a Canadian. See R. Davies, Enjoying and enduring. in A *Voice From the Attic*.

17. Token economies clothe an old technique with a new name. Inmates in institutions, ranging from schools to prisons, to state mental hospitals, win points for good behavior. These points then may be redeemed for cigarettes, candy, or even free time.

18. This fashionable phrase comes from M. E. P. Seligman, *Helplessness*.

6. The Ethos of Contemporary Psychology: II. Social Psychology

1. I have already cited McDougall and Ross in chapter 4, but I have not yet mentioned Le Bon. Not quite so much a darling of conservative thinkers as Edmund Burke, nevertheless, his analyses of human society provide a bone-chilling view. His principal work is: G. Le Bon, *The Crowd: A Study of the Popular Mind*. Despite his political conservative bias, he, using the notion then current in French psychology of suggestion, arrives at a deterministic view of mass human action, and therefore he may be regarded as an intellectual forebear of all that I find objectionable in this chapter.

2. F. H. Allport, *Social Psychology*.

3. S. Koch, The nature and limits of psychological knowledge: Lessons of a century qua "Science." *American Psychologist* (1981), 36:257–259.

4. R. E. Nisbet and T. D. Wilson, Telling more than we can know: Verbal reports as mental processes. *Psychological Review* (1977), 84:231–259.

5. The field experiment is: I. M. Piliavin, J. Rodin, and J. A. Piliavin, Good Samaritans: An underground phenomenon? *Journal of Personality and Social Psychology* (1969), 13:289–299. The laboratory experiment is: J. M. Darley and B. Latané, Bystander intervention in emergencies: Diffusion of responsibility. *Journal of Personality and Social Psychology* (1968), 8:377–383. Latané and Nida attempt a labored explanation of the "boundary conditions" for the group size and helping relation. See B. Latané and S. Nida, Ten years of research on group size and helping. *Psychological Bulletin* (1981), 89:308–324.

6. See, for example, the treatment in E. R. Hilgard, R. L. Atkinson, and R. C. Atkinson, *Introduction to Psychology*, 7th ed., p. 520ff.

7. R. E. Nisbett and T. D. Wilson, Verbal reports.

8. J. Darley and E. Berscheid, Increased liking as a result of the anticipation of personal contact. *Human Relations* (1967), 20:29–40.

9. E. Aronson, *The Social Animal*, 3d. ed.

10. C. Haney, C. Banks, and P. Zimbardo, Interpersonal dynamics in a simulated prison. *International Journal of Criminology and Penology* (1973), 1:69–97.

11. The best of many possible references is to a book: S. Milgram, *Obedience to Authority: An Experimental View.*

12. E. Aronson, *The Social Animal*, p. 48.

13. He borrows the example from P. Zimbardo, E. Ebbeson, and C. Maslach, *Influencing Attitudes and Changing Behavior*, 2d ed.

14. I confess to having confined myself to textbooks and monographs. Except for those which I describe in some detail, I have avoided reading accounts of experiments. They are simply too tedious.

15. On the other hand Aronson also identifies the irrational with maladaptation. See E. Aronson, *The Social Animal*, p. 109.

16. *Ibid.*

17. J. Kagan and E. Havemann, *Psychology: An Introduction*, 4th ed., p. 535.

7. The Ethos of Contemporary Psychology: III. Psychohistory

1. B. Mazlish, ed. *Psychoanalysis and History.*

2. *Ibid.*, p. 182.

3. K. D. Keele, *The Evolution of Clinical Methods in Medicine.*

4. See E. D. Phillips, *Aspects of Greek Medicine.*

5. See B. Inglis, *A History of Medicine.*

6. *Ibid.*, p. 43.

7. T. S. Szasz, *Law, Liberty, and Psychiatry.*

8. News story in the *Washington Post*, March 26, 1982.

9. E. Jones, *Hamlet and Oedipus*, p. 7.

10. *Ibid.*, p. 9.

11. Each of these figures might have been cited, however, I have chosen to

cite the monumental work: J. Bowlby, *Attachment and Loss*. Vol. 1, Bowlby cites both Spitz and Ainsworth.

    12. Allport borrowed the distinction between nomothetic and idiographic from the German philosopher W. Windelband, but he made it well known to psychologists. See G. W. Allport, *Personality: A Psychological Interpretation*, p. 22.

    13. E. H. Erikson, *Young Man Luther*.

    14. *Ibid.*, p. 72.

    15. *Ibid.*, pp. 122–123.

    16. *Ibid.*, p. 248.

    17. *Ibid.*, p. 22.

    18. S. Freud and W. C. Bullitt, *Thomas Woodrow Wilson*.

    19. *Ibid.*, p. 12.

    20. *Ibid.*, p. 26.

    21. *Ibid.*, p. 44.

    22. *Ibid.*, p. 283.

    23. There is another psychoanalytic study of Wilson, not so full of animus but scarcely less extravagant: A. L. George and J. L. George, *Woodrow Wilson and Colonel House*.

    24. B. Mazlish, *In Search of Nixon: A Psychohistorical Inquiry*.

    25. *Ibid.*, p. 24.

    26. *Ibid.*, p. 51.

    27. *Ibid.*, p. 140.

    28. *Ibid.*, p. 152.

    29. *Ibid.*, p. 153.

    30. G. Wills, *Nixon Agonistes*.

    31. One of the major controversies in recent years in American history has concerned the psychological and sociological interpretation of the statistical data on American slavery.

    32. H. James, *The Portrait of a Lady*, p. 19. The text is from the 1906–1907 New York edition.

    33. W. Cather, *Youth and the Bright Medusa*. p. 201.

    34. *Ibid.*, p. 205.

    35. V. Nabokov, *Lolita*, p. 13.

8. Objectivity and Subjectivity in Social Science

    1. Scientific fraud is not unknown, and in recent years there has been an epidemic, particularly in medical research involving clinical trials.

    2. R. Naroll and R. Cohen, eds. *A Handbook of Method in Cultural Anthropology*.

    3. R. Benedict, *Patterns of Culture*.

    4. D. Freeman, *Margaret Mead and Samoa*.

    5. W. H. Goodenough, Margaret Mead and Cultural Anthropology. In Letters to the Editor, *Science* (1983), 220:906–908.

    6. *Ibid.*, p. 906.

7. Ibid.

8. J. Deese, Psychology as Art and Science.

9. E. A. Hammel, ed. Formal Semantic Analysis: Special Issue of American Anthropologist (1965), 67:no. 5.

10. See I. Rossi, ed. The Unconscious in Culture: The Structuralism of Claude Lévi-Strauss in Perspective.

11. C. G. Jung, Studies in Word Association.

12. M. Harris, Cultural Materialism: The Struggle for a Science of Culture.

13. Ibid., p. 75.

14. S. J. Brams and P. C. Fishburn, Approval Voting.

15. D. J. Olson and P. Meyer, Governing the United States: To Keep the Republic in its Third Century, 2d ed.

16. N. Nie, S. Verba, and J. R. Petrocik, The Changing American Voter.

17. P. H. Rossi, Four Landmarks in Voting Research. In E. Burdick and A. J. Brodbeck, American Voting Behavior.

18. S. A. Rice, Quantitative Methods in Politics.

19. Never mind that the same "naive" conception appears in an important work published in 1976. See N. Nie, et al., The Changing American Voter.

20. R. M. Unger, Knowledge and Politics.

21. I am indebted to Professor Kurt Bergel of Chapman College for pointing out to me the need to deal with this issue, given the context of this book.

9. Our Conceptions of Ourselves

1. The original investigations were done by S. B. Sells, a graduate student with R. S. Woodworth. The most frequently cited publication is R. S. Woodworth and S. B. Sells. An Atmosphere Effect in Formal Syllogistic Reasoning. Journal of Experimental Psychology (1935), 18:451–460.

2. Any good textbook on animal behavior will provide the background for my remarks. My favorite, because it is so balanced, is nearly twenty years old. It is R. A. Hinde, Animal Behavior: A Synthesis of Ethology and Comparative Psychology.

3. Even manuals for bird watchers carry this information. See J. Bull and J. Ferrand, Jr., The Audubon Society Field Guide to North American Birds.

4. The biologist is, of course, E. O. Wilson.

5. This issue has led to something of a Harvard family feud, with E. O. Wilson and Charles J. Lumsden on one side and with a larger range of Harvard biologists on the other, including Stephen Jay Gould, Jonathan Beckwith, Ruth Hubbard, and Richard Lewontin. The debate does not extend to questions of the material determination of human action, which both sides seem to take for granted, only to the issue of heredity versus environment.

6. C. J. Lumsden and E. O. Wilson, Promethean Fire: Reflections on the Origins of Mind.

7. Ibid., pp. 117–118.

8. *Ibid.*, p. 174.

9. *Ibid.*, p. 182.

10. In my youth I so regarded the material in G. A. Dorsey, *Hows and Whys of Human Behavior.* Dorsey was an anthropologist who wrote several popular books on what broadly could be construed as the social sciences. *Hows and Whys of Human Behavior* went through twelve printings in an extraordinarily short time. It seems utterly to have disappeared.

11. R. S. Peters, *The Concept of Motivation.*

12. A recent determined effort to argue to the contrary is embodied in what in my view is an extraordinarily bad book: V. Hamilton, *The Cognitive Structures and Processes of Human Motivation and Personality.*

13. F. Rauch, *Psychology: Or a View of the Human Soul.*

14. C. L. Hull, The mechanisms of the assembly of behavior segments in novel combinations suitable for problem solving. *Psychological Review* (1935), 42:219–245.

15. H. A. Simon, Decision making and administrative organization. *Public Administration Review* (1944), 4:16–31.

16. L. M. Blumenthal, Logic. *McGraw-Hill Encyclopedia of Science and Technology,* vol. 7.

17. E. T. Bell, *The Development of Mathematics,* 2d ed.

18. Many citations are possible. I mention a largely neglected work. Its neglect stems both from its intemperate language and the obscurity of the publisher. It is: K. Dunlap, *Mysticism, Freudianism, and Scientific Psychology.*

19. Richter is by far the more important figure, but P. T. Young's book on motivation was very influential. See P. T. Young, *Motivation of Behavior.*

20. This was so announced in F. S. Keller and W. N. Schonfeld, *Principles of Psychology.*

21. R. B. Cattell, *A New Morality From Science: Beyondism.*

References

Allport, F. H. *Social Psychology*. New York: Houghton-Mifflin, 1924.

Allport, G. W. *Personality: A Psychological Interpretation*. New York: Holt, 1937.

Aronson, E. *The Social Animal*, 3d ed. San Francisco, W. H. Freeman, 1980.

Becker, C. L. *The Declaration of Independence: A Study in History of Political Ideas*. New York: Harcourt, Brace, 1922.

Bell, E. T. *The Development of Mathematics*. 2d ed. New York: McGraw-Hill, 1945.

Benedict, R. *Patterns of Culture*. In a new edition with a preface by Margaret Mead. Boston: Houghton-Mifflin, 1958.

Bettenson, H. ed. *Documents of the Christian Church*. 2d ed. London: Oxford University Press, 1963.

Blumenthal, L. M. Logic. *McGraw-Hill Encyclopedia of Science and Technology*, vol. 7. New York: McGraw-Hill, 1977.

Bowlby, J. *Attachment and Loss*. New York: Basic Books. Vol. 1, 1969, vol. 2, 1973.

Brams, S. J. and P. C. Fishburn, *Approval Voting*. Boston: Birkhausen, 1983.

Brenkert, G. C. "Freedom and Private Property in Marx." In M. Cohen, T. Nagel, and T. Scanlon, eds. *Marx, Justice, and History*. Princeton, N.J.: Princeton University Press, 1980.

Bridgman, P. W. *The Logic of Modern Physics*. New York: Macmillan, 1927.

Bull, J. and J. Ferrand, Jr. *The Audubon Society Field Guide to North American Birds*. New York: Knopf, 1977.

Carnegie, D. *How To Win Friends and Influence People*. New York: Simon and Schuster, 1937.

Cather, W. *Youth and the Bright Medusa*. New York: Knopf, 1920.

Cattell, R. B. *A New Morality from Science: Beyondism*. New York: Pergamon Press, 1973.

Cohen, D. *J. B. Watson, The Founder of Behaviorism: A Biography*. London: Routledge and Kegan Paul, 1979.

Coleman, F. M. *Hobbes and America: Exploring the Constitutional Foundations*. Toronto: University of Toronto Press, 1977.

Commager, H. S. *The American Mind: An Interpretation of American Thought and Character Since the 1880s*. New Haven, Conn.: Yale University Press, 1950.

Darley, J. and E. Berscheid. "Increased Liking as a Result of the Anticipation of Personal Contact." *Human Relations* (1967), 20:29–40.

Darley, J. and B. Latané. "Bystander Intervention in Emergencies: Diffusion of Responsibility." *Journal of Personality and Social Psychology* (1968), 8:377–383.

Davies, R. *A Voice from the Attic*. New York: Knopf, 1960.

Deese, J. *Psychology as Art and Science*. New York: Harcourt, Brace, and Jovanovich, 1972.

Dorsey, G. A. *Hows and Whys of Human Behavior*. New York: Harpers, 1929.

Dunlap, K. *Mysticism, Freudianism, and Scientific Psychology*. St. Louis: Mosby, 1920.

Ericcson, K. A. and H. A. Simon. "Verbal Reports as Data." *Psychological Review* (1980), 87:215–251.

Erikson, E. H. *Young Man Luther*. New York: Norton, 1958.

Esper, E. A. *A History of Psychology*. Philadelphia: Saunders, 1964.

Fearing, F. *Reflex Action: A Study in the History of Physiological Psychology*. New York: Haffner, 1964 (reprint of original edition of 1930).

Freeman, D. *Margaret Mead and Samoa*. Cambridge, Mass.: Harvard University Press, 1983.

Freud, S. *The Complete Psychological Works*. Vol. 6 (1901): *The Psychopathology of Everyday Life*. London: Hogarth, 1960.

Freud, S. and W. C. Bullitt. *Thomas Woodrow Wilson*. New York: Houghton-Mifflin, 1966.

George, A. L. and J. L. George. *Woodrow Wilson and Colonel House*. New York: Day, 1956.

Goddard, H. H. *The Kallikak Family*. New York: Macmillan, 1913.

Goodenough, W. H. "Margaret Mead and Cultural Anthropology." *Science* (1983), 220:906–908.

Greenwald, A. G. "Sensory feedback Mechanisms in Performance Control." *Psychological Review* (1970), 77:73–99.

Hamilton, V. *The Cognitive Structures and Processes of Human Motivation and Personality*. Chichester, England: Wiley, 1983.

Hammel, E. A., ed. "Formal Semantic Analysis." Special issue of *American Anthropologist* (1965), Vol. 67, no. 5.

Haney, C., C. Banks, and P. Zimbardo. "Interpersonal Dynamics in a Simulated Prison." *International Journal of Criminology and Penology* (1973), 1:69–97.

Harcum, E. R. *Serial Learning and Paralearning*. New York: Wiley, 1975.

Harris, M. *Cultural Materialism: The Struggle for a Science of Culture*. New York: Vintage Books, 1980.

Hartley, D. *Observations on Man*. London: Richardson, 1749.

Hilgard, E. R., R. L. Atkinson, and R. C. Atkinson. *Introduction to Psychology*, 7th ed. New York: Harcourt, Brace and Jovanovich, 1979.

Hilgard, E. R. and D. G. Marquis. *Conditioning and Learning.* New York: Appleton-Century, 1940.

Hill, N. *Think and Grow Rich.* Cleveland, Ohio: World, 1938.

Hinde, R. A. *Animal Behavior: A Synthesis of Ethology and Comparative Psychology.* New York: McGraw-Hill, 1966.

Hull, C. L. "The Mechanism of the Assembly of Behavior Segments in Novel Combinations Suitable for Problem Solving." *Psychological Review* (1935), 42:219–245.

Hull, C. L., C. I. Hovland, R. T. Ross, M. Hall, D. T. Perkins, and F. B. Fitch. *Mathematical-Deductive Theory of Rote Learning.* New Haven, Conn.: Yale University Press, 1940.

Humphrey, G. *Thinking: An Introduction to Its Experimental Psychology.* London: Methuen, 1951.

Hyman, S. E. *The Tangled Bank: Darwin, Marx, and Frazer as Imaginative Writers.* New York: Grosset and Dunlap, 1966. (Original edition, 1959.)

Inglis, B. A *History of Medicine.* Cleveland, Ohio: World, 1965.

Jaensch, E. R. *Eidetic Imagery and Typological Methods of Investigation.* Translated from the 2d ed. by O. Oesser. London: K. Paul, Trench, Trubner, 1930.

James, H. *The Portrait of a Lady.* Norwalk, Conn.: Easton Press, 1978. The text is from the 1906–1907 edition.

James, W. *Pragmatism and Other Essays.* New York: Washington Square Press, 1963. (Original edition, 1910.)

———. *Principles of Psychology.* New York: Holt, 1890.

———. *The Will To Believe, and Other Essays in Popular Philosophy.* New York: Longmans Green, 1905.

Jones, E. *Hamlet and Oedipus.* Garden City, N.Y.: Doubleday Anchor, 1949.

Jung, C. G. *Studies in Word Association.* Translated by M. D. Eder. New York: Moffat, Yard, 1919.

Kagan, J. and E. Havemann. *Psychology: An Introduction,* 4th ed. New York: Harcourt, Brace, and Jovanovich, 1980.

Kantor, J. R. *The Scientific Evolution of Psychology,* vol. 1. Chicago: Principia Press, 1963.

Keele, K. D. *The Evolution of Clinical Methods in Medicine.* Springfield, Ill.: Charles C. Thomas, 1963.

Keller, F. S. and W. N. Schonfeld. *Principles of Psychology.* New York: Appleton-Century-Crofts, 1950.

Koch, S. "The Nature and Limits of Psychological Knowledge: Lessons of a Century qua 'Science.' " *American Psychologist* (1981), 36:257–259.

Küng, H. *On Being a Christian.* E. Quinn, tr. Garden City, N.Y.: Doubleday, 1976.

Ladefoged, P. and D. E. Broadbent. "Perception of Sequence in Auditory Events." *Quarterly Journal of Experimental Psychology* (1960), 13:162–170.

Latané, B. and S. Nida. "Ten Years of Research on Group Size and Helping." *Psychological Bulletin* 1981, 89:308–324.

Le Bon, G. *The Crowd: A Study of the Popular Mind.* London: T. Fisher Unwin, 1896.

Lumsden, C. J. and E. O. Wilson. *Promethean Fire: Reflections on the Origins of Mind.* Cambridge, Mass.: Harvard University Press, 1983.

Malone, D., ed. *Dictionary of American Biography,* vol. 8. New York: Scribners, 1935.

Marx, K. *Capital, The Communist Manifesto, and Other Writings.* New York: The Modern Library, 1932.

Mazlish, B. *In Search of Nixon: A Psychohistorical Inquiry.* Baltimore, Md.: Penguin Books, 1973.

Mazlish, B., ed. *Psychoanalysis and History.* Englewood Cliffs, N.J.: Prentice-Hall, 1963.

McDougall, W. *An Introduction to Social Psychology,* 14th ed. Boston: Luce, 1921 (original edition, 1908).

Meyer, M. *The Psychology of the Other One.* Columbia, Mo.: Missouri Book Co., 1921.

Milgram, S. *Obedience to Authority: An Experimental View.* New York: Harper and Row, 1974.

Moore, G. F. *History of Religions.* Vol. 2: *Judaism, Christianity, Mohammedanism.* New York: Scribners, 1948. (Original edition, 1919.)

Nabokov, V. *Lolita.* New York: Putnam, 1958.

Naroll, R. and R. Cohen, eds. *A Handbook of Method in Cultural Anthropology.* Garden City, N.Y.: The Natural History Press, 1970.

Nie, N., S. Verba, and J. R. Petrocik. *The Changing American Voter.* Cambridge, Mass.: Harvard University Press, 1976.

Nisbet, R. E. and T. D. Wilson, "Telling More Than We Can Know: Verbal Reports as Mental Processes." *Psychological Review* (1977), 84:231–259.

Olson, D. J. and P. Meyer. *Governing the United States: To Keep the Republic in its Third Century,* 2d ed. New York: McGraw-Hill, 1978.

Patterson, M. M., C. F. Cagavske and R. F. Thompson. "Effects of Classical Conditioning in Hind-limb Flexor Nerve Response in Immobilized Spinal Cats." *Journal of Comparative and Physiological Psychology* (1973), 84:88–97.

Peters, R. S., ed. *Brett's History of Psychology.* Abridged ed. Cambridge, Mass.: MIT Press, 1953.

Peters, R. S. *The Concept of Motivation.* London: Routledge & Kegan Paul, 1960.

Phillips, E. D. *Aspects of Greek Medicine.* Cleveland, Ohio: World, 1965.

Piliavin, I. M., J. Rodin, and J. A. Piliavin. "Good Samaritans: An Underground Phenomenon?" *Journal of Personality and Social Psychology* (1969), 13:289–299.

Pratt, C. C. *The Logic of Modern Psychology,* New York: Macmillan, 1939.

Rauch, F. A. *Psychology, or a View of the Human Soul Including Anthropology.* New York: M. W. Dodd, 1841.

Rice, S. A. *Quantitative Methods in Politics.* New York: Knopf, 1928.

Ridgeway, A. N., ed. *The Selected Letters of Robinson Jeffers.* Baltimore, Md.: Johns Hopkins University Press, 1968.

Robinson, D. *Psychology and Law: Can Justice Survive the Social Sciences?* New York: Oxford University Press, 1980.

Rokeach, M. *The Open and Closed Mind: Investigations into the Nature of Belief Systems and Personality Systems.* New York: Basic Books, 1960.

Ross, E. A. *Social Psychology: An Outline and Source Book*. New York: Macmillan, 1915. (Original edition 1908.)

Ross, W. D., ed. *The Student's Oxford Aristotle*. Vol. 3: *Psychology. De Animal, Parva Naturalia*. London: Oxford, 1942.

Russell, C. *Acres of Diamonds*. N.D.

Sabato, L. *The Rise of Political Consultants*. New York: Basic Books, 1981.

Seligman, M. E. P. *Helplessness*. San Francisco: Freeman, 1975.

Sherrington, C. S. *The Integrative Action of the Nervous System*. New Haven, Conn.: Yale University Press, 1906.

Simon, H. A. "Decision Making and Administrative Organization." *Public Administration Review* (1944), 4:16–31.

Skinner, B. F. *The Behavior of Organisms*. New York: Appleton-Century, 1938.

Skinner, B. F. *Beyond Freedom and Dignity*. New York: Bantam, 1972.

Skinner, B. F. "The Concept of the Reflex in the description of Behavior." *Journal of General Psychology* (1931), 5:427–458.

Spengler, O. *The Decline of the West*. C. F. Atkinson, tr. New York: Knopf, 1926.

Stone, I. *Jack London: His Life, Sailor on Horseback*. Garden City, N.Y.: Doubleday, 1977 (original edition 1938).

Szasz, T. *Law, Liberty, and Psychiatry*. New York: Collier, 1968 (original edition, 1963).

Twain, M. *The Mysterious Stranger*. New York: New American Library, 1962. Also see No. 44, *The Mysterious Stranger*. Berkeley: University of California Press, 1969.

Unger, R. M. *Knowledge and Politics*. New York: Free Press, 1975.

Young, P. T. *Motivation of Behavior*. New York: Wiley, 1936.

Watson, J. B. *Behaviorism*. New York: Norton, 1925.

Watson, J. B. "Psychology as the Behaviorist Views It." *Psychological Review* (1913), 20:158–177.

Watson, J. B. *Psychology From the Standpoint of a Behaviorist*, 2d ed. Philadelphia: Lippincott, 1924. (Original edition, 1919.)

Williams, H. H. The Will. *Encyclopedia Britannica*, vol. 28, 11th ed. New York: The Encyclopedia Britannica Co., 1911.

Wills, G. *Inventing America: Jefferson's Declaration of Independence*. New York: Vintage Books, 1979.

Wills, G. *Nixon Agonistes*. New York: Houghton-Mifflin, 1970.

Woodworth, R. S. and S. B. Sells. "An Atmosphere Effect in Formal Syllogistic Reasoning." *Journal of Experimental Psychology* (1935), 18:451–460.

Zimbardo, P., E. Ebbeson, and C. Maslash. *Influencing Attitudes and Changing Behavior*, 2d ed. Reading, Mass.: Addison-Wesley, 1977.

Index

Critical Assessments of Contemporary Psychology
Daniel N. Robinson, Series Editor